MW01633713

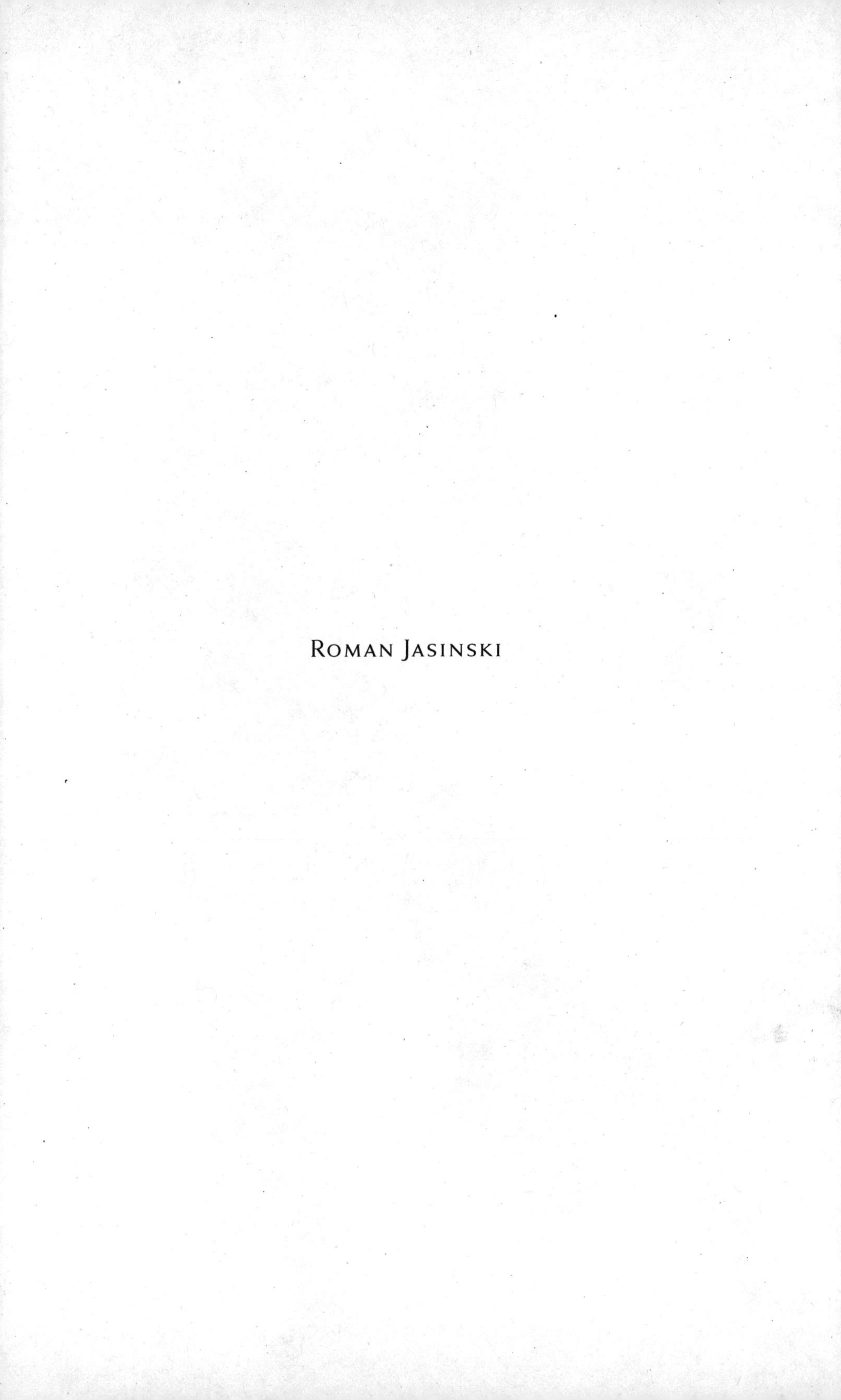

Roman Jasinski

TULSA BALLET THEATRE, INC.

To Mary! Happy Reading! Cheryl & Georgia

# Roman Jasinski

## A GYPSY PRINCE *from the* BALLET RUSSE

CHERYL FORREST AND GEORGIA SNOKE

All proceeds from this book benefit the Roman Jasinski Fund, an endowment formed to preserve Tulsa Ballet, the company founded by Roman Jasinski, Moscelyne Larkin, and Rosalie Talbott.

© 2008 by Cheryl Forrest and Georgia Snoke

All rights reserved

International Standard Book Number 978-0-615-22160-1

PUBLISHED BY

**TULSA BALLET**

1212 EAST FORTY-FIFTH PLACE SOUTH

TULSA, OKLAHOMA 74105

918.749.6030

www.tulsaballet.org

DESIGN, EDITING, PROJECT MANAGEMENT:

CAROL HARALSON, SEDONA, ARIZONA

PRINTED IN CANADA

ON 100% PCW RECYCLED PAPER USING VEGETABLE-BASED INKS

FRONTISPIECE: Roman Jasinski in the title role of *The Prodigal Son.*

Photo by Thorlichen, Buenos Aires. Private collection.

WE DEDICATE THIS BOOK TO

CZESLAW ROMAN JASINSKI

OUR JASHA

OUR MENTOR

OUR TEACHER

OUR FRIEND

*Cheryl Forrest and Georgia Snoke*

## CONTENTS

## III
## The War Years 1939–1947



## IV
## Life in America 1948–1991



## Epilogue: Tulsa

# ACKNOWLEDGMENTS

So many individuals have aided us in our effort to recount the story of Roman Jasinski. First and foremost: a thousand thanks to our patient families. Cheryl's husband John and Georgia's husband Ken waved us away on adventure after adventure, cheerfully surviving on their own while we explored Monte Carlo, Paris, London, and New York, relentlessly ferreting out information. Many thanks to our children, Bennett and Stephanie Forrest, and Heather Snoke Pohl and Kelsi Snoke Neill, who viewed their mothers with amazement and pride.

We owe a debt of gratitude to our editors: Diane Seebass, our intrepid copy editor, who also provided encouragement and enthusiasm during the long process; and Carol Haralson, our editor-in-chief, who took our efforts and made them sing.

We gratefully acknowledge Moscelyne Larkin, Artistic Director Emeritus, Tulsa Ballet, for relaying countless tales of life with her husband Roman Jasinski in the Ballets Russes and beyond; and Roman Larkin Jasinski, former Artistic Director, Tulsa Ballet, and son of Roman Jasinski and Moscelyne Larkin, for the many interviews concerning his late father and for sharing scores of documents. Others who played a pivotal role in this endeavor were Jack Anderson and George

Dorris, dear friends and dance writers extraordinaire, for their encouragement and guidance over many years, and for permission to reprint Mr. Anderson's poem, "A Gift to the Plains."

Also Stéphane Boudin-Lestienne, Historien d'Art et d'Architecture, Villa Noailles, Hyères, France, for a guided tour of the villa and information pertaining to the Noailles' life there; Yvonne Chouteau, Miguel Terekhov, Frederic Franklin, the late Pablo de Madalengoitia, and the late Alexandra Danilova, for interviews; Dr. Eugene Gaddis, Archivist and Curator of the Austin House at the Wadsworth Atheneum, Hartford, for assisting and advising along the way; and Dr. Sharon-Michi Kusunoki, Head of Gallery, Archives, and Collection, The Edward James Foundation, West Dean College, Chichester, England, for allowing us access to Edward James' materials relating to Jasinski.

Additionally, Sue Whyte, former Archivist, Royal Opera House, London, for patiently researching the presumed last performances of the unfortunate Eugene Lapitsky; Rebecca Quinton, former Curator, and Eleanor Thompson, Curator, Costume and Textiles at the Royal Pavilion and Museum, Brighton and Hove, England, for information pertaining to Les Ballets 1933; Veronique Fabré of the Patrimoine Historique, Archives Société des Bains de Mer, Monte Carlo, for access to Ballets Russes materials; Lee Christofis, Curator of Dance, National Library of Australia, for assistance on various topics; the staff of the Royal Air Force Museum and Roy Hemington of the Commonwealth War Graves Commission for aiding in the search for the wartime efforts of Felix Rolo; and the late DarJalane Priybl of Cannes, for sustenance, a roof over our heads, and encouragement.

Also, Alice Standin of the Jerome Robbins Dance Division of the New York Public Library for the Performing Arts at Lincoln Center; and the staffs of the Bibliothèque-Musée de l'Opéra and the Bibliothèque de l'Arsenal, both in Paris, for patiently guiding us through their collections and for granting our many requests; and Mrs. Bjarne Holm, Dr. Robert Hudson, Christopher Jean-Richard, Ann Dee Lee, Susan Lively, John McCormack, Jon Petersen, Ron Seymour, and the staff of Tulsa Ballet.

This has been a true labor of love, a deep obeisance to our mentor, and we give profound thanks to those who have made its publication possible: Billie and

Howard Barnett, Adrienne Lee Barnett, Allison Michelle Barnett, the late Bisser and Bud Barnett, Ludmila and Frank Robson, Hannah and Joe Robson, Jenk Jones Jr., Kathy Kraft Hilti, Ana Maria Lloyd-Jones, Lindsay Alexander, Dale and Ron Roberson, Mollie Williford, Ramez Hakim, and Terry and John Williams.

And finally, authors Patty Floyd and Lili Livingston for their steadfast belief in the project; Mary Forrest-Doyle and Philip Doyle for proofreading; Jerri and Jenk Jones Jr., David Jones, Ana Maria Jones and the late Jenkin Lloyd Jones for advice on the manuscript; and Laurence Yadon, for encouragement and advice on publishing.

CHERYL FORREST AND GEORGIA SNOKE

TULSA, OKLAHOMA

AUGUST 2008

# Gathering Jasha's Stories

Who was Roman Jasinski? When I was a young dancer, this question was prompted by the sights and sounds around me: photos and posters from around the world, the mixture of English and Russian resounding between my artistic directors, the promenade of world-famous dancers through my young onstage life.

The curiosity remained long after I left the company, and upon my return to Tulsa it was my privilege to sit by Mr. Jasinski's side recording hundreds of hours of anecdotes and observations concerning his life in dance. Our last interview took place three weeks before his death, and even from his hospital bed Jasha ("Yasha") continued to add to his tales. His voice was stilled on 15 April 1991.

Years passed. Life and its demands intervened. Finally, I asked my longtime friend Georgia Snoke to join me in preserving and sharing the tale of Roman Jasinski's life. An accomplished dancer, a resourceful writer, and in Jasha's words, "an artiste" (his highest praise!), Georgia brought her considerable talent, dedication, and creativity to the project, and together we sought the answer to the question.

Our search left astonished but supportive husbands and children at home to fend for themselves while it carried us to the cities of Monte Carlo and Paris one summer; to Chichester and Brighton, England the next; to New York several times; to London. Our adventures were sometimes embarrassing, sometimes astonishing, always intriguing. We think Jasha would have loved them.

Jasha spoke many languages, English the last among them, haltingly and heavily accented. We have attempted to retain his charming manner of communicating, while adding research findings and general historical detail to his recorded narrative wherever appropriate to provide context.

It has been our great joy—and the great adventure of our lives—to discover just who this quiet, modest man really was, and to share his story.

—CHERYL FORREST

ALTHOUGH I CAME INTO THIS PROJECT LATE, I suppose it could be said I've been preparing for my part in it for decades.

In 1956, Jasha and his beautiful wife Moussia, my teachers in Tulsa, decided to create a civic ballet and I was one of the eighteen students selected to dance in the corps. Today's fully professional company, Tulsa Ballet, stands squarely on the shoulders of that first endeavor, and I am proud to have been a minor cog in its creation.

And so it began. . . Because of the professional stature of these two gifted people, the greatest dancers of the time came to Tulsa to perform. Through the years we students danced behind the five Oklahoma Indian ballerinas, luminaries such as Markova and Fonteyn, McBride and Mazzo, and a whole new generation of artists who came to learn vintage ballets from "the J's."

As a young adult I was Jasha's partner for one of his last professional performances, and even though I matured and my priorities changed, my love for ballet and for the Jasinskis never wavered. Roman Jasinski became "brother" to my husband and "Uncle Jasha" to our dancing daughters. We traveled together, laughed together, grew misty-eyed over beauty together. How could I not join Cheryl's project?

His was a life to learn from, to marvel at, to celebrate. Thank you, Jasha, for indelibly altering and enriching so many lives. This book is our tribute to you.

—GEORGIA SNOKE

# Prologue: Warsaw

*Everything happened a miracle in my life.*

IT WAS SUMMER IN WARSAW.

Clouds of heat and grownup party chatter swirled around a ten-year-old boy who was sitting idly on the grass. As he stretched out a leg and wriggled one dusty bare foot in the air, a girl turned casually in his direction. Suddenly she shrieked and rushed to kneel beside him.

"Look at that instep!" the girl cried. "Look at that arch! Oh! There are auditions for the ballet school in a month. With a foot like that, you must come!"

From such small moments are miracles born.

The girl was from the Warsaw Opera Ballet and the foot that so entranced her was eventually to carry that young boy around the world as a ballet star of international acclaim.

It would lead him to a career of promise and passion, to the joy of an enduring autumn-spring marriage, and to thousands of students half a world away whose lives he would indelibly alter.

One glance. One life-changing moment.

This is that young boy's story.

Everything happened a miracle in my life. I went to the audition and it was very serious. If I were accepted, the government would spend money on me and give me an education. A director was sitting there watching carefully. They turned me all around and looked at my spine and how I was built. Then they said, "Open your feet. Now wider. Now, can you close them?" I was able to do what they asked right away. Perfect.

The boy, Czeslaw Roman Jasinski, was accepted immediately at the school of the Warsaw Opera Ballet. Thirty-five boys were selected in all, but as the years rolled by more and more were sent home. "You'd better go and make cookies. Go be a shoemaker. Ballet is not for you."

That casual, cruel dismissal never came the young Jasinski's way. Dancing was easy for the gifted boy. His body adapted well; his legs turned out naturally. He was in love with ballet from the first day.

It was a love that would become a passion, a pinpoint focus that would divert and isolate him from many of the world's distractions. His life would both narrow and deepen into single-minded devotion. In a sense, that devotion led to a sort of wise naiveté—wise in terms of the human emotions and aspirations that create great artists, wise in the canny street sense that comes with living by one's wits, naive in the understanding of the "real world" politics that surrounded and shaped his art. But that was to come. First the young Jasinski had to develop. Despite burdens of physical and scholastic training that few were offered or could endure, there were pluses to his training. The education was painstaking, comprehensive, and, most important, free of charge, and he was given a technical grounding that would lead him ever higher in his career.

Some say the Warsaw Opera Ballet is the oldest ballet school in Europe. I walked three miles to the school and back, twice daily. I was at the school by nine in the morning, then I walked home, ate my mother's soup, and walked back. We studied geography, history, all the school subjects, from three in the afternoon to seven at night, and then I walked home again. I did this for years. Saturdays, too.

Ballet was taught differently in Warsaw than now in America. My teachers built up my body very carefully, very steadily. We mastered control before we learned to jump. We didn't move too fast. They thought we should have time to stretch our legs, make them strong, develop them. I had already walked three miles before class so I was warmed up and ready to work hard.

We didn't do long classes, either. Here in America, class can be two and a half hours long and can move very fast. All kinds of steps are put into combinations. Your brain works as hard as your body. When I was in ballet school, we never made combinations like we do in America. Because we went slowly, I never had accidents like so many dancers do. My body was strong and prepared.

Even as a child, the young Jasinski showed the elegance and regal promise of a prince. He had long legs, a finely proportioned body, and a bright, handsome face that would one day make him a favorite among the ladies. His teachers were quick to spot his talents and carefully prepared him for a classical career.

I was about eleven or twelve years old when I began to perform in operas and ballets. In FAUST there was a big kettle with fire coming out and every time the fire came out a little devil came out with a pitchfork. I was one of the devils. And I was a frog in SWAN LAKE, a beautiful frog with a big, green head. We frogs were very cute!

I finished school in the afternoon and went straight to the theatre. When I came home everyone would be asleep except my mother, who was listening for me. When I came to the door she let me in. She never slept. Then I had to study. I used candles, or I would work under the moon shining through the window. And in the morning I had to get back to school. My mother woke me at seven because I had to be back at nine.

Worst was the wintertime. When winter came I was shaking to death. I walked in the snow. "How will I get through? How will I survive this winter?"

How did he survive? By scavenging newspapers from the streets, stuffing them in his shirts, and using them to cover the holes in the worn soles of his shoes.

> The snow was so heavy! When I came home there was no one else on the streets. The theatre was dark. Everyone was gone. I walked bent over, hunched, and so cold!
>
> Sometimes I ran to class because I was late, or I rode the tram, which was a little wagon pulled by horses. That was hard because I had to pay. Sometimes we poor boys would jump up on the steps, but when we saw the conductor coming we would jump off. During snow, they changed to a sleigh. For five months it snows in Warsaw, starting in November. I walked almost all the time because my family didn't own any horses. It was our legs that took us where we wanted to go.

He walked. Studied by moonlight. Performed. Shivered in the bone-fracturing cold of Warsaw winters. It was a hard life, brutal. But now the young Jasinski had a life with a purpose.

> Before I joined the school I had never even seen a ballet. The ballet was for people who had money. For poor people like us, there was no way for you to go. If you were not rich in Poland then you didn't have any chance at all.
>
> My mother was happy that I was in the ballet and would come to the matinees when she could, but she couldn't come very often. She didn't have time. She worked all day in the kitchen to feed the family.
>
> I danced in reviews and clubs here and there in the summertime. I remember one club called Morskie Oko, "The Eye of the Ocean." We students went there to make extra money. Two hundred Polish zloty! Good money! It was kind of a review, like the Folies-Bergères or Casino de Paris. Morskie Oko brought all kinds of numbers from the United States, from France, from Europe, from everyplace. The acts stayed one month and then the shows would change. We gave two shows every night, so I wasn't through until midnight.

This was the first time we ever saw black people. They were tap dancers from America and they taught us tap. Fantastic! We knew from our school that Africans are black and Indians are gold-brown, but here we actually saw them for the first time. We loved them, these three tall guys, and learned how to say "Good morning" in English.

I also danced in an open air theatre in the summertime. We boys from the Ballet danced a Bacchanalia and I was the Bacchus, covered with a big fat costume. Because I was young, sixteen or seventeen, they made me old with special makeup. I had to dance with champagne corks in my cheeks. They would say "Cork him!"

By then, the boy was coming into his own. His ballet studies were progressing; he was watching, learning, absorbing his art; he was making performance money on the side. Life seemed better and better—until the day his good luck plummeted.

When I was seventeen I did a very stupid thing. I lost one whole season of training because of it.

The director of the Ballet, Piotr Zailich, had lots of girls, and every girl thought she was going to sleep with him, that she was going to get parts. One day when I was sitting near his office, one of the girls rushed out and ran away. Zailich saw me sitting there, and from then on it was clear there was something about me he didn't like, although I was always very polite and would bow to him.

The time came when we poor boys in the ballet school wanted some money for the tram to go back home at night. The other boys asked me to speak for them. They said, "You are very important to the Ballet. They will not throw you out. If we ask, they will throw us out, but not you." So we went to Zailich together to ask for the money.

Zailich was a terrible man. I didn't even try to tell him the whole story. I just tried to tell him that we were poor boys from poor families. He jumped like the devil from his seat and yelled, "Get out!" Then he started to come at me. I turned my head and I was the only one there. We boys had come in together but as he screamed they all ran and I was all alone.

Then he called to his secretary, "I want this boy out at this moment. I do not want him in the ballet school any more."

My teachers and professors could not understand. They went to Zailich and said, "He is such a talented boy. Why did you do this to him?" All the first dancers, the principals, went to him and asked him not to do this to me. But he said, "No! I don't want him!" He was not human. It was terrible.

Sliwinski, the director of the Opera and Ballet, was very rude. "I'm sorry. I cannot see you. I am very busy." My mother cried! "My God, you have lost so many years!" She was so despairing. I had a friend whose father was a lawyer. He wrote a registered letter to Sliwinski and then I had a telephone call. Sliwinski wanted to see me. He said he could not do anything about it, but they had done a certain damage to me and maybe they could give me some money. They gave me about two hundred zloty. This was good money. At this time the dancers were making maybe fifty zloty monthly.

I went back to the review at Morskie Oko, but to me this was the lowest life. I wanted to go up with my life. They paid me well, but it was not what I wanted. One whole season passed.

Then something very strange happened.

The Opera Ballet fired Zailich and immediately called me back to the theatre. My teachers had asked for me. Zailich had been lazy. He didn't work the corps de ballet at all. Some of them even rehearsed in their street clothes. They walked through rehearsals, never dancing full out. The new choreographer was there only two or three months. The others didn't like him because he worked them too hard. He started to make a ballet where monkeys climbed ropes. We were all monkeys. I was very good, very quick on the ropes. The others couldn't do this. They were fat with big stomachs; they couldn't do the choreography. The new man was the choreographer, ballet master, director of the Ballet, everything.

Finally they threw this director out, too. He worked the dancers too hard. But by then I was already in the corps de ballet on salary and they had given me good roles. Everyone wanted the old director back, the mean one, Zailich, so he came back. He saw me when we stood and bowed. "You are here again?" He tried to get me fired again, but he couldn't.

I was never at ease with Zailich. Never! There was a Polish general who used to come to rehearsals; he was Zailich's friend from his army days. This man was a very great general and I was afraid of him. His chest was covered with medals and all the women were crazy about him. He was a good looking man. Tall. Impressive. Even for me he was impressive. When he came to rehearsals all the women put on lipstick. You knew "someone" was watching rehearsal. But Zailich could have said at any moment, "I don't like this boy. Put him into the army," and the general would have done it. I was always uneasy with Zailich.

I graduated from the Warsaw Opera Ballet School with highest honors in May 1928. I was almost twenty-one. Our graduation performance started in early afternoon in the Grand Opera. My father was out of Warsaw at the time and my mother was too busy with cooking to come, so my friends Ludovic Matlinsky, Yurek Shabelevsky, and I graduated by ourselves and then went to a bar to celebrate.

I remember it was a Friday and we ordered vodka and tripe.

But you know, when I came back to Poland after six years as a dancer, I never once put my foot in that theatre. I would have liked to see the other people but on account of Zailich I would not go. But he gave me a good lesson for my life. If someone in later years wanted me to go to the director for them I would say, "You go and enjoy. Not I!"

It was a lesson Jasinski never forgot. For the rest of his life he focused on ballet alone—performing, training, teaching—choosing to ignore company infighting, politics, and personalities. If, from the distance of decades, his life seems insular and self-protective, it is the legacy of an angry man named Zailich whose career-killing power was never forgotten.

What did those three young boys discuss that graduation day? Formal schooling was behind them. They had immersed themselves in classical technique, learned all the ethnic dances dear to their profession, and each had choreographed his own graduation variation.

Should they try to stay with the Warsaw Opera Ballet?

Could they avoid the Polish military duty that threatened every young male's career? Or could they, should they, go somewhere else, anywhere else, to dance? Their future held as many fears as hopes.

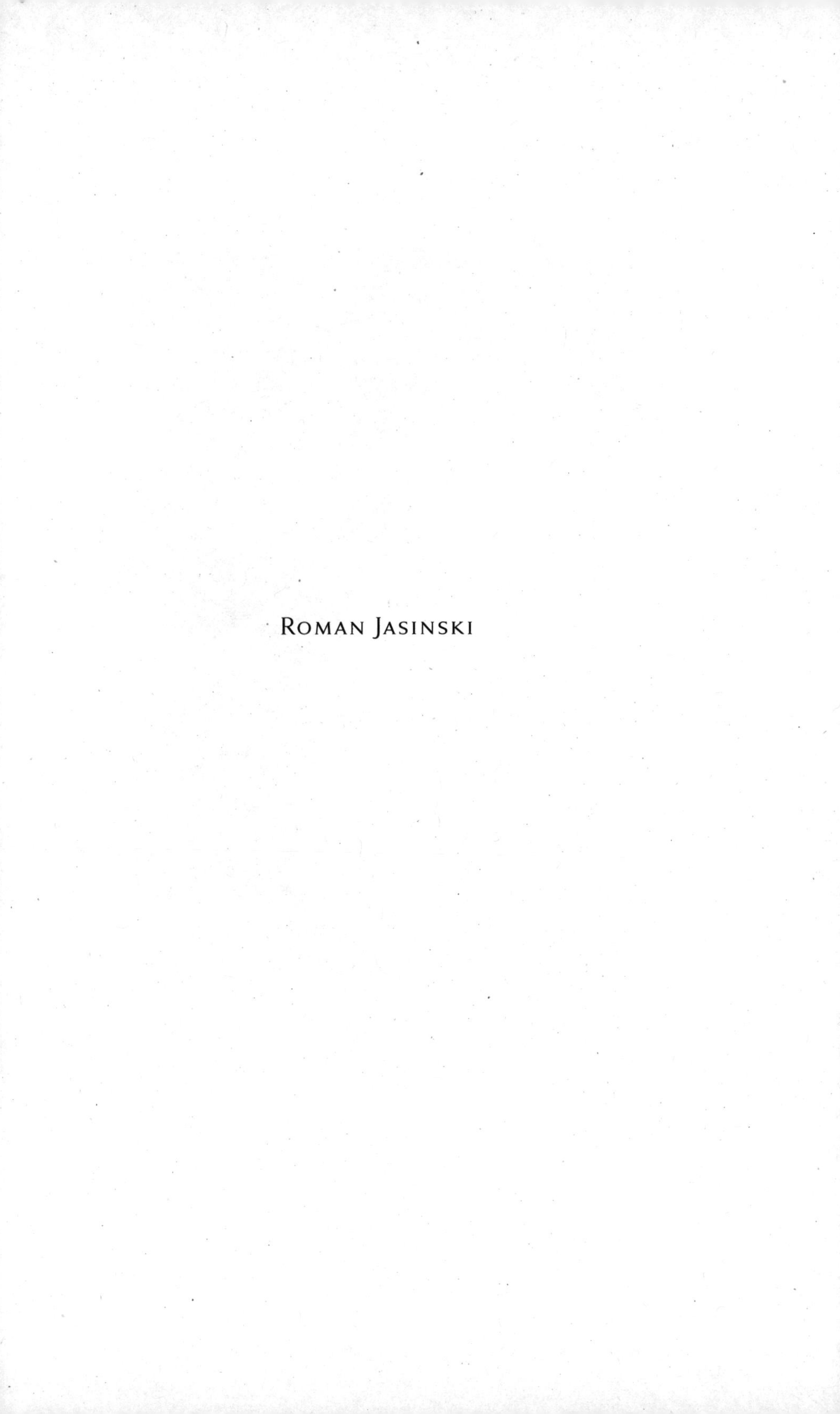

Roman Jasinski

ROMAN JASINSKI AS A YOUNG DANCER IN PARIS

Photo by Studio-Iris, Paris. Private collection.

# I

# A Gypsy in Europe

1928–1932

CHAPTER 1

# 1928: Setting the Stage

*I had in my life a certain destination.*

That there was a future at all for dancers in the twentieth century is due, primarily, to one man—the extraordinary Russian impresario Serge Diaghilev—and his dance company, the Ballets Russes.

Diaghilev developed a vision for the troupe, selected its dancers, oversaw its productions, monitored composers, storylines, sets, and wardrobe, and saw to it that top-flight publicity pulled the public in. He had an instinct for creating popular artistic taste and was blessed with a staff that was studded with genius.

The western world had never seen anything like Diaghilev's Ballets Russes. It was an amalgam of imaginative scenarios, colorful costumes, lavish sets, compelling music, and a level of soaring Russian technique hitherto unseen. Through the influence of the Ballets Russes, ballet as an art form became the toast of Europe, and Diaghilev's audiences went wild.

Brightest of the stars in Diaghilev's star-spangled company was a young man with uncanny charisma and a leap that became—and remains—legendary. His name was Vaslav Nijinsky.

Lesser known, but ultimately to have a greater impact on the world of ballet, was Nijinsky's sister, also briefly a Diaghilev dancer. Tough, demanding, smart, and shrewd, Bronislava Nijinska was securely her own woman. In time she combined in her compact person the roles of teacher, choreographer, and impresario, and she was fiercely competitive and successful in each.

Another of Diaghilev's dancers was Ida Rubinstein, a woman of exotic beauty and exceptional intellect, blessed (or perhaps cursed) with a vivid, dramatic sense of self. Born to a wealthy Jewish father with interests in railroads, Ukrainian grain, and international finance, Ida Rubenstein was a wealthy woman in her own right and had the means to pursue any interest. She grew up in St. Petersburg well-educated, well-versed in the arts, speaking several languages, and consumed with a yearning for the stage. She was plucked by Diaghilev from relative obscurity and featured in roles where her jaw-dropping beauty all but obscured her lack of versatility.

Audiences loved to behold her, and they often beheld almost every unclothed inch of her. An early, enraptured admirer gushed after her portrayal of Cleopatra that "Her long. . . peculiarly angular body seemed to have just descended from an Egyptian bas-relief, and her marvellous Eastern profile with narrow almond eyes was very appropriate to the rôle."

"Marvellous" she may have been, but, unhappily, the lady displayed more talent for self-promotion than for the art of dance.

Still, Rubinstein possessed just the right combination of aura, audaciousness, and scandal to make audiences adore her. Mistress to the extremely wealthy Walter Moyne, son of an English earl and heir to the Guinness fortune, Ida Rubinstein was flush with ego, ambition, and unlimited funds, and she was angered by the artistic restraints she felt were imposed upon her by the great Diaghilev.

Ida Rubinstein wanted to star—to *star*—in everything. So she severed her ties to Diaghilev and entered upon the world stage to exploit what dramatic and dance talents she could muster.

In 1928 she called upon former Diaghilev associates Bronislava Nijinska and Léonide Massine to create original ballets for her. Her goal was to form a whole new company—choreographers, dancers, set-designers, composers—that would perform throughout Europe, Les Ballets de Madame Ida Rubinstein. To stock its store of talent, she would seduce away from Diaghilev the choreographers, dancers, set-designers, and composers he had personally selected, trained, and promoted.

Predictably, Diaghilev was outraged.

From a distance of many decades, one wonders how much of this turmoil contributed to the famed impresario's decline and death a year later. He had created a star and, in his eyes, she had turned on him and become a monster.

Still, the stage was set. Three young graduates from the Warsaw Opera Ballet yearned for careers. A ferocious choreographer sought new talent. An aging egoist's company was open for business.

It was time for Jasinski's curtain to rise.

CHAPTER 2

# Paris!

*Coffee and croissants! Delicious!*

MY MOTHER BELIEVED IN DREAMS.

One day I found her crying. She said she had seen a woman, a stranger, in her dream. This woman pulled me away while Mama tried to hold fast to me. Mama loved me, but this other woman took me away.

Very soon after this dream one of my teachers received a letter from Paris. Bronislava Nijinska wanted dancers for a new company. The teacher came to Shabelevsky, Matlinsky, and me and said, "Would you like to go to Paris?" Can you imagine? Paris!

You know, my mother always knew in dreams what was going to happen.

Nijinska, like Diaghilev before her, often turned to the Warsaw School of Ballet for male dancers, believing that the best male dancers were Polish and the best female dancers were Russian. Jasinski thought they saw something distinctive in the temperament and training of Polish male dancers that supported their visions. And it was vital that he and his two friends be plucked out of Poland at just that moment because within months they would be called to army duty.

I didn't want the Polish army to catch me and make me a soldier. It's not like here in America today where you join the army and it is very good. The army in Poland in 1928 didn't feed you. In the morning you got black coffee, a piece of bread, and out you would go for the day to run and run. For two years you would have to run and run. What would happen to a dancer's legs? I was a classical dancer; my legs were important. If I went to the army for two years, my career would be finished.

By then my sister Janka was married to a doctor who was a major in the army. He helped release me from my service for two years. But when the two years were over, I was always afraid I would be called to duty.

It was a threat that was to haunt the young Jasinski for the next decade of his life. How could he protect himself from conscription into the Polish military? Paris was a means to escape that threat, at least for the moment, but between Paris and Jasinski lay an odd hurdle.

Jasinski had graduated at the head of his class at the Warsaw Opera Ballet School. His body and mind were trained to perform. He had already created his first choreographic piece and was in superb physical condition. And yet, at twenty-one, he looked very young. Dark hair and eyes glowed. A strong, straight nose and firm chin presaged the matinee idol looks to come. The winsome mouth smiled easily, winningly. But, no doubt about it, he looked boyish. A bit unformed, a bit baby-faced, immature. What could he do to seem dashing and debonair, an asset to sophisticated Parisian theatre?

He had a portrait photo made. The image showed a handsome young man with a false moustache penciled above his lips and a face darkened not by a haze of whiskers but by the shadows cast from a large sombrero. The ruse worked. Nijinska accepted Jasinski and his comrades.

My brothers and sisters had learned Russian in school but I did not, so I had to ask my brother, Feliks, to write Madame Nijinska in Paris. In just one week I received a letter back. Shabelevsky, Matlinsky and I were hired! Soon Nijinska sent train tickets and money for our trip. Everyone came to the train station. My mother cried and cried. "Mama, don't cry. I love you. And you still have four boys at home. I want to dance so I can help you. I will make good money and send it to you."

I was hanging out the window of the train and Mama was standing below me, crying. And then the train began to move away.

Czeslaw Roman Jasinski was to see his mother only twice more in his life, but he never lost his reverence for her. Throughout the years he lit candles to her memory. His voice softened at her name.

But at the age of twenty-one, on the brink of high adventure, his thoughts flew to the future, obscuring the people of his past as surely as the steam clouds of the departing train enveloped and concealed their diminishing forms.

We went directly to Paris in about twelve hours. My sister Janka had given us a bottle of French wine. In Poland the wine is sweet because it is from apples. This French wine was probably a good white wine, but it seemed sour. We didn't have any glasses so we had to drink from the bottle. "Too sour!" we said, and threw it out the window. In Paris we arrived at the Gare St-Lazare. Nijinska's husband was supposed to meet us at seven in the morning but it was only six.

I said, "Come on. Let's go get some hot coffee." It was a cold, rainy day. We saw a cafe, sat down and I said, "Garçon!" (I remembered "garçon." I had had three years of French in school.) "Garçon, s'il vous plaît, trois cafés au blanc!" He brought us three glasses and a bottle of wine. Can you imagine? Why did he do this? He brought white wine—blanc! We didn't know that the working people in France, first thing in the morning, drink wine. So we looked at the wine with our empty stomachs and said, "Oh, Jesus!" Then we said, "Let's have a little drink to us!" It was the vin ordinaire, very sour. We couldn't drink this—maybe half a glass. And we were hungry; we hadn't eaten anything. So we called him back for coffee.

"Garçon—"

"Oui, oui, monsieur!"

"Garçon, trois cafés au blanc s'il vous plaît!"

When we saw that he was coming with the bottle of wine and three glasses again, the three of us jumped up like tornadoes. "No, no, no! Stop, stop, stop! Café au blanc!" and he said, "Oui, oui, monsieur." Then I took him by the arm and showed him the big machine that served the coffee and milk. I said, "Café au blanc." And he said, "Non! Café au lait." I said, "Oh. Oui, oui, monsieur." That's when I saw the croissants. "Oh yeah, trois this, too!" Finally, we had coffee and croissants. Delicious!

After their first taste of food in many hours, with coffee and wine chasing the chill from their bones, the three boys were ready for the next big step.

Nijinska's husband couldn't believe Jasinski looked so young when he first saw him at the station. The other boys looked older. "What are we going to do with you?" he said. "You look like a little boy!" But there he was. So the three young dancers took their suitcases and followed.

We didn't have much. I had only one suitcase and it was only half full. I had some books and just a few clothes. One suit was on me and a black suit for church was in the suitcase along with one pair of shoes and a few shirts. That's all.

Nijinska's husband brought us straight to rehearsal in a taxi. When we came to Madame Nijinska I bowed very low and kissed her hand. "How young you are!" she said. I was scared to death she would send me back to Poland. Instead she let us leave, all three of us, because we didn't have proper rehearsal clothes. She said to come back that afternoon for our first day of rehearsal.

Two of Nijinska's dancers, Eugene Lapitsky and Serge Unger, were sent along to help us. They spoke Polish and knew what we needed. For rehearsal in Poland we wore a type of shorts with stockings and socks. In Paris everyone dressed differently. We had to buy black tights made of wool that came to the ankle, white T-shirts, socks, belts, and different ballet shoes. In Poland our shoes were canvas. In Paris they wore shoes made of leather.

The hotel they chose for us was only two or three blocks from the studio. We left our bags and then Lapitsky and Unger took us to see some sights of the city.

Rehearsal began at three. And, with it, their new life.

Lapitsky and Unger, the Polish-speaking dancers Nijinska put in charge of the three newcomers, were older than Jasinski. Both had danced with Diaghilev's Ballets Russes. They were to become Jasinski's companions and guides, taking the neophyte under wing and teaching him to maneuver venues already overcrowded with dancers desperate for a meal and a stage.

Serge Unger, born in Russia, had worked his way from Riga to Europe in his youth. His long friendship with Lapitsky stemmed from Kiev where the two young men and their colleague, Serge Lifar, were once Nijinska's students. When Diaghilev needed to replenish his roster of male dancers in 1923, Nijinska recommended that he take the three boys. Diaghilev paid for their travel and visas from Warsaw, but first they had to get through war-torn Eastern Europe to Poland.

The road was not an easy one. Armies roamed everywhere throughout Eastern Europe. Suspicion of strangers lay heavy in every averted eye. Official papers were repeatedly demanded, and failure to produce them could end in a casual bullet to the brain.

When the three succeeded in reaching Paris and joining Diaghilev's company, their technical achievements were received with a large and dismissive yawn. Sniffed Serge Grigoriev, Diaghilev's assistant, "We were disappointed to find them very weak and inexperienced. The best of the party was E. Lapitsky. The worst was a boy named Serge Lifar." How wrong he was! Serge Lifar was to become, in time, one of the greatest stars of the ballet world, and a mentor, employer, and inspiration to Roman Jasinski.

The Parisian ballet world at this time was still reeling from the effects of the Russian Revolution. Russian émigrés and escapees had fled to Paris for their lives. Former counts drove Paris taxi cabs. Impoverished ballerinas opened tiny dancing schools. All considered themselves lucky to be alive and safe from the horrors of that Russian holocaust. Such was Paris on the rainy autumn day of Jasinski, Matlinsky, and Shabelevsky's arrival. Three Polish boys had to learn different cultures, different languages, different ways of dressing, rehearsing, coping.

Young and unestablished, filled with insecurity, the boys were grateful just to be given a chance to dance. And dance they did. Constantly.

> Nijinska's ballet classes in Paris were very strange to me. Arms here and arms there in different exercises from the ones we had learned in Warsaw. No one today can believe the work we did! We started class each morning at nine o'clock, rehearsed from ten to one, lunched until three, rehearsed again until six, took dinner until eight, and then from eight until eleven o'clock in the evening had the last rehearsal of the day.
>
> And what rehearsals! Nijinska was choreographing new ballets. We worked full-out every rehearsal every day. We could not walk or mark the steps. For months we rehearsed like this!

Nine new ballets were created in all—seven by Nijinska and two by the famous choreographer Léonide Massine. Massine was given the eight o'clock to eleven o'clock evening slot, after the company had worked intensely all day with Nijinska. What an exhausting introduction to the professional world of ballet—working with two great artists, two indefatigable egos, two insatiable slavedrivers of limitless energy. The all-encompassing memory for the overworked dancers of this first Rubinstein company was of bone-numbing, mind-blotting fatigue.

> Now when my students say, "It is too hard," I say, "My Lord! You don't know what work is!" Nijinska rehearsed us nine hours a day. I was happy just to come back to my hotel and fall down on the bed!
>
> In those early days I took everything so seriously. I was learning Russian and French at the same time—French because I was living

BRONISLAVA NIJINSKA

Nijinska as she appeared in the 1936 program of Col. W. de Basil's Ballets Russes, Royal Opera House.

in Paris and Russian because that is what the company members spoke. When I came to France I had had three years of French in school, but you know how they teach you: "S'il vous plaît." "Donnez-moi." "La table." "La chaise." It was a big help to already know these words but when we came to Paris I made lots of mistakes. It took some time, but after a while I learned to think in French. I didn't speak Russian when I left home, but I learned it very quickly because it is so close to Polish.

I danced with the corps de ballet at first. Then Nijinska gave me some better parts and that caused problems with some of the other dancers who had been there longer. They called us three Polish guys "boys." But Madame said, "Anything I give them they can do."

On the other hand, we were not at all alike. Matlinsky was very strange. He would never work. Maybe it's because his mother always used to bring him breakfast in bed! They would tell him to work and he would say, "A horse needs to work. I am not a horse!" But if it was something easy, he would do it.

Shabelevsky worked as hard as I did, but he never sent any money home to his mother. My mother told Shabelevsky's mother that I sent money from my salary to her all the time, so Shabelevsky came to me and said, "My mother is so angry! Tell your mother not to tell my mother about the money."

Between the exhaustion and stimulation, the young Jasinski still had time for acute observation. Severed from his own close family, he was transported into an unfamiliar realm of incessant demands and odd ways. His gratitude to his employer never weakened his sense of fair play, and he instinctively recoiled from the verbal abuse he heard every day.

Madame would shriek at her husband in front of everyone, and he would come running. It embarrassed me a little. I didn't like it. He was some kind of military officer, very handsome. He was also a dancer with us, although he was not very good—corps de ballet only—and a kind of official in the company, too. He would call, "Madame Nijinska is coming. Everybody come out!" and we were all expected to come right away.

Still, I liked Nijinska, although she always stayed apart from the dancers, never close. I could speak Polish with her and her husband.

We never saw Miss Rubinstein for the first three months that we worked. She was there only at the end. We rehearsed with Nijinska alone. We heard stories about Madame Rubinstein, of course, but we never saw her.

In fact, members of the Rubinstein corps de ballet often joked that the company should have been called "La Compagnie des répétitions de Madame Ida Rubinstein." It never seemed to get beyond the "répétition" (rehearsal) stage. Rubinstein herself worked in private with Nijinska. Classes and rehearsals were conducted separately, leaving the curious corps to speculate wildly about the woman paying their wages and way.

Then one night, Nijinska came and said, "Tonight Madame Rubinstein will come and see the company. Please, boys, clean socks tonight, clean shirt. Girls, everything perfect." With Nijinska, boys and girls didn't sit together. Boys on one side, girls on the other.

We heard the announcement "The limousine has come!" A red carpet was rolled from the limousine down the street, down the hall, and into the rehearsal room.

Nijinska said, "Everyone stand up!" We all stood, holding our heads down respectfully, and Miss Rubinstein entered on the red carpet. "All right, everyone can sit down now." We applauded very politely and then we sat down.

How furtively the young Jasinski must have eyed the polished elegance of the wealthy woman before him. Born poor, haunted by the threat of military conscription, charged with ambition and a consuming love of dance, the young man knew that his future depended upon pleasing these two women: the self-indulgent performer and the commanding choreographer. How different their worlds from his own!

> As a dancer, Miss Rubinstein couldn't even stand on her toes. But she had lots of money! Nijinska worked hard to represent her the best way she could. In one classical ballet, Miss Rubinstein had to go on pointe. It was very hard for her so Nijinska told the girls to get around her to hide her foot.
>
> Then Nijinska choreographed BOLERO. In a Spanish ballet, you don't need to be a trained classical dancer. Nijinska placed Rubinstein on top of a big table and had all us boys around it, grabbing at her ankles. Nijinska liked the way I had so much expression as I moved. One day her husband said, "Everybody, act like this boy. Make this face! Madame likes this expression!" Nijinska was always laughing at me, but she liked what I was doing, that I had so much feeling.

The "feeling" that captivated Nijinska rose from the soul. Throughout his life Jasinski was ruled by music and story, his body responding instinctively and expressively to the choreographer's message. That can neither be taught nor bought.

Poor Ida! Surround herself as she might with expensive and extravagant spectacle, her lack of balletic talent was still painfully clear. She sought to rival Diaghilev but the final result was, to be charitable, "uneven." The "star" could not live up to the firmament surrounding her. A dancer in one of Rubinstein's later companies recalled that "as a static Goddess she was admirable; but as a dancer, no." Even Nijinska was heard to mutter, "Madame Rubinstein can do anything—but without virtuosity."

All the hours, the exhaustion, the "répétitions" without cease, had an ending at last on 26 November 1928 when the curtains opened on Les Ballets de Madame Ida Rubinstein. As an attempt to add lustre to the Rubinstein mystique, the company was a questionable success.

Nonetheless it launched some outstanding careers. Former students became professional performers in that Paris Opera premiere. They were rehearsed by a remarkable and renowned choreographer, performed with a woman of undeniable stardom, and entertained an audience of discernment and sophistication. Composer Maurice Ravel was in the pit, conducting his *Bolero* for the very first time. The greatest set and costume designers of the era contributed their gifts. Despite the downside, these were heady days for young, unpolished performers.

That first Rubinstein season combined the sublime and the ridiculous. Rubinstein's lover, the earl's son, is said to have spent over a million English pounds on her touring career. Yet despite all her money and all her beauty, Rubinstein suffered agonies of onstage insecurity. She was forty-three years old. Her stage fright before each performance was of the cowering, quaking kind. She must have been aware that her friends tittered through her performances, and yet there seemed no way she could calm the fierce desire to perform.

A disgruntled Serge Diaghilev, in the audience at her debut, dismissed her efforts as "astonishingly provincial, boring and long-drawn-out," but Diaghilev was hardly disinterested. She was a formidable rival to his Ballets Russes.

THE IMPRESARIO: Serge Diaghilev (1872–1929)

Painting by Valentin Aleksandrovich Serov.

Critics sneered that Nijinska had sold her talents to support Rubinstein's self-promotion. As for Rubinstein herself, Serge Lifar complained that she "had nothing of the dancer, and the role that she attributed to herself—that of prima-ballerina of her troupe—could only compromise the success of the performances."

Every aspect of Rubinstein's fledgling company underwent scrutiny. One of Diaghilev's more scathing descriptions read: "The theater was full, but as for success—it was like a drawing room in which someone has suddenly made a bad smell."

By this time, Diaghilev had reached the end of his legendary verve and energy. He was exhausted, disillusioned, in poor health, and yet the show—his show—had to go on. He was genuinely terrified of any success Rubinstein might have that would filter audience away from his company. He had "created" Rubinstein. Now this "static goddess" whom he had brought to life was using his choreographers, his set designers, his composers, and even some of his dancers, in more original works than his own company could produce. He ridiculed her costumes ("like a Pavlova swan, specially got up for some Moulin Rouge performance"), but beneath the sharpness of his rhetoric lay enormous anxiety. The woman could afford anything! He and his Ballets Russes could not.

Of the nine new ballets, *Bolero,* written just for Rubinstein, was the greatest success. It must have been mesmerizing. An enthralled viewer later wrote, "With an almost demonic indifference, Ida Rubinstein turned without pause . . . on an immense round tavern table, while at her feet the men, expressing an unleashed passion, struck themselves until they bled." *Bolero* was considered by some critics to be the best production of the season.

Reviews of the overall effort were mixed. Negative reporters pointed fingers at Rubinstein's self-aggrandizement and lack of technique, while supporters said she "was treading in the steps of Diaghilev." What she accomplished, one wrote, was "an art so expressive, so simple and grand, that [it left] tears in the eyes."

In fury Diaghilev wrote to Lifar: "Stravinsky was seen in Ida's dressing room, where it appears he said: 'Delightful: I say it from the heart: charming.' . . . But the morning after the show Stravinsky rang up to say how disappointed he had been, how indignant the whole thing made him."

The much anticipated performances continued, and then, within days, were over. The whispers and sneers, the accolades and applause, all faded. Ahead stretched a new road for the young Polish trio of Jasinski, Matlinsky, and Shabelevsky—touring with Rubinstein to some of Europe's most glamorous cities.

> We were in Italy two months at least, going first to Milan at La Scala and then to Naples. At that time it was the rule in European ballet companies for the corps de ballet to travel by third class on the train, the soloists by second class, and the principals and directors by first class. By then I was a soloist. They had moved me very fast. Any place I danced, they quickly moved me to soloist.
>
> The company paid us more when we were on tour. Instead of 1,300 francs a month, they paid us 1,800 francs. Miss Rubinstein wanted to pay us more still, but Nijinska was against this. She made so much money she didn't need to worry, but she didn't want her dancers to make much money. "When you give dancers more money they will spend it drinking in a café and come in drunk the next day. That's why we don't pay them."

All was new, all exciting, to the young and impressionable company. Only a year before, the boys from Poland couldn't afford a tram ride to their Warsaw theatre. Now they were dancing in Monte Carlo, Rome, Vienna, and Brussels, with more Parisian performances to come in May 1929. Jasinski was escaping the Polish army and sending what he could to help out at home.

Then, in May 1929, it was suddenly over.

> Miss Rubinstein simply said, "I am tired. Good-bye." But she was a very sweet lady. She gave Shabelevsky, Matlinsky, and me second-class tickets back to Poland and one month's extra salary.
>
> We didn't use the tickets—we traded them for money. I already knew I would rather die than to go back to Poland. I wanted to help my family and I could do that only by dancing. It would be a disaster to go into the Polish army.

> Nijinska told Unger and Lapitsky, "Take care of this boy. Find him a job." That was what this woman arranged for me after the Rubinstein company was over. I will never forget what she did for me!

Nor did he. It was Nijinska who brought him out of Poland, who saw something unique in his talent. It was Nijinska who acted as a remote sort of mentor. Jasinski was to dance for her many times in his career. She had given him the chance to leap from the familiar into the future, and his loyalty to the woman would never waver.

> I went to the Polish consulate and got permission to stay for another year. I was so afraid of being sent back. I saw my future in Europe, not in Poland.

CHAPTER 3

# The Gypsy Years

*For me, it was heaven just to eat.*

In the dance world, a "gypsy" is one who travels from show to show, company to company, always competing for a job, a salary, a place.

By mid-1929, big ballet companies were scarce. Diaghilev reigned with his Ballets Russes, and elsewhere choreographers cobbled together ephemeral groups that toured hand to mouth, performing wherever and whenever they could.

Jasinski was resourceful and intelligent and had already begun to make friends in this dog-eat-dog world. His gypsy life began.

> A Polish man named Kruczewski organized a tour. I didn't like him. He made a small company using Polish dancers in Polish costumes, but everything he did was very cheap, not very good. I liked working in a better way, but there was nothing else to do. Shabelevsky, Matlinsky, and Matouchevsky, a dancer from Diaghilev's Ballets Russes, were in the company. Unger and Lapitsky were not on this tour because they were from Russia.
>
> We rehearsed in Kruczewski's Paris apartment, moving tables and chairs so we could dance. Sometimes he gave us something to eat, but I remember that there was a very small restaurant nearby that

prepared the best mussels with cream of anyone in the world. Mussels and cream and French bread!

We went to Italy with Kruczewski. I had a hard time getting a visa. Italy didn't want to give us visas at first. Kruczewski was always busy, running around to get visas and passports. Somehow he managed all this.

I don't remember where we went or what we danced. It was not a very good company and I was anxious to get paid and get back to Paris with my money.

I never had enough money to pay my hotel bill before I left for tour. Each time I would show the concierge my ballet contract and she would say, "Leave your suitcase. Then I'll know you'll come back to pay me." I would have to leave the suitcase and go just as I was dressed.

When we came back from the Kruczewski tour the concierge just said, "Your suitcase is gone!" Just like that! Everything important was in this suitcase—programs and pictures and all my books—everything. All my earliest memories—gone. I still feel this loss.

But this is how I lived, from little tour to little tour.

For the next three years Jasinski led a vagabond's life, searching for, and bouncing from, one itinerant company to another across Europe. He eluded the ever-present threat of army service in Poland, learned his craft, and began to make his mark.

I went to Vincennes, an area of the poor in Paris, and took an apartment with Matlinsky and Shabelevsky. We lived together on the money from Rubinstein's tickets to Poland.

I would go to the market but I told them, "I'll buy the food, but all of us need to cook because I don't want to cook all of the time." The Matlinsky boy didn't have the slightest idea about cooking. We tried his mess and then he was out. Shabelevsky was a better cook. But I was lucky. Unger and Lapitsky took me for work. A Russian woman in

Paris set this up and I left my friends some money and the apartment because I had paid for it in advance.

We sailed from Marseille, renting chaises longues on the top deck for ten francs. In the morning we arrived in Africa for this job.

The three of us danced for one month at a casino in Fort de l'eau, an Algerian resort on the Mediterranean coast. The customers played the casino, dined in a fine restaurant, went to a theatre, listened to singers in a nightclub. For us, it was like a vacation. We swam all day and worked only at night. We were given both money and food and did a Russian dance with jumps and knee bends on a hard stone floor. Here in America dancers complain if the floor is too hard but I danced there because I needed to eat.

In Africa we made little trips to Tunis, Algiers, and Casablanca. Casablanca shocked me! The streets were very dirty, very narrow, and they smelled. We went up and down all these steps. And so many prostitutes! Two men took us there, one in front and one behind. They walked with us and they had guns because it was a very dangerous place. If anyone killed us our bodies would never be found.

When our stay was over, we took an overnight boat back to Marseille. I paid ten francs for a chair on the deck and lay down. It was a beautiful night and I fell asleep right away. Suddenly I woke to darkness and wind. There was tremendous rain. The boat was up and down, up and down. Everywhere screaming and terrible panic. We were all afraid the boat was going to sink. I tried to go downstairs but there was an awful smell there where people were pressed together and sick in the corridors.

I ran back up. Lapitsky, Unger, and I belted ourselves to a canopy pole to keep the wind from blowing us off the boat. There were no lifeboats—not even life preservers. All the chairs were gone into the sea. I fell asleep standing belted to the pole. The captain turned from the storm and headed towards the Canary Islands. At last the sea was beautiful and calm. You could look down and see the bottom. We were able to turn again and go back to Marseille.

After Africa, I had another little job. The Russian woman who got us the job at Fort de l'eau took us to Malaga, Spain. We traveled on a freight train. Back then, if people didn't have far to go, they sat in the baggage car. We were in with the chickens and cows. The train did not go directly to Malaga; it went here and there to leave off packages. But after four days we reached Malaga and danced all kinds of numbers in the "toros" place, the arena where they fight the bulls.

I had these little jobs constantly—Italy, Africa, the south of France. Other times I didn't dance at all. I would have one month, maybe, without a job, but I was very economical. I knew how to live on little.

On 19 August 1929, shocking headlines hit all the French papers. Serge Diaghilev, the most successful impresario of his day, had died suddenly in Venice. With him died his Ballets Russes—audacious, provocative, challenging arbiter of balletic taste and talent for the past twenty years. Diaghilev's company had been rich earth, nurturing creative forces of all kinds. Upon his death, seasoned dancers, musicians, and artists found themselves abruptly uprooted and unemployed. Many of the major influences on Jasinski's later professional life were suddenly "at large." Luminaries such as Alexandra Danilova, George Balanchine, Alicia Markova, and Serge Lifar were suddenly on the streets scrambling for jobs. Not much was left for a young Polish dancer with only a year's experience.

Some years later, ballerina Alexandra Danilova told Jasinski that Diaghilev had seen him dance with Rubinstein and had said he wanted him for his company. It would have given the young man the established ballet home he longed for, knowledgeable mentors to guide him, colleagues of taste and talent. But Diaghilev died and it was not to be.

I was always dreaming maybe one day I, too, could be part of this company, like lots of other of Polish men. I never met Diaghilev but he was in the audience once when I danced. He had his eye on me.

Danilova told me later that Diaghilev had said good-bye when their contracts ended in May and told them how beautiful everything would be the next year, that they had a very good contract. And then in the paper came the big headline, "Death of Diaghilev."

Diaghilev's longtime assistant Serge Grigoriev received the telegram: "Diaghilev died this morning. Inform company. Lifar." "I read this terrible telegram over and over again," said Grigoriev. "I could not take it in. Diaghilev dead! The idea seemed nonsensical. And then, as the truth was borne in on me, I grew dizzy, and for the first time in my life I fainted."

The ballet world was shattered.

Those years were very hard. Many outstanding dancers were suddenly without jobs. I didn't know what was going to happen but I knew that I would come out somehow from all these problems. I was lucky. Most of the dancers were sitting, doing nothing. I would just go around from place to place. I was not capricious; I needed to eat. There were many little companies dancing wherever they could. Here, now, people could never dance like this in America. They need a special floor. They must have this, they must have that. They could never survive the way I survived. I danced to eat.

We found out about jobs at a certain cafe on Place d'Italie. There was a Frenchman, Leo Staats, who was the ballet master and choreographer at the Paris Opera. He needed dancers for a movie, LES MISÉRABLES. When I heard this I ran to the Opera, found the people who were hiring and said, "I need to dance! Please!" They hired me.

By now I was living on Rue Pigalle and had to walk a long way to meet the bus. It came at six in the morning to the Opera and about thirty people boarded. We were driven to Fontainebleau, a beautiful château where the kings once lived, about twenty-five miles from Paris. There were no stars there; we were just a background waltz for a scene in a ballroom hung with great chandeliers.

It was cold and I was very hungry. I had thought maybe I could get an advance but the man said, "No, we will pay you at the finish. Three days."

I don't know how I survived sometimes.

Paris at this time was the center of dance in Europe. Flooded with aristocratic refugees from the Russian Revolution and studded with unemployed artists from the disbanded Diaghilev company, it seethed with poverty-stricken energy and ambition. One of its principal teachers was Princess Troubetzkoy, better known as Lubov Egorova, a former ballerina with the Imperial Ballet in St. Petersburg and Diaghilev's Ballets Russes. To her studio on Rue de la Rochefoucauld flocked the talented poor. She salved their hunger and ambition by serving them hot tea and hard technique. Her wealthier students subsidized the poorer ones by paying full fees.

At Egorova's studio the stars of the future came and crossed and congregated: David Lichine, Boris Kniasev, Oleg Tupine, Roman Jasinski—and, most important to our tale, Serge Lifar, who appeared again and again like a shining thread in Jasinski's darkest moments, pulling him steadily toward life, freedom, and fame. With a nudge here and a hand there, Lifar saved Jasinski time and again and set him on his way. Egorova's studio was just the beginning.

I took class with Egorova. Her studio was very small, like all the other studios in Paris. There were barres all the way around the room and a little mirror in the middle. Everybody tried to get in front of the mirror.

I was always hungry in those years—and exhausted, too. But I will never forget a certain moment. There was rain. It was cool. Serge Lifar was giving the class. . .

An English dancer who later came to know that studio well described it as "the Black Hole of Calcutta . . . with a linoleum floor, no ventilation and the thermometer mounting towards 90°F." For Jasinski, however, the chance to receive expert teaching for free and to associate with others of like mind overrode any discomfort. He never uttered a word of complaint.

Madame Egorova was an awfully sweet lady and everyone came to her. In the morning when I got up I had not even one franc for food. I walked from my apartment in Vincennes, and it was very far. That is when I moved to Rue Pigalle. Egorova knew that everyone was hungry. She put on hot water and we had tea and two little sweet biscuits. That was all. For me, it was heaven just to eat! Every day we went and got hot tea and two biscuits and then went to work. Egorova was sweet because she knew we had no money. She made money from her French students. There were some good students from the Paris Opera who came and took class. Some of them had rich men to support them.

Hot tea and sweet biscuits, too soon consumed, forged an enduring, lifelong sense of obligation in the hungry student towards his generous teacher. He never forgot Egorova, repeatedly sending books, food, and mementos from the United States to her Paris home in gratitude for her generosity.

Her studio was a creative crossroads.

Egorova's studio is where I came to know Kniasev, a really crazy guy. I would dance in his company three or four times in the years to come. Serge Lifar gave adagio class to the boys, and David Lichine was in the studio all the time taking class. He had been with me in Rubinstein's company; it was before he became a soloist. He was from Russia and somehow changed his name from Lichtenstein to Lichine. I met Oleg Tupine there, too, who later became one of my greatest friends. He was a Russian boy who was also poor, so he didn't pay, either. His mother came to the studio sometimes to sell meat pies because she needed the money. They were dough with meat, or sometimes cabbage or potatoes inside. This was Russian. You bought it for a franc or so.

I also took class with Alexandre Volinine, a first dancer, who was once the partner of Anna Pavlova. I can never forget him. He had a school in Paris with lots of girl students but not enough boys to partner them. He gave me free classes because I stayed after class and partnered these big, rich American girls. Lots of Americans came to Paris and studied with him because he was very well known with Pavlova.

These American girls were kind of fat because they had the money to eat. I was thin, you see, like skeleton. I remember a pain in my shoulder. It started to hurt because I lifted them up and down. I'd finish with one and run and pick up another. I don't remember if they were good dancers. I was so hungry, I didn't notice. My business was to lift them!

An enthusiastic visitor a year or two after Jasinski's time wrote, "The girls wear bathing suits to prevent possible accidents. . . . The skill with which quite recent beginners catch their partners after a grand jeté is a remarkable tribute to all concerned." Our hungry Polish boy had quite another point of view.

Whew! How I would shake! When I finished the class I was worn out. This man gave a strong class. But this is what is kind of sad: he never ever asked if I was hungry or would like a piece of bread. And the smell of the soup! I could smell the soup coming from the kitchen and my stomach would cramp from the hunger. My nose was telling my stomach to go to the kitchen, but this man never asked if I would like to eat something after class.

And after this, I walked, walked, walked home. It was a very long walk. His studio was far, but to get a free class I went there.

Many years later, I met Volinine here in the United States, but he didn't remember me. I talked to him but never mentioned that I was the hungry student from Paris. Everything had changed. At this time he was not so successful and I was already "somebody." My feeling was not to embarrass him. Now he was in that down position and I was going up. You see, in life, funny things.

I worked anyplace I could find a job. Most people couldn't find work but I was lucky. My two friends from Poland often didn't have any work. It was thanks to Nijinska and the two boys she had looking after me that I could find jobs.

In spring 1930 Nijinska asked me to join a company with a very great Russian ballerina, Olga Spessivtzeva, at the London Coliseum. Nijinska choreographed PAYSAGE ENFANTIN for her. We dancers called it "the bug ballet." Spessivtzeva was the night bug and we were the little bugs, termites, who ate the tree. I wore a cylinder around my body, black tights, and black shoes and I had a little stick for our dance.

Once again, Jasinski, Unger, and Lapitsky were working with Nijinska, along with Jasinski's fellow Poles Shabelevsky and Matlinsky. In addition to "eating the tree," Jasinski played the part of the "Ant Don Juan," Lapitsky was "the Musician Grasshopper," and Unger was "the Tenor Bird." The ballet has long since been lost to time, probably mercifully, but Jasha's memory of the great, gifted, doomed Spessivtzeva remained with him to the end of his life.

Spessivtzeva was really a fantastic ballerina. I had never seen a dancer like her. She seemed to be in the air all the time, never touching the floor. There was something strange about her, though. I remember her laughing—sort of hysterical—after she finished the performance. Her dressing room was not far from ours and I would hear this loud high laughter through the walls. Later I heard she went a little bit crazy.

The "little bit crazy" led to eventual insanity. The fine line between genius and mental instability was crossed too easily, but the impact of Spessivtzeva's genius remained.

This is where my life changed again. That summer Boris Kniasev found out that I was back in Paris and asked me to join his company. I had met Kniasev at Egorova's studio. He was a choreographer, dancer and director—kind of a crazy guy.

Yurek Shabelevsky was also in the company. We had been together most of the time since coming to Paris from Poland. Lichine was there, too, from Ida Rubinstein, and this is when I worked first with Paul Petroff.

I started to work for Kniasev for food only. We rehearsed without money. He didn't pay you, but he took you to a restaurant and paid for your food. Once a day. We would come together at nine o'clock in the morning, but no one wanted to work. We would say, "We didn't have coffee." And Boris would order someone, "Bring us coffee and croissants!" and we would have coffee in the morning.

He started then to give a class, followed by rehearsal. It took Kniasev hours before he actually did some steps, and then he would change them. It was a big mess!

We worked like this until six. No lunch! And then we would say, "Boris, we are tired. We need to go and eat!" And he would say, "No! Once more. Once more!" He was crazy! He could work without stop for twenty-four hours. He was excited about his work but all we were thinking about was food.

Then he would take us to a restaurant. We'd get a couple of tables and order anything we wanted, and he'd pay for it. I would eat and eat. But since he didn't have any money either I don't know how he arranged to do it. Somehow he always found someone to borrow the money from. This was kind of an adventuresome life. Not everybody can do it. You must have talent, too.

In 1930 a conductor from Italy, Carolus-Duran, came to Paris to form a small company of about five people. Kira Stcherbatcheff, a very pretty girl, was my partner. We danced together often. Lapitsky was there, too, and because he spoke a little Polish, he was a big help to me when everyone else in the company spoke only French and Russian.

We went on tour to the south of France for one month because it was always warm there. It was at this time that my name was changed. I had been dancing under the name of "Czeslaw Jasinski" until then. The director asked, "What is your name?" "Czeslaw." He stared at me and said, "Czeslaw? What kind of a name is Czeslaw? How can anyone spell Czeslaw? Do you have another name?" "Well, yes. I am Catholic. We have many names. I am also 'Roman.' "

"All right. You are 'Roman' from now on!"

And so I became Roman Jasinski, but Nijinska and others who knew me in those early days continued to call me Czeslaw. "Jasha" was my nickname from Jasinski. No one but a Pole could say Czeslaw.

Not only could no one spell or say "Czeslaw" but there seemed widespread difficulty in spelling "Jasinski," as well. Throughout his performing career most programs listed him as "Jasinsky," with a Russian "y"—perfectly appropriate for a Russian ballet troupe—but in the latter, American, part of his life, Jasha preferred the Polish spelling of his name with an "i." So we have "Jasinsky" and "Jasinski," both of which are correct. However, in his youthful dancing days when he was listed haphazardly in various small companies, we found him as "Jasinskiy," "Jassinsky," and "Yassinsky," among others, and even on occasion "Yazvinsky," an obvious confusion with an older dancer. In deference to Jasha's wishes, we write the Polish spelling of his name unless we make a direct quote.

With this tour, the Tournées de Charles Baret, we traveled all day on the train. We left it only to dance. We didn't have hotels; we slept in the theatre. Sometimes they brought some beds from schools and put them in the dressing rooms and we slept there.

We lived like this for one month or so, dancing for Baret, even though, by then, we could pay for beds. I was making good money—one hundred francs daily. But you see, it was a resort area and there were no rooms for us. Rich people would rent rooms in private homes two or three years ahead. Every year the same people came there. Since I couldn't rent a room, I made 3,000 francs on this tour!

I ate three times a day for twenty-five francs. The rest was cash. Then one day there was no hotel and no bed in the theatre either—they didn't want to keep us in the theatre. They put the girls someplace and we boys slept on benches in the park. We had our suitcases with us and we slept there. When it started to rain we put newspapers on our faces. My friend said, "Let's go to the train station." We thought the train station would be open, but it was closed. It was about four or five in the morning and the station didn't open until six.

Later in the morning we went to work again. We were so exhausted! The director wanted to make a longer tour but I told him, "I don't care how much you pay me. I just cannot do it!"

I caught cold, I remember, and I coughed. In the Pyrenees toward the end of the tour I was so exhausted I fell asleep on the train and you know, they couldn't wake me up, I was asleep so strong! They took me by the arms and legs, took me outside, and put me on the platform, still sleeping. Somehow they finally woke me. We finished the tour and I came back to Paris.

After the tour I had a sickness in Paris and the doctor told me I would die.

I never thought that I would die; that had never occurred to me. I had a friend—a girl—who helped me. She brought me food and the doctor came every evening. I paid him ten francs and he said to her, "There is a chance that this boy will die. I cannot save him."

What? Die? He is crazy! It turned out I had the Spanish flu—the sickness that killed people all over Europe.

Overworked, scrimping to send money home, battling constant hunger and frequent cold, the young Jasinski was in dangerously fragile health. His stamina was shattered. It was one thing to forge grimly ahead when feeling robust, but when the outlook was bleak and the future dim, how must that sick and saddened boy have longed for rest, warmth, a little casual kindness.

Later that summer I had another job with my partner from Baret, Kira Stcherbatcheff. There was a Russian lady, Nevelska, who had a little studio in Cannes. Kira and I couldn't pay her for classes because we didn't have any money so we had the idea to go to the casino at Cannes and see if we could get a job.

Nevelska had a very good heart. She choreographed all the numbers to help us and then she rehearsed us. The director liked what we did and took us.

I was supposed to be there one month, but I was there only one day. I remember it was so hot that I dripped with sweat. After the first dance, I was supposed to change to boots but I sweated so much I could not put the boots on. When they called me for the next dance I was naked. They called me to the stage, but I couldn't go and I missed my entrance. Kira went on to dance without me, dancing anything that came to her mind. The director came to me and said, "Fired!" Just like that! "Fired!" I tried to explain about the boots but he didn't want to listen. He said, "She can dance without you." Then he threw me out of there. I was very unhappy that I lost my job.

A funny thing though. Some fifty years later when my company, Tulsa Ballet Theatre, was touring in California, a lady from the audience met my son, Roman. She had seen his name, "Roman Jasinski," in the program and wondered if it could really be me, how I could look so young! She wrote me a note, and it was signed, "Kira Stcherbatcheff"!

CHAPTER 4

# Kniasev: Not Crook But Magic

*It was a struggle just to survive.*

AND SO THE PICK-UP JOBS CONTINUED. A week here, a month there, doing hand-to-mouth work that barely sustained body and soul. But bit by bit Jasinski was learning his craft, and bit by bit he was becoming known.

Kniasev had no money. I don't know how he arranged anything. I would say he was kind of—I don't know what you call people like this—not crook, but magic.

There was an American lady who supported him. She paid for the rehearsals and the bills in the restaurants, and he pretended he was in love with her.

This lady had a daughter that I partnered. She was blonde and beautiful, but not a very good dancer. Kniasev told this lady he would make a ballet for her daughter called UN FAUNE and they would film it for a movie. Kniasev was the faun, I was the shepherd, and the daughter was the shepherdess. We had a couple of sheep. It was kind of a dirty story. I went with the girl to do love in the forest and the faun jumped from tree to tree, watching us. Kniasev spent lots of the lady's money on this film. He brought a whole army to Fontainebleau with cameras and sandwiches. We spent about three days filming there. The American woman was rich and she paid for everything until we finished.

Later, I was working near Rue St-Lazare and saw the Russian director who made the film. "Hello. When can we see this movie?"

"Movie? What movie?"

I looked at him, thinking maybe he was the wrong man. "What do you mean? We were three days making this movie!"

"Yes, you spent three days. But there was no film inside the camera!"

Kniasev took the money from the American lady so we could have three days of sandwiches!

Although Jasinski's recollections of Boris Kniasev were accompanied by the fond nod of a young admirer for an engaging rogue, Kniasev was a serious dancer who partnered many of the world's great ballerinas, and a serious director of many ballets. His career as a dancer was long; his career as a teacher, longer. Critics and reviewers used such words as "elegance" and "poet of the dance" to describe Jasha's "crazy guy." Beneath Kniasev's charming, quixotic, opportunistic exterior a serious artist lived, employing whatever means were necessary to further his work. He also could provide an occasional kindness to an eager young dancer.

I came back to work too soon after the Spanish flu. Somehow on a bus a cold wind blew on me and for three weeks I was sick again. My face became crooked. I couldn't talk or anything. Oh gosh, I couldn't eat. I would put the spoon in my mouth and all the food would fall out. It was terrible. Kniasev took me to his doctor. The doctor said I had a nerve spasm—Bell's palsy. I was very weak. I went to this doctor for three weeks and he gave me an electric massage to straighten my face. Beep, beep, beep, beep, beep. It was very old-fashioned. There was a wire and a pump and your whole face shook. But it worked! After two weeks I was better and eventually my crooked face was gone. Then the doctor told me, "For two years you must not get in a draft. Don't open the window or, if the windows are open, sit someplace where there is no window." I was very careful for two years and this finally passed. Really, sometimes I don't know how I survived. I thought God was probably testing just how much one human being can take.

In Italy, we had a performance one day in Rieti, not far from Rome. There were only four people in the audience. I remember the windows were broken and snow fell down on the stage. It was cold. There was no heat, nothing. I was running in place on the stage to keep my muscles warm while the snow kept coming in. Finally, we dancers said, "Excuse us. There are only four people in the audience. We cannot do this performance." And we left the theatre.

Not far from our hotel was an empty restaurant run by a nice Italian man. He made lots of spaghetti for us and gave us everything else to eat—sausage, vino, everything. I ate about four plates of spaghetti! The next day when we needed to leave he was such a sweet man, he made us breakfast free in the morning.

It was in Rome that I received a telegram that my father had died. He was seventy-four years old and his intestine had closed. I didn't even have the money to go home to pay my respects. It was a struggle just to survive.

I was also with Kniasev when he made some kind of connection with Monte Carlo. Oh, it was so beautiful there! Blue sea, blue sky, clear air. Fantastic! We gave four performances in January of 1931, and I met René Blum, the Monte Carlo theatre director. I was to know him well in later years. We lived in a very good hotel there, having anything we wanted—dinner, lunch, anything! It was a beautiful hotel. At the end of this tour, Blum paid Kniasev the money the company had earned—and Kniasev went to the casino at Monte Carlo and lost it all! The whole company had no money to go back to Paris! We had no money for our beautiful hotel! We moved from the hotel and started hunting for Kniasev. He was missing for three days. Finally,

René Blum gave us tickets back to Paris and he said, "Boris Kniasev never never put your foot in the Monte Carlo casino again!"

Truth to tell, Boris Kniasev did put his foot again in Monte Carlo, and the man who hired him was René Blum, proving that even in the ballet world expedience can take precedence over experience. But in spring 1931, when Jasha and the rest of the Kniasev company were reeling from lost wages and lost respect for their chagrinned and chastened leader, the dancers could do nothing but retreat to Paris.

BORIS KNIASEV AND ROMAN JASINSKI

Kniasev is at center, with the diagonal dark band; Jasinski is over his left shoulder, in profile.

Courtesy Jerome Robbins Dance Division, The New York Public Library for the Performing Arts, Astor, Lenox, and Tilden Foundations.

CHAPTER 5

# A Chance to Dance

*A big new company was being formed.*

A STUDY OF PARISIAN DANCE PROGRAMS from the early 1930s shows an amazing wealth of companies. Whether they survived by artistry or chicanery, were serious efforts or egotistical exploitations, they provided sporadic work and sporadic pay for eager performers looking for a chance to dance.

In the summer of 1931 Jasinski, Lapitsky, and Unger found themselves united once again with Nijinska and Rubinstein, dancing with Les Ballets de Madame Ida Rubinstein in both Paris and London. Again, they pawed at Ida's ankles in *Bolero* with Ravel conducting in the pit. Again, they presented new and old works by Massine and Nijinska. And again, they worked with costumes and sets created by the best artistic minds in Paris. Rubinstein's talents were limited, but her funds were not. As the ballet critic André Levinson lamented in reviewing the season of 1931, "How sad that Mme Rubinstein, who stages so many important productions, persists in spoiling everything by becoming a star."

The seasons were short. By 18 July the London performances were over, and after one more brief tour with Kniasev, Jasinski rejoined his friends Lapitsky and Unger. Together, they seized the chance for a month-long "vacation" in the south of France with minimal work amidst maximum luxury. They did not know that of the three who went, only two would return.

The Russian lady in Paris—the one who sent Lapitsky, Unger, and me to Africa and Malaga—prepared a little company of about eighteen dancers for a job in Nice. There was a marquis there who had an enormous villa, three floors high with maybe forty rooms. He would invite fifty or sixty friends every year to spend a vacation there. Some would leave and others would take their places. There were always new guests.

We signed a contract for one month. The marquis didn't pay us much, just enough to live on, but the food was fantastic. French cooking! We ate the same food as the guests, but at a separate table. First we had wine, then we danced.

The tables were in the villa's park and they built a place where the guests could dance in the center. They had an orchestra, cocktails, champagne, and then they served dinner. They had forty cooks there! We were the entertainment. They built a special outdoor stage for us.

In the mornings we would go to swim. Three of us boys and two girls rented a villa not too far from the beach for not much money. The boys' job was to go to the market where the peasants brought food and sold it. They had good fresh vegetables but the meats were covered with lots of flies—not like here in America where our meat is refrigerated. The girls cooked whatever we brought home and washed the dishes.

Then, in the middle of the month, a relative of the marquis died and he closed his villa. He gave the order that everyone had to leave. He paid us for the whole month, although we had danced for probably only two weeks. We stayed there in our villa for the rest of the month because we had already paid and were on vacation.

And then Lapitsky went to swim in the ocean. Everyone told him not to go far out because it was dangerous. Big rocks were hidden under the water and the waves were strong; the waves took him up and crashed him down. I remember how Unger searched all night up and down the beach in the dark, calling, calling his name.

Eugene Lapitsky probably died in late summer or early fall of 1931. His name was in the Rubinstein London cast list of July, but seems to disappear from all programs thereafter.

A photograph from the Ida Rubinstein program of 1928 shows a stocky man, older than Jasinski, in a stylized tunic and bloomers. Lapitsky was a soloist, one of Nijinska's most reliable dancers. It was an honor to be featured in the Rubinstein program, for Ida Rubinstein was the focus, founder, and funder of her company, and she did not encourage competition.

Many young artists from that company went on to fame in the decades following. Lapitsky may well have joined them, but for one careless moment in the waves of the Mediterranean.

When he was interviewed, Jasha was curiously reluctant to talk about Lapitsky's death. He simply shook his head, muttering, "I needed to work on myself." It was his lifelong means of coping, turning away sadness and getting on with life. The phrase became his mantra for each sorrow meted out by fate. "I needed to work on myself."

And how does a dancer "work on himself"? By throwing yet more effort and energy into his art.

It was probably during the Rubinstein tour in July 1931 that choreographer Léonide Massine tapped Jasinski for another job. There was to be a month of rehearsal in London, followed by a waiting period that Jasinski ever after referred to as "the spaghetti months."

> Massine needed boys to go to Italy. We rehearsed his ballet BELKIS in London for about a month and I signed the contract there. That is when he made the choreography. BELKIS was opera and ballet together and he was engaged to do this at La Scala in Milan. When we finished with him in London, there was a wait. He didn't take us until two or three months later. I thought, "It is now September. We don't start our tour until January. How can I survive?" I had only £10 left when I finished rehearsals in London. I had to live for three months in Paris on those £10: October, November, December. I changed my English pounds to francs and planned how much I could afford to spend.

I bought a little burner that used wood alcohol so I could cook for myself in the hotel. I knew if they found out I was cooking in the room, I would be thrown into the street, so when I finished cooking I hid everything in my suitcase. For three months I cooked spaghetti—no sauce, no meat, just spaghetti. In the mornings I would have something like Ovaltine and a piece of bread before my class with Egorova. Then, spaghetti, twice a day. For three months I lived like this!

I lived in a hotel on the Avenue de Wagram but I couldn't pay for the hotel. I told the nice lady, "I don't have any money," but she let me stay anyway.

I remember that each time I passed the kitchen I smelled—oh—such smells! And I had to live by myself. My friends would have eaten my spaghetti! On Sundays I could go to a museum because on Sundays all the museums were free. I spent most of my time in the Louvre. I would wander from room to room looking at the art, happy to be dry and warm. Then I would get a little bite in a cafe. A croissant or something once a week.

Jasinski patiently endured each long, sterile, pasta-fueled day, studied with Egorova as he could, and hoarded his spaghetti, trusting that eventually January would come, and with it Italy, *Belkis,* and an income. But before year's end a truly bright spot appeared on his horizon. A major ballet company, the newly formed Ballets Russes de Monte-Carlo, offered the young dancer a position.

Before we left Paris for Italy with Massine we heard that a big new company was being formed. This was to be like a second Diaghilev company. Its stars were from Diaghilev and it would be called "René Blum and Colonel de Basil's Ballets Russes de Monte-Carlo."

De Basil and René Blum were co-directors and had already heard about me from Nijinska. Maybe Blum remembered me from the time Boris Kniasev lost our money in Monte Carlo and Blum had to send us back to Paris. I don't know. Anyway, I went to the office, was sent to the theatre to audition, and they took me right away. I went back to the office to sign the contract.

Finally, 1932 came. Only a few people went to La Scala with Massine: Jan Hoyer, David Lichine, Shabelevsky, another Russian boy, and Jasinski.

They left for Milan in January. It was snowing.

There was a festival scene in *Belkis,* with much dancing. Drums were brought in and the boys jumped up and danced atop the drums. Jasinski was covered with black paint. "Sticky!," he would later describe it. They danced like this for nearly a month, and people said, "The five Nijinskis have come to La Scala."

DAVID LICHINE

Lichine as he appeared in the 1936 program of Col. W. de Basil's Ballets Russes, Royal Opera House.

Photo by Maharadze, N.Y.C.

SAVOY

THEATRE :: STRAND, W.C.2

EVENINGS at 8.45 MATINEE: WEDNESDAYS at 2.45

EDWARD JAMES

presents

THE BALLETS OF 1933

Choregraphy by GEORGES BALANCHINE

with

ROMAN JASINSKY

Art Director:

BORIS KOCHNO

FULL SYMPHONY ORCHESTRA

Under the direction of

CONSTANT LAMBERT and MAURICE de ABRAVANEL

JASINSKI STARS IN BALANCHINE'S FIRST SOLO COMPANY

Poster, London. Private collection.

# II

# The Ballets Russes and Balanchine

1932–1939

CHAPTER 6

# De Basil's Ballets Russes de Monte-Carlo

*I was in the very first performance.*

UNTIL NOW, I HAD GRABBED ANYTHING that came to me, to live. But I always thought that one day there would be a big company to join. Somehow I knew that the Ballets Russes of Blum and de Basil would be a serious company. I felt absolutely at home right away. It gave me a kind of security. Rehearsals started at the beginning of 1932, and as soon as BELKIS was ended in Italy I joined the company in Monte Carlo. I felt like a man with a future.

Jasha's future was to be bound up closely with Monte Carlo: the polished marble of its tiny theatre, the warm applause of an enthusiastic clientele, the sun-struck beauty of sea and sky. Monte Carlo was to become his European home for the next few years, and ever after he remembered its elegance and intimacy with nostalgia.

Surrounded by scenic beauty, alight with ambition and hope, it was time for Jasinski to acquaint himself with the newly-gathered personalities who would become his surrogate family. More important, he had to prove he was a young man of promise to the strange, driven man known as Colonel de Basil.

I didn't know anything about this man, de Basil. His real name was Colonel Vassily Grigorievitch Voskresensky and he had been a Cossack in Russia, cutting off Bolshevik heads. I saw one of his swords once, a sabre. "You see this?" he would say, showing the muscle in his grip. "This muscle is from cutting off heads."

There were lots of stories that de Basil himself had been a dancer—that he had danced in Paris, maybe in the Opera. That he danced when he was young with his first wife, but he kept it a secret. He had some kind of past but he never wanted anybody who knew about it to work for him.

Whatever that past, de Basil would give the future a formidable ballet company, and yet the Diaghilev influence was everywhere—in the choreographers, the scene and costume designers, the established dancers who brought to the new Ballets Russes the lustre they had first achieved with the old.

Diaghilev's early Ballets Russes had swept through a culture unaccustomed to thinking of dance as art. Artist, impresario, choreographer, and musician had come together to brainstorm, create scenarios, squabble, laugh, scream, throw things, dare mightily—and to produce balletic miracles that opened whole new artistic horizons.

Although de Basil lacked Diaghilev's elegance, poise, wit, and self-proclaimed superiority, he shared his passion, vision, and organizational cunning. A big, bluff, blunt man, he nonetheless fought a wily fight that created a company that would last for nearly twenty years.

De Basil may not have had a good artistic background but he really loved the arts. And you know, when he saw a good dancer he could almost smell success. One thing I know is true. Russian people have great feeling. They see things that other people can't see. De Basil could see talent. He tried to keep people with special talent in the company and if they left he would try to get them back. I liked de Basil. He was not a great dancer, but he could see that this boy, Jasinski, had talent. He did great things and built a great company.

> Some people say de Basil was a crook, the way he went after money, but he talked with you and explained things to you, explained the situation. Call him anything you want, but he had seventy people to care for. He would do anything to support us. De Basil once told me, "I need to sacrifice and be a crook. I need to be smarter than other people." He used his army training in running the ballet. He always told me how he prepared to get what he needed. "I will attack these people as though I have tanks and a whole army. If they move against me, I will win."

De Basil put all his Cossack training to work for the move to Monte Carlo in his position as co-director with René Blum. He had to outflank conflicting egos, juggle entrepreneurship with day-to-day minutiae, finagle to find financing.

Blum was the company's artistic director in name, but his real importance lay in the fact that, as director of ballet, it was he who secured the engagement at Monte Carlo. According to Jasinski, de Basil gave him his title in exchange for a five-year contract there.

Blum was de Basil's ballet director in Monte Carlo only, where he also produced opera and engaged other ballet companies. Jasinski recalled Blum as a man with great knowledge in all the arts and very different from the Colonel.

> When de Basil hired dancers he didn't give them a name like "first dancer" or "soloist." He just signed them for five years or for three—the length of time, not the position. I danced in the corps de ballet sometimes and then maybe I would dance a solo. Wherever he needed me, that is where I danced.
>
> It was with the Ballets Russes that I first met George Balanchine when he came as ballet master. Balanchine was very pleasant to work with. The ballets COTILLON, LA CONCURRENCE, and LE BOURGEOIS GENTILHOMME were all created by Balanchine in Monte Carlo at this time. I was in the very first cast of LA CONCURRENCE and LE BOURGEOIS GENTILHOMME as well as Massine's JEUX D'ENFANTS, but not in Balanchine's COTILLON. Later, I danced it many times.

GEORGE BALANCHINE'S *LA CONCURRENCE*, 1932

Roman Jasinski is on the left.

Copyright ©Archives Monte-Carlo SBM.

I danced in some of the operas in Monte Carlo before the ballet season opened, but what was really important—I was in the very first performance of the Ballets Russes de Monte-Carlo!

Roman Jasinski was to call this company home for fifteen years. His tenure spanned most of its performing life. The association was neither smooth nor uninterrupted, but it was the forge that shaped his raw talent into mature and tested artistry. He grew to treasure the company and the company grew to treasure him. His greatest performing days paralleled those of de Basil's Ballets Russes.

This is also when I met Serge Grigoriev. He was the regisseur general who rehearsed the ballets. This position, "regisseur general," doesn't exist any more, but in the Russian ballet, a regisseur rehearsed the ballet and also auditioned, hired, or fired the dancers. Grigoriev had very strict discipline. He kept the repertoire—all the steps to all the ballets—in his head. He had been the regisseur for Diaghilev, and Grigoriev's wife, Tchernicheva, was a former Diaghilev ballerina. At that time, the difference between the regisseur and ballet master was that the ballet master was the choreographer. Grigoriev, as regisseur, had to remember every single thing that the choreographer did in every single ballet the company performed.

When Grigoriev and de Basil first met to discuss the company, Grigoriev said, "I want my wife to teach the company and to dance, and Vova, my son, to be secretary." This way, his wife would get a second salary and Vova would also be paid. That is how de Basil got Grigoriev to work for him.

The company began to take shape. Excitement, enthusiasm, and hope were in the air. More and more dancers were hired to flesh out the company and support its stars. Mature and Diaghilev-tested talent assembled in Monte Carlo, but the greatest attention swirled around three young girls brought in by Balanchine. Tatiana Riabouchinska was fifteen years old, and Tamara Toumanova and Irina Baronova were a couple of years younger. All three were fresh, young, beautiful, and technically astounding. Their adoring press quickly dubbed them "the baby ballerinas," and they became a major factor in the new company's outstanding success, despite their warring and vociferous mothers who juggled for the primacy of each gifted child.

Older ballerinas found themselves overshadowed by the formidable threesome. This was a gnawing embarrassment to established ballerinas already accustomed to accolades and acclaim. Alexandra Danilova, in London, heard that Balanchine thought she and other Diaghilev ballerinas were "too old" to be hired. This did not sit well, particularly as it came from Balanchine, her former colleague and lover, and she didn't join the company until 1933. "Mature" ballerinas continued to dance, of course, but the balletic buzz and excitement were all on the side of dewy-eyed youth.

IRINA BARONOVA

Baronova as she appeared in the Original Ballet Russe program, 1940–1941.

Photo by Maurice Seymour courtesy of Ron Seymour.

I was a little bit in love with Baronova. She was very popular with all the boys. Riabouchinska was popular, too. Lichine was after her and wanted to marry her. He was married to someone else at the time but was fooling around with Riabouchinska. With Toumanova, Mama was there. You couldn't get too close; Mama was there all the time between Tamara and everyone else.

These girls could dance anything. That's why Balanchine took the three of them—Toumanova, Baronova and Riabouchinska. They were very different. Tamara Toumanova was more aloof, Baronova was warm, and Riabouchinska had great feeling.

TAMARA TOUMANOVA

Toumanova as she appeared in the 1936 program of Col. W. de Basil's Ballets Russes, Royal Opera House.

Photo by Maurice Seymour courtesy of Ron Seymour.

All of these personalities found a new home in Monaco and left their collective mark on the sunlit city of Monte Carlo. It is easy to understand Jasha's love for this city, a place more Italian than French in food and feel. Today's Monte Carlo spills down from a high semi-circle of surrounding slopes in a curve toward the Mediterranean Sea, and is ablaze with ruby bougainvilleas and stately palms. White marble walls are bordered by blossoms of lemon, cerise, and orange, their flowers curiously odorless, as though all of their energy is focused on color instead of scent.

This was to become Jasinski's home away from touring for three years, and its beauty endured in his memory for a lifetime. He knew the city in the uncertain era between two world wars when Monte Carlo was a magnet for those with money to burn at the casino and a lodestar for those with a thirst for the performing arts.

The theatre in Monte Carlo held only five hundred people so the company could perform the same ballet for two weeks or a month at a time. It was also beautiful and sublimely intimate. Built in the 1870s by Charles Garnier, the architect of the more-restrained Opéra in Paris, the Monte Carlo theatre was contained within the casino, a prime example of nineteenth-century neo-Baroque architectural extravagance. All those cherubs. All those voluptuous naked goddesses in plaster. All that gilt, crystal, and red velvet opulence! It was a tour de force in imagery and in fashionably overblown elegance.

On one side of today's casino there is a small plaque which adorns a modest side gate. It marks the theatre entrance for the troupes of Blum, Kniasev, Diaghilev, de Basil, and other legendary impresarios. This was where some of the greatest artists of an era turned to enter, rehearse, perform.

Jasha's descriptive speech was sparse but it is possible to sit near the theatre and imagine the elegance of Monte Carlo seventy years ago and its enormous contrast to the poverty of Jasha's native Poland. One can almost see the slow metamorphosis of an itinerant young "gypsy" into the "prince" that was to be, formed by his times here, burnished by this place, this Monte Carlo, and the cosmopolitan company which adopted its name.

TATATIANA RIABOUCHINSKA

Riabouchinska as she appeared in the Original Ballet Russe program, 1940–1941.

COLONEL DE BASIL

De Basil as he appeared in the Original Ballet Russe program, 1940–1941.

Photo by Maurice Seymour courtesy of Ron Seymour.

> Everyone in the company spoke French and Russian. If anyone spoke Czechoslovakian I could understand a little because it is very close to Polish. Same thing with Yugoslavian and Bulgarian. But Romanian? No! Not for me. By 1932, I was speaking French as well as Polish, and my Russian was getting better all the time.

And so this amazing multi-lingual, multi-talented company was launched. It sounded ideal: an international company, brilliant dancers, a cosmopolitan venue, a gem of a theatre. It offered much, if only the possessiveness of warring personalities could be kept at bay.

A breach in company loyalties occurred when Léonide Massine, Jasinski's acquaintance from the Rubinstein and *Belkis* days, arrived to muddy the choreographic waters. The arrival of Massine, who was an expert dancer and superior choreographer, both angered and threatened the younger Balanchine. The rivalry between the two took a bitter twist when the ballet *Jeux d'enfants* was assigned.

> There was trouble about this ballet. You see, de Basil had promised it to Balanchine and then gave it instead to Massine. That was really big trouble. Joan Miró, the designer of the sets and costumes, was very Spanish. The costumes he designed for the Amazons were kind of shocking—it looked like one breast was cut off. Some of the girls hated to dance like this! They were ashamed. I remember myself, I didn't like it, but this ballet was very successful. Lots of dancing, lots of variations.
>
> Massine later set other ballets with stories like LE TRICORNE, BEAU DANUBE, and LA BOUTIQUE FANTASQUE. Diaghilev had spent years teaching Massine how to do the story ballet.

Story ballets such as *Jeux d'enfants* were central to ballet companies of the day. Dance for the simple sake of dance was rare. Balanchine was also story-bound at this early stage of his career, although the winds of change were already beginning to blow as he created *Cotillon*. It would take his later move to America to bring his mature, abstract, plotless ballets to the fore.

The two rival choreographers now divided the company into two rival camps. Young Jasinski, just four years out of Poland, found himself in a hotbed of creativity and angst, working with first one genius and then the other, hard upon the heels of the equally demanding Nijinska and Kniasev. It was a tightrope he was to walk for years, balancing the requirements of the greatest choreographers of the age, learning from them, absorbing their styles, analyzing their techniques, inhaling their passions.

> When Massine arrived in the company there was a different atmosphere. Some people liked Massine; some people liked Balanchine. The company was split. I liked Massine all right but thought he was more for money than for art. He was not a man that you could easily like. In rehearsal he would scream hysterically, but he was a very talented choreographer.
>
> By now, though, Massine was more famous than when I first knew him in rehearsals for DAVID and BELKIS. He had started to be nicer with people. De Basil was very careful because Massine had just started with the company. He knew that Balanchine and Massine didn't like each other. He knew that when Massine came Balanchine would probably leave. I was told that Balanchine and Massine had had a fight in Diaghilev's time. If so, their anger went back a long way. I think that Balanchine was upset because Massine could really dance.
>
> I watched Massine carefully. I made movements my way but I used Massine's sharpness. He had strong movements of the head, the body, everything. He had his own style.
>
> Some dancers stayed in the dressing room and never watched the great stars. But I was different when I was dancing. I was never "jealousy." If someone great went on the stage I would always go and look. I would always try to learn from them.

The Ballets Russes de Monte-Carlo opened to the public at the Théâtre de Monte-Carlo 12 April 1932. The opening program consisted of *Les Sylphides, La Concurrence,* and *Cotillon,* the latter two choreographed by Balanchine.

*Cotillon* broke new balletic ground. Dancers flowed on and off the stage without a clear, comprehensible plot line. Parts of the ballet were mysterious, parts merely puzzling, but underlying everything was the sense that at last dance had come into its own and was sufficient unto itself. Decades later, Jasinski would revive its lost pas de deux, "Hand of Fate," for his own company, Tulsa Ballet Theatre—a revival greeted with enthusiasm by New York's major critics.

In its first season, the Ballets Russes de Monte-Carlo was hailed as a grand successor to Diaghilev's company. Monte Carlo critics cheered, audiences applauded wildly, and Paris awaited its arrival with breathless anticipation. From 9 June– 21 June 1932, the Théâtre des Champs-Elysées in the City of Lights became a magnet for artists, poets, society mavens, and critics as the works of Balanchine and Massine marched across the stage to appreciative accolades. But Balanchine and Boris Kochno, Diaghilev's imaginative librettist and right-hand man, were in the process of severing their connection with de Basil, and instead were deep into negotiations for Balanchine's own company. Their dispute with de Basil was both artistic and political and they dreamed of a company where Balanchine would hold the artistic reins and Kochno would provide the intellectual inspiration he had once shared with Diaghilev.

> Balanchine just said he was leaving the company. He refused to work anymore and called de Basil a crook. I don't think that Balanchine wanted to work with Massine in the company because while Balanchine was a choreographer, Massine was both a choreographer and a dancer and Balanchine couldn't dance any more. He had a bad lung. Kochno went with Balanchine because they were better friends. You know, the artistic director is everything to a company.
>
> Kochno was not a choreographer but he spent his lifetime in museums. When he started talking I was like a baby listening. He knew everything that existed on this earth. De Basil probably wanted Kochno to stay, but Balanchine and Kochno left together.

When the Paris season of the Ballets Russes ended and its hoopla and applause subsided, Jasinski briefly collaborated once again with his old friend Boris Kniasev. Again he rehearsed without pay, waiting for performance to put money in his pocket. Kniasev entered his ballet *Légende de Berioska (The Birch Trees)* in an international competition, Le Concours International de Danses Artistiques, which opened in Paris 2 July 1932. Once again Jasinski was haphazardly listed in the program. This time he was renamed Jacques Yassinsky.

> Lots of companies came to this competition—they came from Paris and Belgium and Germany and all over Europe. I think someone even came from Poland. The competition was for the best ballet. It was held at the Théâtre des Champs-Elysées and Knasiev was sure that we would win. A girl represented a birch tree and we boys were the branches. A wind came and took away one branch and then came again and took away another branch. Kniasev was the wind in the ballet.
>
> When we didn't win Kniasev was very upset. Kurt Jooss won the prize with THE GREEN TABLE, which is not dancing, really, it is more pantomime, but it is very beautiful. I was sorry for Kniasev that we did not win. I liked working with him—he was kind of a crook, a crazy guy, but with a very good heart.
>
> Then came the fall tour with the Ballets Russes. We went to the Netherlands, Germany, and Switzerland by bus because it was cheaper. Oh my God, that was a disaster! That tour was very hard. In one city, we would give a matinee, come back, sleep in the bus, and then perform a soirée. Then we would go to another city. We sometimes slept in the bus because we needed to save our money to eat. The whole company, thirty or forty people, was traveling on the bus. We had stagehands with us, too, and musicians. We didn't rehearse very much; there was no time.

For six cold weeks, from 14 October to 1 December, the ballet "gypsies" rolled across Europe, costumes strapped to the top of the bus. From time to time the bus would stop and the company would tumble out to take barre, clinging to fences by the side of the road. A matinee here, an evening performance, or soirée, there. Little time to rest. Little time for respite. Bouncing endlessly between food, theatre, bus, and lodging.

> We would arrive on the bus in the center of the town at one, two, three o'clock in the morning and everybody would take his suitcase. We needed to look for hotels.
>
> Imagine! It was dark. Nobody had any money. Ten people stayed here and ten people stayed there. We tried to get cheaper boarding houses, renting a room with no water, no basin. It was terrible.
>
> The worst was when we came to the Netherlands. We arrived about midnight and everyone started to look for a pension. The room that a woman gave to me was in the basement. Nobody had slept in it for years. There was so much water in my bed! My God, it was wet! You know how I slept? In my coat! With shoes and everything, because it was so cold. Even the walls were wet. I was afraid of the damp; I was afraid to be sick again. In the morning I got up and I was so cold! But when I went upstairs in the morning I remember that there was a long table, and on this table was any food I wanted. It was a fantastic breakfast with all different kinds of food.
>
> We went to a couple of cities in Germany and had a very strange time. A man was killing women, just like Jack the Ripper. In one town in Germany, Frankfurt maybe, nobody came to the theatre at all. The people were afraid. We were supposed to perform, but nobody was there to watch. This "Jack" had already killed a couple of people before we came.
>
> Once I remember the bus arrived about two in the morning and stopped at the center of a city in Switzerland. As usual, everybody had to go look for a pension. There was no organization, like there is in touring today. We had to take care of ourselves. In this city we didn't know what to do with our suitcases. There was a policeman, I remember, standing there. We went to him and said, "What do we

do? We need to look for a pension." And he said, "You can leave the suitcases here on the street. Nobody will touch them."

You know, they would cut off the fingers of thieves there. You could leave your things—even for twenty-four hours—and nobody would touch them. It was fantastic. You could come the next day and the suitcases would still be standing there.

After six weeks the tour ended. The autumn season of Les Ballets Russes de Monte-Carlo was over. Everyone was brought back to Paris.

Then the announcement came that Balanchine was starting his own company and the long-anticipated defections began to take shape and substance. Rumors were rife as to who would be lured from de Basil to join the visionary Balanchine.

Jasinski was one of the first to leave.

CHAPTER 7

# BALANCHINE AND LES BALLETS 1933

*I trusted Balanchine.*

WHEN BALANCHINE discovered where Jasinski was living in Paris, he sent Dimitriev to him. "Mr. Balanchine wants you to join his company! He wants you to be his first dancer!"

I decided right away that I would go. And I left, just like that! I left and de Basil knew that I was going with Balanchine. It was very open, without intrigue, but I didn't go to de Basil and tell him that I was leaving, so de Basil sued me. Some dancer said he had heard me say that I was going to stay with de Basil the next year. He was lying. De Basil just didn't want to lose me.

But I lost the lawsuit. I don't know how much Balanchine and Dimitriev had to pay to settle it. Still, at this time Massine was with the Ballets Russes so it was not so bad for de Basil that Balanchine was gone.

I left de Basil because it was always interesting for me to dance new works. I trusted Balanchine. I didn't know that he didn't have any money. I just went. They told me that Tamara Toumanova was coming with them, too, and lots of girls from Egorova's school. You can do crazy things like this only when you are young.

It was Vladimir Dimitriev who caused big trouble for Balanchine. He wanted to make a name for himself, to be the director. He simply took Balanchine over. Dimitriev talked for him, signed his contracts, collected his money, everything. He had been hired by de Basil because he was Balanchine's friend and because he signed Balanchine's contract. One of the things that caused trouble between Balanchine and de Basil was that Dimitriev wanted to be the director. It was Dimitriev who had brought Balanchine, Danilova, and some others out of Russia, and Balanchine remembered that.

So once again I was living in Paris. I know the number: 35 Rue Pigalle. I went back there always. My Polish friends Shabelevsky and Matlinsky were in Les Ballets 1933 with me, but Shabelevsky left. He was a little bit jealous because Balanchine took me as premier danseur and not him, so he left after one or two months and went back to de Basil.

The Balanchine bubble would burst too soon, but despite the hardships that followed, Jasinski remained proud all of his life that he was Balanchine's first "first dancer." He loved Balanchine's work, trusted his genius and threw himself enthusiastically into Balanchine's imaginative maelstrom. They all did. A handful of young, impressionable, eager artists left ballet schools and professional companies to provide the clay for Balanchine's creativity. He worked with each, promoted the best features of each. They cheerfully accepted physical hunger and ongoing uncertainty, and each would look back on those days as high points in their lives.

We were free all day and rehearsed at Egorova's studio in the evenings. Egorova's classes started in the morning and went all day. We would take class and then about 7:30 at night she would give up her little studio and we would start to rehearse. She let Balanchine work there for free.

You know, I worked all this time with the Balanchine company but they did not pay me. Every four or five days Dimitriev and

Balanchine bought me a meal. In between, I would eat a crust or something—coffee or a croissant. They gave me ten francs or so every now and then, but it was not a salary. The company had about fifteen dancers, but only four were boys. Everybody rehearsed without money.

Actually, there was some money. Ten prominent artists and balletomanes, including Coco Chanel and Cole Porter, promised to kick in ten thousand francs each. It was a hand-to-mouth affair. The whole gifted company—artists, dancers, musicians, and all—donated their talents to the dream. Even so, there wasn't enough money to hire a hall. Painter André Derain quipped that he would build a cart and they would caravan around the countryside, dancing at county fairs as "Les Ballets Ambulants." It would be painted in the style of Toulouse-Lautrec, and would be a whimsical way of bringing itinerant ballet to the people.

Everyone asks me, "How was Balanchine as a dancer?" Balanchine was very good. He was a very high jumper. When he jumped, he held himself in the air and landed in a nice, soft plié, like a cat. This was what he taught all of us in class.

I liked Balanchine's classes. When I was in his company Balanchine was a normal teacher and the classes were like in Russia, normal classes. Good combinations, interesting steps, all these things. Exciting. Anything he gave, you tried.

Mama Toumanova made some problems, I remember. Mama always wanted something special for Tamara, and one day, Mama was so happy! On this day Tamara was wearing a white leotard, very nice, and Balanchine was going to give her a special variation. Balanchine put the whole variation on the floor and Tamara became black with dirt! Balanchine wanted her to look like everyone else—dressed in black. In rehearsal, Balanchine would come and create all the steps on us, what we could do best. He was a pianist, so he knew how to listen to the music. He listened and then would start to choreograph. He didn't prepare anything before rehearsal.

One day a girl was running to me for some kind of lift. I think it was in LES SONGES when I danced the part of a big rat. The lift was hard for me and I hurt my shoulder but I never told Balanchine. I just worked it out by myself. I would try to do anything he showed me. Maybe I didn't do it exactly the way he showed, but I know he was happy with me.

Everyone struggled, worked, dreamed. Hopes were high, although funds were short. And then came the announcement that the impossible had suddenly become possible.

I remember the day Boris Kochno came to rehearsal and said, "We have found someone to buy this company! We are going to perform!" Before this, we didn't even know where, or if, we were going to dance.

An Englishman called Edward James had bought the company. There was a rumor he was the illegitimate son of Edward VII. He wanted to buy the company for his wife, Tilly Losch, who was singing and dancing as a nightclub entertainer in Germany. Without James, I don't know. Maybe this company would never have danced. We didn't have any place to perform, or any money!

When Edward James bought the company, there was no scenery, nothing. He needed to pay for it all. It was like an explosion. All the musicians, the composers, the painters—André Derain and Pavel Tchelitchev—came to the rehearsals and planned together. Barbara Karinska made the costumes and there were many theatrical effects—spectacle, lighting, decor.

I heard that James paid a million francs, maybe more for all this. Nobody paid me for the months I had worked without money, but now they started to pay us a kind of salary.

It was almost as though Diaghilev had been resurrected. The atmosphere was charged with excitement. Kochno was in his element, writing scenarios, overseeing everything. Balanchine tried this, tried that, sought ways to showcase his dancers effectively and unusually. James and his all-important checkbook gave the company a fighting chance to succeed. That there was a serpent in the wings was unknown. The dancers danced, elated and exhilarated. Jasinski, too, was transported with hope, but when a chance for a personal fortune came his way, he was far too human to pass it by.

> It was through the scene painter Tchelitchev that I met my friend, Felix Rolo. Rolo led me into one of the craziest adventures in my life. He was an Egyptian who loved art and always went to the ballet, but Rolo was kind of an unhappy man. He enjoyed my company because he said I was different. He said when he sat with me at dinner it relaxed him and his happiest moments were when we could talk together. I always told him, "Felix, when I become a good dancer and make more money, I will invite you to dinner many times. I will repay you some day."
>
> I always thought that I would succeed in my life and that I would repay those who had helped me at the beginning.
>
> Rolo was a rich man, very rich. His father was with a bank in Cairo. I talked with him in French and he also spoke very good English. He had finished school—at Oxford, I think—and he lived on the Champs-Elysées at a very good hotel. I remember one favorite restaurant where he took me. They served chicken. They put butter on the chicken and broiled it. I could eat a whole chicken! I ate soup, vegetables, salad, and a whole chicken! And the next day I could work all day. It brought satisfaction to him that he was helping my career by giving me something to eat.
>
> But you know, when I knew him, Felix was kind of a gambler. In France they already knew that he was a rich boy. He spent money like water in the casinos in Paris. He just signed the papers and the casinos knew they would get this money from his father.
>
> I never went gambling with him, but when I was first dancing with Balanchine, Rolo came to me and said, "Jasha, would you like

to make ten thousand francs?" "Ten thousand francs! I've never seen more than 1,300 francs in my life!"

"In the south of France there is a girl who wants to be married. Her father died and left a will, but for her to get the money she needs to marry." The arrangements were like this: I would go there, and if I decided not to marry I had no obligation. I was so poor that I went to meet her.

They put me in this beautiful hotel in Cannes. They gave me tickets and money for both ways and extra money for traveling. We had cocktails on the terrace where we could see the ocean. Three men were there. One was her lawyer and the others, I think, were her brothers. They gave me papers to sign and then I came down the hotel stairs to meet this girl.

She came into the room and we were introduced. She was not very pretty! I thought, "Oh, my Lord!" I was scared to death. I shook hands with her and she looked at me constantly; she never took her eyes from me. She asked where I was from and I told her where I was born and showed her my passport. I would probably have had to become French because she was a French citizen. That worried me. The papers said I would be married to her for one month, and then she would divorce me. That worried me, too.

She asked me what I was doing in Paris. I told her about Balanchine and the company. She didn't ask too much. The other men talked among themselves kind of quick when I wasn't with them and then they talked to her. They knew her well, it seemed.

When we finished dinner two of the men said, "We want to talk with you now." They asked me how I liked her and I said, "She is not very beautiful." One said, "Would you like to marry her?"

Suddenly, when I examined all this, I didn't want any money or anything. I thought of all I had been through in my life, and then I made a very smart decision. I just wanted to go back to Paris. I told him, "You know, I don't think I can go through with this. I thought I could, but now I can't."

And you know, these people were very nice to me. One man said, "Don't worry. You can go home tomorrow."

After dinner I said good-bye to her. She didn't know when we said good-bye that I would not marry her. I don't remember her name. At that time I didn't even want to think about it again. I think she was older and at this time I liked only the young, pretty girls. I've told my wife, Moussia, that I had a chance to be married, but it was a kind of dishonesty to myself to marry for money. When I went there something in my conscience was telling me, "No!"

I never saw her again. She probably married somebody else. I think they thought a different type of man would come. They wanted somebody—maybe a French guy—and I was Polish. I never wanted to be a French citizen—only American. And the girl—she was looking for someone, but maybe she didn't want to ruin my life, either. Maybe she was not happy to marry me. She was watching me closely. Maybe she was looking for a gigolo. She was surprised that I was a different type of person.

If I had married her, I would have needed to divorce her—that is another thing that I remember. I needed to stay married a certain amount of time so that they could collect the money and then I needed to divorce her.

I started to think about things. That later I might want to marry again and I would have been divorced. Or maybe I would be stuck with her. "What will happen if she doesn't divorce me?" I was a little bit afraid. At this time I didn't speak French very well. Like my English right now. Maybe these characters—I don't know—maybe they were gangsters.

I was gone two or three days to Cannes. Balanchine had given me time off from rehearsal, but he never knew why. I never told him. Only Rolo knew, who knew these people. He was not surprised when I told him I said "no."

He only said, "That's your decision."

So I didn't make ten thousand francs.

> Later I appreciated what I had done with my life. I was looking for some pretty girl like Moussia. So I came back to Paris and I was so happy and relieved that I hadn't married. I had thought I could marry this girl in Cannes. Ten thousand francs! This way I could get some extra money. I never thought I would ever have so much. But I also felt kind of guilty. Guilty to God and dishonest to myself. I said to God, "You need to excuse me, but I have nothing to eat."
>
> Later, when England declared war on Germany, Rolo was one of the first to volunteer. He was Egyptian, you see, but he had a home in England. When I came to Paris after the war I tried to find him but couldn't. Felix Rolo was another one who helped me that I was never able to repay.

Once back in Paris, Jasha found the company in turmoil. Before Edward James's arrival, Balanchine had created three unusual ballets, *Mozartiana, Fastes,* and *Les Songes,* all led by Jasinski and Tamara Toumanova. When James's wife, Tilly Losch, was brought into the mix, company dynamics changed abruptly. There was no room for Toumanova in the newly created *L'Errante, The Seven Deadly Sins,* or in the short-lived *Les Valses de Beethoven,* and Toumanova's role in *Fastes* would have to be shared with Losch when the company went to London. James was promoting his wife above all others and the cat fight began. "Our ballerina was not very happy because Tilly Losch took her parts," remembered Jasha.

Poor Toumanova! It must have been galling for this much admired "baby ballerina" to be upstaged by a woman of equal beauty and lesser talent. Who, of these two, was to reign?

In all, Balanchine created six pieces for the company. Some combined pantomime, unusual visual effects, and avant-garde music; all were so varied they could have been created by six different choreographers.

Money flowed endlessly from the deep pockets of Edward James. Composer Igor Stravinsky was hired but eventually withdrew. Designers Tchelitchev and Derain whisked about the stage adding wild, imaginative set designs to the overall effects. A small, select audience was allowed to observe the creative

MOZARTIANA, LES BALLETS 1933

Jasinski and Toumanova in George Balanchine's original production of *Mozartiana.*

Photo by Studio-Iris, Paris. Courtesy Jerome Robbins Dance Division, The New York Public Library for the Performing Arts, Astor, Lenox and Tilden Foundations.

process, but despite vague promises of financial backing from a select few, in the end, James bore most of the expense. Of greatest importance to the dancers, they were being paid.

As to that lurking serpent in the wings, it could only be defined as love. The whole James enterprise was designed to save a rocky marriage, and the whole premise was that Tilly Losch must be showcased. Like Ida Rubinstein before her, Tilly was a gorgeous exotic, ever the center of attention, ever the "star." But English corps de ballet member Tamara Finch remembered that Losch "danced with fussy hand movements and violent body jerks. What we could see we envied—her beautiful face, fascinating, with large eyes seemingly full of innocence and devotion. Fabulously dressed she would sweep in and out of rehearsals as she pleased. . . . Tilly had the ability to mesmerize everyone."

The ability to "mesmerize" and the ability to dance are not the same. Another young corps member recalled that Tilly "was the despair of Balanchine." Not that he should have been surprised! He had worked at least once with Losch in previous years and knew her to be a star of limited lustre. It was no doubt a tradeoff—without Tilly there was no company, so her place in his creations was a necessary evil.

When inspiration is blocked one turns to special effects. The new sets and costumes were dramatic, expensive, splashed with color, or ominous in shade on shade. Weird monsters occasionally roamed the stage. Storms raged. Costumes billowed. With a greater dancer, less emphasis might have been placed on effect, but Tilly's limitations dictated design. Balanchine exploited her beauty, emphasized her originality, and trusted to the rest of the creation to make it all work.

One of the more unusual ballets was *Les Sept Péchés Capitaux (The Seven Deadly Sins),* a dual role between Losch and the German cabaret singer, Lotte Lenya, danced to a dissonant score by Lenya's husband, Kurt Weill. The success of his *Three Penny Opera* and its signature tune, "Mack the Knife," was already behind Weill, and while the score for *The Seven Deadly Sins* was far less popular than its predecessor, it survived Les Ballets 1933. The revival of *The Seven Deadly Sins* in 1958 by Balanchine's New York City Ballet was "hugely acclaimed" and is still considered an important work today.

I liked the singer Lotte Lenya. I met her on the stage when Balanchine presented me. Her husband, Kurt Weill, conducted the orchestra. She was very simple, very pleasant, and Mr. Weill was very nice also. They were friendly people.

We would come in the morning, shake hands and begin to work. In Europe, you know, we were more formal when we worked. Very disciplined! It is not like here, with first names, casual. In Europe we take time before we can be open to each other.

The cast was assembled. Everyone had an opinion on everything.

Boris Kochno, the artistic director of Les Ballets 1933, watched all the dancers and corrected them. He had great knowledge of ballet.

One day Balanchine was working on my solo when Kochno came in and Balanchine said, "Let's show him your variation." I showed him, and Kochno said, "It's no good." Balanchine was so mad! "Rehearsal is finished! I am going home." I had never seen him mad or lose his temper before; he was always under control and he didn't care what satisfied others. "Kochno doesn't know what he is talking about. What I stage now I stage for twenty years in the future!" But the next day he changed the variation.

For all the time I knew him, Boris Kochno was very intelligent, very helpful. Many years later, he came to me one evening and said, "Jasha, I was watching SWAN LAKE. You look like 'Romeo' instead of the 'Prince.' You think about this." And I thought about it. I asked myself why he said this and I found that he was right. The next time he came to me, he said, "Ah, today was different." I had changed the way I did it. I always changed if I thought a criticism was right.

Finally, after months of planning, creating, rehearsing, the moment of truth was upon them. It was 7 June 1933.

Our first opening was in Paris—the Théâtre des Champs-Elysées. I liked this theatre; I liked its location. It was a very beautiful place on a very beautiful street. Trees were growing there and a cafe was opposite the theatre. If you came too soon you could wait at this cafe. The theatre was for both rich and poor, a mixture. It always was popular because it was open for any group that came there.

The Théâtre des Champs-Elysées was the inaugural home of Les Ballets 1933. With a starkly modern exterior and black-and-white interior, it was a fitting venue for a young, ambitious, imaginative choreographer's first solo experimental works. For an account of the company's premiere, we turn to an ambitious writer for *The New Yorker* with the pen name Genêt, who, tongue firmly tucked in cheek, exercised her wit and pen: "*Les Ballets 1933* was presented by Edward James, new optimistic British art patron, at a cost of a million francs. The program consisted of six Balanchine ballets, only half of which, or around five hundred francs' worth, the public appeared to enjoy."

LES SONGES, LES BALLETS 1933

Jasinski as the "Rat" ("Monstre") and Toumanova as the "Ballerina" in Balanchine's *Les Songes*. By the kind permission of the Trustees of the Edward James Foundation.

Of the new works, the least successful was *Les Valses de Beethoven*. Jasinski was its star, but was not in the least unhappy when it was shortly dropped from the repertoire. He felt much the same about *The Seven Deadly Sins,* although it remained a staple during the company's short life. "It was kind of a success, but the ballet, the story, the music—everything was different, like pantomime. I didn't especially like it." *Les Songes,* which starred Toumanova, was quite different. It gave full creative license to the designer and librettist André Derain, and allowed Balanchine's imagination to soar.

In *Les Songes* Jasinski performed the roles of "Monstre," "Acrobat," and "High Life." "Monstre" was a giant rat, performed with a massive rat's head and a stiff triangular coat that fell to the floor. Beneath the coat was another costume, garnished with awkward hoops. When freed from the rat regalia, he had to reappear with large hoops in his hands and smaller hoops circling arms and legs. The hoops had a tendency to catch between his legs, nearly causing him to fall.

It is also to André Derain, lover of antiquity, that *Fastes* can be credited. This ballet took place during an Etruscan festival peopled by gods, priests and pagan worshippers. Jasinski took the part of a priest who illustrated the three ages of man—"Youth," "Maturity," and "Old Age." London's *Morning Post* of 29 July would call it "by far the most ingenious dance of the evening, admirably carried out. . . by Roman Jasinsky."

Was the "most ingenious dance of the evening" performed nearly nude, as one writer suggests? Jasinski certainly never said so in his reminiscences, but a sketch by Derain makes it a possibility, and nudity was not unknown in the theatre of that day.

The ballet *L'Errante* turned out to be a triumph of elaborate sets, billowing costumes, and creative lighting. A silken train, said to be twenty feet in length, embellished the costume of Tilly Losch and became part of the choreography, twining sensuously about her body. The final falling cloudburst of silk, so inventive in its time, is still used by choreographers today.

A famous photo from this ballet shows a passionate Tilly, Jasinski reclining at her feet, her silken train flying dramatically behind her. What it does not show is Balanchine hidden behind the train, clutching its silken folds high overhead with both hands to achieve its sculptural effect.

L'ERRANTE, LES BALLETS 1933, POSTCARD

Roman Jasinski and Tilly Losch. A concealed George Balanchine holds up the train of the dress from behind.

Photo by Sasha, London. Courtesy Archives, Tulsa Ballet.

Balanchine's first *Mozartiana* consisted of pure classical dance in yet another enigmatic setting. Critic Edwin Denby wrote that he couldn't get it out of his mind, while the *Evening News* would report from London, "Tamara Toumanova and Roman Jasinsky danced brilliantly a series of intensely difficult movements." Jasinski only commented, "This was the best one for me because there was lots of dancing. Very classical." The die was cast. The dream was launched. A tiny company sought to test itself against well-known rivals. That the company was small was understood by all within. Only the audience in attendance was truly ignorant of its size, for it seemed, on stage, to be much larger. Corps members played multiple roles, dashing from one side of the stage to the other, shedding cloaks and scarves as they ran, whisking on other pieces of costumes and reappearing back on stage within mere moments to portray yet another dancer or character. Timing was everything. Pressure was everywhere. Everyone danced and danced hard.

Parisians had their choice of companies to enjoy that June. Serge Lifar was at the Paris Opera and Jasinski's old comrades from the Ballets Russes were opening at the Châtelet. Still, Balanchine's innovations were received with initial enthusiasm and the Who's Who of Parisian society, including Igor Stravinsky, Serge Lifar, and Coco Chanel, attended his fledgling performances with interest.

As for Jasha, the *Paris Weekly* of 9 June 1933, wrote, "Roman Yasinsky [sic] [has] daily been making such strides of progress that he promises before the year is out to become a dancer of a quality not less than a Serge Lifar."

Hopes within the youthful company were high. Boris Kochno later wrote, "From the moment of our debut, the theater of the Champs-Élysées was packed. Applause and accolades greeted the company, and we were convinced we had a brilliant future."

Alas! That brilliant future was not to be. Although Balanchine was his own master at last, his first company would quickly crumble and disband in discord. Nonetheless, it presaged a grand choreographic career that would soon take root across the ocean and permanently change the face of twentieth-century ballet. This metamorphosis was on the way, awaiting an onstage accident and an introduction from the audience to materialize.

During that fateful summer, shuffling from performance to performance was a young American looking for the answer to a dream: the establishment of an American ballet company. His name was Lincoln Kirstein, and as he watched, compared, and evaluated rival choreographers, Balanchine's Les Ballets 1933 slowly succumbed to infighting, intrigues, and jealousies.

> Dimitriev was always the problem. Dimitriev wanted to be the business director but he didn't know anything about business. His mind was always working on how to make money, how to cheat somebody, how to go to James and get more money from him. James paid for the costumes, the painters, the scenery, everything. A fortune was spent on this. Without James they couldn't have done anything. Balanchine was the choreographer, Boris Kochno was the artistic director, and James was the owner, the director, but Dimitriev wanted to be the director.

> After our opening in Paris we came to London, but we brought our problems between James and Dimitriev with us.

Problems there may have been, but there were also pluses. The *Daily Telegraph* of 29 June 1933 commented that Les Ballets 1933 "introduced us to a brilliant male dancer, M. Roman Jasinsky."

> Our company was very small, about fifteen people, and we performed at the same time as de Basil's company in London. We were at the Savoy and they were at the Alhambra, which was larger. That was murder! We couldn't compete with the Ballets Russes. They had a tremendous repertoire and were enormous competition. We had had success in Paris but not so much in London. I wasn't able to see the de Basil company because I was performing every day, but I know they had a fantastic season.
>
> In London, Serge Lifar joined our company as a guest artist. Edward James insisted. Alicia Markova did too, although Lifar made it very plain he preferred to dance with Toumanova. James brought Lifar in because he had had a big name ever since he danced for Diaghilev. Lifar was a great dancer as well as ballet master and choreographer with the Paris Opera, but the kind of dancing he did was very different from Balanchine's choreography. Lifar liked Balanchine, he had worked with him before, but somehow Lifar was set against James. Lifar wanted to influence the company, too. I remember some problems—maybe even a fight.

A fight there was. And words. And even the threat of a duel. Tamara Tchinarova Finch, in her reminiscences of Les Ballets 1933, said Lifar slapped James in the face, "calling him 'nothing but an amateur.' " Poor James. It was one more indignity to be endured in this thankless, unforgiving world called "ballet."

Lifar danced *Le Spectre de la Rose* and *L'Après-midi d'un faune,* two Diaghilev pieces that contrasted sharply with the modernism of Balanchine. All this succeeded in doing was to dilute the vaunted experimentalism of the company, its sole reason for being, and to ultimately lose the identity and soul of Les Ballets 1933. Consternation and conflict reigned. The stage was set. Now came the little moment that was to culminate in bringing Balanchine ballet to the United States.

> In LES SONGES I had to turn on my knee on the wooden stage and I drove a splinter deep inside. Usually, if you are hurt, nobody knows—you just go on anyway—but Balanchine and Edward James had to take me in the car to the emergency room in the London hospital. I had an infection on my knee and the doctor had to cut and clean it. He said, "You will be all right, but you cannot dance tomorrow." Balanchine said, "Then I will dance for him." So for that one day I didn't dance, although I danced the day after.

Sitting in the London audience that night was a young man on a mission. Lincoln Kirstein had followed the ballet migration from Paris to London, and after waffling between Lifar, Balanchine, and Massine for weeks, Kirstein had found his man. The night Balanchine danced Jasinski's role was the night that Balanchine and Kirstein met. Dance in America—and dance worldwide—would never be the same.

> They introduced me to Lincoln Kirstein. Balanchine said, "This rich man here wants to bring us to America. I would like to have you and Tamara come so we can build a company on you." He didn't want the whole company, you see. "We are going to America." America! It had always been my dream! We finished the season. I think we had two or three weeks in London, and Balanchine and Kirstein had meetings all the time. Because of these new plans, Edward James came and asked me to stay. He still owned the company with all its sets and costumes. His wife, Tilly Losch, would go back to Germany if I didn't stay. I was her partner, you see. "If you stay, Tilly will stay, and you will save the whole company." All these dancers were now without a job. James thought that we could work in Paris and that we could tour.

When James asked me to stay with his company and Balanchine asked me to go to America, Boris Kochno came to me and said, "Jasha, stay. You stay with Mr. James and I will help you. Don't go with Balanchine. You will never get this kind of fortune. Later, if this company doesn't exist, I will try to help you choreograph."

James had money and offered me a contract for one year at £50 a week! Then Kochno went to Balanchine and said, "Don't take this boy. This is his only chance to make money. Let him go. Look at the big money he can make for one year."

Fifty pounds a week! A contract for one year! These were unheard-of riches for the impoverished young man from Warsaw.

But I just turned my back. Somehow I trusted Balanchine. I trusted that he had made arrangements to pay a salary to us. I didn't ask how much he would pay; the money didn't mean much to me if I could survive somehow.

I loved Balanchine's creations. I liked working with him. Balanchine was interesting to me and I was interesting to him and we wanted to work together. I was young and I didn't think about any money. Maybe it was foolish, but it was more interesting to me if I could dance with Balanchine.

It seemed that Balanchine wanted to be rid of Kochno, that he didn't want him to come to America, although they had been very good friends in the Diaghilev and de Basil companies. That's why Kochno planned to stay with James.

Kirstein gave Balanchine and Dimitriev the opportunity to go to America. That's what gave them the nerve and they said now they didn't need James anymore. If Kirstein had never shown up, James's company would still have been there. Balanchine didn't have anything else to do. What could he do? He didn't have any costumes or anything.

GEORGE BALANCHINE

Photo courtesy Archives, Tulsa Ballet.

And so Les Ballets 1933 folded. It was, wrote Boris Kochno more than fifty years later, a "short, adventurous and passionate spell. . . . like a beautiful dream suddenly interrupted. . . ." Jasinski, always looking for the positive, had another perspective: "This company was too short, but it made me more famous. I think always that what happens in your life happens for the best."

However, what happened for Jasinski's "best" was not the best for Edward James. His marriage fell apart very publicly and vituperatively, and his dreams for his company died with Jasha's departure. And yet James never seemed to blame the young Pole. He remained, in their rare meetings, both cordial and kind. As for Jasinski:

I was Balanchine's first premier danseur. I was the only one who was really with him in this period of time.

When Balanchine had this proposal to come to America from Lincoln Kirstein, Kirstein didn't have any money either. I don't know if I would dare to try something if I had no money, but Kirstein went to the United States and started to collect. He had a hard time. He collected $6,000 dollars or something, just enough to buy some tickets. He was a rich boy, but his parents had all the money.

Kirstein, indeed, had a hard time raising the money, but the idea of an American company with American dancers had been with him since he was a Harvard undergraduate. What he lacked in dollars he made up for in passion. Moreover, he had already inspired his great friend, A. Everett ("Chick") Austin, director of the Wadsworth Atheneum in Hartford, Connecticut, with the same extraordinary vision and passion. Kirstein wrote Austin from London:

BATT'S HOTEL,
DOVER STREET, W.1
July 16: 1933.

Dear Chick:

This will be the most important letter I will ever write you as you will see. My pen burns my hand as I write: words will not flow into the ink fast enough. We have a real chance to have an American ballet within 3 yrs. time. When I say ballet—I mean a trained company of young dancers—not Russians—but Americans with Russian stars to start with—a company superior to the dregs of the old Diaghilev Company which will come to N.Y. this winter and create an enormous success. purely because though they aren't much they are better than anything New york will have seen since Nijinsky.

. . . . We would have to do a little theatrical camouflage at first. A few leaps by Jasinsky or a few fouettés by the adorable Toumanova will lift a room full to their feet, cheering. I wish to God you were here: that you could know what I am writing is true—that I am not either over enthusiastic or visionary.

> Please, Please, Chick if you have any love for anything we do both adore—rack your brains and try to make this all come true.

As page flows upon page, Kirstein extols George Balanchine, his dancing and his choreographic works, decries the "decadence" of the Ballets Russes, and sings the praises of the two dancers Balanchine wants to bring with him to start this uniquely American company. The timeline for the rise and fall of Jasinski's fortunes is captured in terse exchanges between the two young American men.

*On 6 August:* Kirstein in Europe receives news from Chick Austin in Hartford that Austin has raised $3,000 to bring Balanchine, Toumanova, and Jasinski to America.

*On 8 August:* A telegram from Chick asks that Kirstein obtain an "iron-clad contract" from Balanchine, Toumanova, and Jasinski starting 15 October, adding, "Can't wait."

*On 8 August:* A cable from Paris to Hartford exclaims: "will arrange everything can I guarantee living expenses Balanchine Toumanova Jasinsky one year no salary necessary. . . most important thing all of us will ever do congratulations=Kirstein."

A day later Chick cables "Guaranteed living expenses up to $6,000."

Then on 11 August, at a meeting where Kirstein, Balanchine, and Dimitriev were joined by Dimitriev's girlfriend, Kyra Blanc, in Paris, it became clear to Kirstein that it was Dimitriev with whom he must negotiate. It was Dimitriev who advised Balanchine on all details of business.

After this, Balanchine made the tactical error of leaving Toumanova and her parents to exist in Paris however they could while he scooped up an exhausted, elated Jasha, and with Dimitriev departed on vacation to Monte Carlo, leaving Kirstein to return to the United States and guarantee more money.

> Tamara Toumanova stayed in Paris. She was to be Balanchine's ballerina, I was to be the first dancer and together we would teach. Then Balanchine said to me, "Jasha, I am going to Monte Carlo. Let's go together on vacation." And I went with him. I would rather wait in Monte Carlo than wait in Paris. The Ballets of 1933 was finished. I just

trusted Balanchine. I was so happy! It was August. We were going to relax for one month and then we were going to America!

Before long Kirstein contacted Balanchine in Monte Carlo "asking him as nicely as possible," as he later wrote, "what the hell Dimitriev did, anyway; was he. . . necessary?" to which Balanchine, on 29 August, cabled in reply, "Await your decision presence Dimitriew is necessary."

So while Jasha sunned and dreamed in Monte Carlo, the hopes he embraced were inexorably and surreptitiously unraveled by those around him.

> After about two weeks in Monte Carlo Dimitriev suddenly came to me and said, "I have very bad news. I have a telegram from Tamara Toumanova and she has signed a contract to go back to de Basil." There had been cables going back and forth but I had no idea. They never told me. They had been working behind the scenes. Balanchine said, "We must go right away back to Paris." I asked him, "What about me?" and he said, "Well, Jasha, we have a little problem here. If Tamara doesn't go with us, you are in trouble because in a case like this, we don't need you right now. Maybe later."
>
> We drove back from the south of France in Balanchine's Pontiac, stopping to visit a French countess in Toulon for about three days. Balanchine was very, very unhappy with what had happened. But you see, there were lots of stories. Mama Toumanova, when I talked with her later, told me that they had been in Paris and didn't have any money to live on. Of Mama, Papa, and Tamara Toumanova, no one was working except Tamara. She made the salary for three people and she needed to support her parents. They wrote a letter to Dimitriev and said, "You must send us some money because we don't have any way to live. We don't have any money and we don't know what to do." But Dimitriev never told Balanchine about this letter. It is very complicated. At least, that's what Mama Toumanova told me.

The cables between Monte Carlo and America had flown thick and fast while Jasha was basking in sunshine and blissful unawareness. A euphoric Kirstein had raised funds on the premise that Jasinski and Toumanova were pivotal to the teaching-performing venture. Indeed, of Jasinski, Kirstein had written: "He is extremely beautiful—a superb body and by way of becoming a most remarkable dancer. . . .Jasinsky works all the time, is a fine mime modest, a bit dumb, but marvelous in an experts hand like Balanchine."

"A bit dumb"? No. Reticent? Yes. Jasinski never leaped into a conversation, particularly with those he considered "above him" in station. He was a modest, quiet, deep man, but one doesn't achieve the success that Jasinski achieved in learning new languages, cultures, choreography, and styles without shrewd and ceaseless brainpower.

Imagine Kirstein's alarm, after all the enthusiasm and euphoria, when he was belatedly informed by Balanchine in Paris on 14 September: ". . .presence Jasinsky and Toumanova not indispensable. . ." A cabled yelp of protest was answered one day later by "Presence now Toumanova Jasinsky absolutely unnecessary. . . ." In other words, Toumanova had been tricked into signing with de Basil, and poor Jasinski, too proud to ask the Colonel for his job back and far from the fortune once offered by James, was hung out to dry by Balanchine and Dimitriev.

> I did not want to go back to de Basil. I had left him when Balanchine offered me a chance to go to America. Balanchine wanted us in America, money or no money. I wanted to do the same thing, money or no money. I wanted to be in America.
>
> Tamara told me later that de Basil came to them in Paris and said, "Tamarishka, I want you to come join the company because I just signed a contract with Balanchine. He is coming back with us, touring." So she signed the contract. When she came to London she said, "Where is Balanchine?" but Balanchine was not there. How true all of this is only two people know—Tamara Toumanova and her mother.
>
> I asked Dimitriev what had happened and he said that it was not his fault. He said it was Toumanova's fault. "We don't know what to

do with you. We will go to America first and we will bring you later." I was left without a choice.

"Balanchine, what is going to happen to me?"

"Oh Jasha, I don't know."

"Before you send for me, what am I going to eat?"

"I don't know, Jasha. You know that I don't have any money. Dimitriev has the money."

That was true. Balanchine was not involved with any money at all. You see, Balanchine was always innocent in these things. I am not blaming Balanchine because he was the kind of man where only the art existed. He didn't care about money; he only wanted to do ballet. But when I talked with him, he said, "Jasha, talk with Dimitriev. He has everything." But Dimitriev said that he didn't have any money. Dimitriev was lying.

I said to Dimitriev, "I don't know what I'm going to do today or tomorrow. Can't I borrow some money and return it later?" I didn't ask for much—just 2000 francs. "Please, to live for a month before I find another job." Dimitriev said, "I'll give you 200 francs." And he took it right then from his pocket. Two hundred francs is nothing! I paid the hotel ten francs daily and restaurants cost ten francs. I already owed my hotel for two weeks. People are always saying something bad about the French people, but I was very lucky. I was always without money and the hotel people still let me live there. I had told the concierge that I was going to America. Big story! No money!

Anyway, before they left Paris for America we had dinner together. Balanchine was living at the George V near the Champs-Elysées. He could afford an expensive hotel because Dimitriev paid for it. I was living in a hotel on the Rue Pigalle in Montmartre. I didn't have one penny. I couldn't even afford the metro to the Champs-Elysées. I had to walk. It was a very big walk.

The "very big walk" spanned more than the center of Paris. It spanned the distance between penury and luxury, desperation and callousness, trust and betrayal.

Jasinski's hotel at 35 Rue Pigalle probably looks today much as it did in the early 1930s. A six-story edifice, squeezed between two buildings from a more gracious era, the Gramont-Eden Hotel proclaims in neon lights the virtues of "Amstel Biere."

A narrow door opens onto a faded green interior with peach and orange accents and a worn teal carpet ascends a narrow switchback stairway. One can easily imagine a dispirited young dancer pulling himself up those stairs towards the cheapest rooms under the roof, his dream in ruins, his very survival in question.

> What they did to me was not very nice. I stayed in my hotel for two weeks. Dimitriev and Balanchine had told me they would write, but they left and I didn't hear one word from Dimitriev. Balanchine wrote two letters. After two weeks all my money was gone. I knew how to live economically but it came to the point where I didn't have a piece of bread. Nothing. It was a disaster. For three days I stayed in the hotel and ate nothing. I thought that was the end of my life. I thought I was going to die.

A room and a bed, far up that long, switchbacked stair. For three days Jasinski lay on his bed without food or hope, in a city where no jobs were to be had for a foreigner with none but dancing skills.

## CHAPTER 8

# My Starving

*My starving did not start when I came to Paris. I was starving long before—in Poland.*

AS A LITTLE BABY I WAS CRYING—always crying. How hard for my mother, all her children crying. We wanted to eat and we didn't have any food, any bread. There were seven children to feed, five boys and two girls. We just barely existed. My mother would say, "Go to sleep quickly. The pain will go away."

My mother, Stefania, and my father, August, met on the day they married. Their parents had arranged this. In time they had ten children. Twice they had twins. It was the way in Poland to have a child every two years. The first twins died. Of the second twins, my sister died and my brother, Stefan, lived. Henryk was the oldest, then Feliks, Stefan, Janka, Leon, Stefania, and me.

I was the last, the baby, born 23 June 1907. My mother didn't want any more children. She didn't even want me, she told me later, but after I was born she loved me. She called me Cenka, or Czesio, for Czeslaw. In the family they called me that, but in the Russian ballet they called me Jasha for Jasinski. They couldn't pronounce any of the other names.

My father was an architect of churches. He was a very religious man. He built churches outside of Warsaw and small, simple homes.

My mother was the most wonderful woman, but with so many children she was always working. She would get up in the morning early, make breakfast, and then clean up after everyone. There was lots to do. Lunch. Dinner. And she needed to wash the clothes. I can still remember how every Friday she washed the sheets and pillows with her hands, and sometimes her hands were bleeding. We would put the laundry on wood under a big heavy box filled with stones and we would roll it with our hands. Press it. You needed to go to a special place to do this and you needed to pay a little bit, not much. I liked to do this. It made me strong. And then the clean laundry was hung under our roof on a line.

When I was a little boy of three or four, a big fire burned a large section of Warsaw. There was only enough time for my family to get out of the house. These were big houses with thirty or forty people in each, and many houses burned. No one was hurt badly but my family lost everything. We were out on the street and it was bitter cold. It was always cold in Poland.

The house we moved to was outside of Warsaw and had no toilet. In the night you had to go down and outside, no matter how cold it was. My mother suffered from this and convinced my father we needed a toilet.

That is when we moved to 54 Wilcza in the center of Warsaw. We had a big house but we only lived in part of it. Other people lived in the rest of the house. Our family had a kitchen, a little hall, and two rooms for seven people. My brothers opened army beds and the rest of us slept two people to one bed.

The heat in our kitchen was from a salamander, a place in the center of the room where you put coals on top of bricks. We had wood and coal and we always had to clean up the coal dust. The salamander was round, high, and you could cook on it. Our water was cold like ice. We did not have hot water, so sometimes we boiled water on top. Everyone just sat around the salamander to keep warm. I was always cold.

We have this very strong river, the Vistula. If you stay close to the shore it's all right. It doesn't have great power. But if you step further it will catch you. One day I was swimming there and somehow I lost bottom and started calling for help. I screamed. The water was choking me, coming into my throat. A man who was walking by saw me. He threw off his jacket, jumped in the water, and pulled me out. I was unconscious. I remember that I saw a long tunnel with a white light at the end. I felt very warm and safe, and wanted to go to the light. There was someone there with open arms inviting me, but suddenly I was pulled back to the world. I didn't want to come back. The man had put me on my knees and was pushing the water out. When I could speak I said, "Pan ("Mister"), let me get a piece of paper. I want to get your name and number." But he went away. He saved my life but I was never able to pay him back. All my life it was my goal to pay back the people who helped me.

When I was older I was in the school all day; I was never home. I started the public school when I was seven years old. I don't remember its name because I don't have very pleasant memories of it. It was very strict. They beat you if you didn't prepare your schoolwork. They hit your hands with a ruler three times. Next time they gave you more hits—six times. It was in an old building, heated, but not by much. We sat on benches two by two—all of us with our coats on.

In the public school the teachers were tough. It was just like the army. They didn't have any pity for you. School was work. My sister Janka had prepared me. I could count; I knew the alphabet. My best subject was geography because I always wanted to travel. Since I was a little boy I was always dreaming of travel.

I loved history, geography, and arithmetic but I remember one time the teacher asked me about one of Poland's kings and I didn't know. He hit me because I hadn't prepared my schoolwork and my arm was red. There was no next time. I couldn't go home and tell that the teacher had spanked me because my father would spank me too. My father told me if they spanked me at school he would double it.

My father was a very strict man.

In Warsaw there were special places where you could do your after-school work. These places had benches like at school and you could sit down and do your work before you went home. After classes I had two full hours of schoolwork to do. The government lit these places with electricity because poor people didn't have electricity. At home at night I had to work under the light of the moon.

Education in Warsaw was different from here in the United States. In my school if you made a mistake you had to correct it a hundred times. But in America, when my son came home from school I would say, "Where is your homework?" and he would say, "I have no homework." I went to the school and they said, "Oh, we want him to enjoy his childhood." What stupid thing is this?

We were all scared of my father. We were so afraid that we didn't like him. When the door opened and he entered the room, we jumped and pretended we were reading. If I didn't want to do something like clean the oil lamps, or bring the coal in the bucket, my mother would say, "Well, I need to tell your father that you don't want to do this." That was enough.

In three years of interviews Jasha seldom spoke of his father, although on one occasion he remarked that his father had hoped his son would become an engineer. The respect he felt for a parent was tempered by the fear he had known as a child and there was little communication between the two. Still, Jasha once told his son, Roman, of the day he turned eighteen. His father took him to a bar, handed him a drink and a cigar, and said, "Today you are a man!"

Long before that celebration, when Jasha, the youngest child, was a still a schoolboy, the family's tight finances began to ease a bit. Habits remained frugal, the older children grew into self-sufficiency, and life became a little less lean.

In the summertime we would go to the market each Friday. Everyone went to the market for chickens, sausage, ham, and bread. And there was Park Agrykola where I went to a summer program.

The government gave the children a piece of bread and a glass of goat's milk. Free! We played football there.

A piece of bread and a glass of goat's milk. Those were the good days before the First World War. To the end of his life Jasha relished sausage, borscht, and bigos. Indeed, there were meals throughout his life that Jasha could recite from beginning to end.

> My mother made pigs' feet, and pigs' feet jello made with carrots. It was very delicious. She also made faworki, a dough that she would cut very thin, roll into balls, and throw into hot oil. They would puff up and she would sprinkle them with cinnamon and powdered sugar. Oh! Delicious! She could do this only for special occasions, but holidays and saints' days would be a time for treats.
>
> My saint's day was 20 July. I was called Czeslaw, but I was named for Saint Roman. For my saint's day my mother would maybe make some cookies too. I didn't get many presents.
>
> We always celebrated Christmas, even if poorly. My brothers would go into the forest around Warsaw, cut the tree, and bring it home. We would decorate the tree with candles and all kinds of stuffed paper. We painted nuts and hung them on the tree or we hung almonds wrapped with gold, red, or yellow paper. And apples, we hung lots of apples. In the night we children would get up and tippy-toe to steal these apples. They never caught me!
>
> There were not many gifts under the tree. I remember once I got a gun with a cork. I was twelve or thirteen. Another time there was a small train on a track. A gun or a knife if you were a scout.
>
> It was a very hard life, but I appreciate my life now. I have everything I could possibly want. Children in America have too much. My God! We ruin them.
>
> When I was still a child, the Russians were everywhere in Poland; they had occupied Poland for a hundred years. My brothers had had to learn Russian in school and when a Russian came toward you on

the pavement, you were supposed to move to the side to let him pass. My brother Leon didn't move one day and a Russian soldier punched his nose.

It was very exciting when my mother's sister went to America with my uncle and their nine children. They came to this country without any papers on a boat that stopped at Ellis Island, and then my uncle got permission to stay. I always dreamed of coming to America when I was little boy, but we couldn't go after the war because my father didn't make enough money. When my aunt and uncle came to America it was open visa—you didn't need papers or money. You came for free. They probably were smart people who had had enough of Poland and wanted to try New York. Many years later I looked for them but could never find them.

They wrote letters about how wonderful it was in America. They had food—lots of food. That's what started my dreaming. I wanted to come to America because there was food here. Then, when I was in school, I read about America and how big and tall the houses were. I saw pictures of American skyscrapers. That was so interesting to me.

Before long the nascent dream of a future in America dissolved into the horrors of World War I.

The war started when the Germans invaded Poland. The Baltic Sea in the north of Poland was very important to them. My father was from the North but I never met my grandparents because both the Russians and Germans had closed the path to the sea.

I remember when the Germans came to Warsaw. My older brother went to the war to fight against Germany, but the Polish army didn't feed a soldier very well. They would give him a piece of bread in the morning to last all day. Sometimes they didn't even do this. Sometimes he had to eat apples before they were ripe. He'd have terrible stomachaches. Another brother, Feliks, fought for Austria because they gave better food. You could also join the French army and fight against Russia. You could choose which army you wanted. Everybody in Warsaw was against Russia and against the Germans too.

This is when Jasha's hard life became harder. The Germans swarmed into Warsaw in 1915. With the Germans came real want, real hunger. Thousands of Poles died of starvation as retreating Russians scorched the earth ahead of approaching German armies. The entire Jasinski family survived—but suffered deeply.

War meant terrible things for us—hunger and death. I remember the hunger most of all. During the war there was no food at all in Warsaw. Farmers outside the city could raise something to eat but war is always tough on people who live in big cities. Warsaw was the worst. When you cannot get bread you cannot survive. My mother could not cook anything because there was nothing there to cook. We ate bread and water. To buy bread we waited in line for hours and hours.

One night after curfew about twenty Polish people jumped from the shadows onto the Germans who carried bread in a big truck pulled by horses. The Polish people threw the Germans out of the truck, opened up the back door and threw the bread onto the street. One of my brothers picked up two loaves and ran home. If they had caught him he would have gone to prison. I was eight or nine when he brought home the bread.

In order to make coffee, my brother Leon would climb an oak tree like a monkey and shake its branches in the autumn. The nuts would fall down and we would take the shells off and cut the nuts in small pieces. Whenever we wanted coffee, we put some in a kettle to get warm, stirring them all the time to keep them from burning. It took a couple of hours to turn them from white to brown. Finally, after they cooled we took a mortar and pestle and ground the nuts into powder This is how we made our coffee. We ate bread and drank coffee or water. No butter. No meat. No vegetables, except sometimes carrots or potatoes. For two or three years we ate like this. There was nothing more. The farmers didn't come into Warsaw because they were afraid the army would take their food.

I remember one time there were some Germans on a truck full of potatoes. We boys yelled at them to give us some. One soldier was so mad that he threw a potato and hit me. I was so happy! I took the potato home and that night it fed my whole family.

When my brothers came back from the war they were covered with lice. The first thing my mother did was burn their clothes.

After the war, we started to receive help from America. The Red Cross sent us sacks of flour. They also gave each family a big can of lard.

Ignacy Paderewski gave lots of concerts for Polish relief in America, donating all this money to Poland. He was Polish—a great composer and a great man. Many, many years later I dedicated my ballet PAS DE PADEREWSKI to him in thanks.

After the war the government gave people little pieces of property where they could grow carrots and potatoes. My mother couldn't have a farm because she needed to prepare food for the family and that took all day, but our neighbor had a little farm and my mother said, "Cenka, why don't you go to her farm? You can walk there and pick some carrots for our soup." Before I came home I had already eaten the carrots. I was so hungry and the carrots were so sweet!

Despite the concern of constant hunger, ballet classes consumed Jasinski's time and passion. The boy grew in knowledge and technique while his older siblings went their ways. Brother Henryk, the eldest, became an alcoholic. In the end he died from exposure, passed out on a park bench in the midst of a Polish winter. The thought of Henryk always saddened Jasha. Their sister, Janka, was both competent and opportunistic. Unlike Jasha, Janka lived for herself, never contributing to the family finances. The young dancer who spotted Jasha's amazing instep at the party that summer in Warsaw had been Janka's friend. Janka took credit for her brother's career and never failed to remind him of his debt to her.

And as for Leon, he was brilliant with figures, adding them in his mind faster than a machine, but he, too, hoarded his pay.

Not so Jasha. Sending money home was both an obligation and a pleasure for the young dancer, so his double failure as provider and performer after the Balanchine debacle must have made those dark days of deprivation in Paris bitter indeed. There was nowhere to go, no one to turn to, no future to plan for.

> For three days I stayed in the hotel and ate nothing. I thought it was the end of my life. I thought I was going to die.

CHAPTER 9

# Lifar to the Rescue

*Oh! What a dancer he was!*

THEN IT WAS LIKE A MIRACLE. Suddenly the concierge came. "Mr. Jasinski, Serge Lifar is here. Come down." I was on the sixth floor. The higher the floor, the cheaper you can live. I ran down those six floors as quick as I could. I saw Lifar and I thought, "My God, maybe I can borrow some money from him!" Lifar said, "Jasha, what are you doing here?"

"Mr. Lifar, I have not eaten for three days. Could you give me one franc? I just want a piece of bread!"

"Jasha, would you like to go with me to America?"

"America? OH YES!"

"Well, I don't have any money. I never have any money. Go to my office at the Place de la Madeleine. Tell them that you need some money. You can sign the contract today."

Here was another man who didn't think he needed money! He was involved with the ballet and he was poor. Well, not poor, but whenever he wanted to take a taxi, he was so famous, the taxi driver wouldn't take money from him. He would say, "Oh, I am so lucky to have Serge Lifar in my taxi!" and would let him ride for free! Everyone knew Lifar in Paris. He was the director at the Paris Opera. When he wanted to buy a tie they gave him the tie. And if he went to eat, the restaurants would say, "Oh, Serge Lifar was in my restaurant!"

I went to his agency near the Place de la Madeleine. They gave me the contract and five hundred francs. I said, "I am so hungry. I need to go eat." And I walked straight across the street to the nearest restaurant.

The contract that Jasinski signed that day is dated 15 October 1933. It is eerie to match an exact date to an exact meal devoured decades ago, but Jasha always affirmed that that visit from Lifar saved his life.

SERGE LIFAR

Photo courtesy Jerome Robbins Dance Division, The New York Public Library for the Performing Arts, Astor, Lenox and Tilden Foundations.

Another original contract confirmed plans for a two-month tour that would end in mid-September 1932, no doubt the genesis of Lifar's later search that led him to Jasinski's hotel, and sent the concierge up that long flight of stairs.

> The first time I came to Paris, I had made a special effort to see Serge Lifar dance. We knew about the Diaghilev company in my school in Warsaw, so I went to the theatre to see him perform. I paid lots of money for my ticket—fifty francs. I didn't see Diaghilev himself, but I saw Lifar in PRODIGAL SON and then in LA CHATTE.
>
> Oh! What a dancer! I never dreamed that anyone could dance like this. I was absolutely standing, screaming. No one in my life had ever made such an impression on me. He was more balletic, you know. He was like lightning on the stage. Pirouette! Pow! Pow! Pow! Sharp! The man was dynamite—fire!
>
> Lifar was a great man. He always tried to help dancers. He asked the other dancers where to find me. Dancers always went to a special cafe at Place d'Italie; it was sort of our information center. Every artist since Diaghilev went there. They drank and played cards there. That is how he knew where to find me, and how he saved my life.
>
> Then, at last, came my first trip to America.
>
> Serge Lifar's company was not big. I would say probably no more than ten people, and I was hired as soloist. For Lifar it was a tour in between opera seasons to make more money.
>
> I remember with Lifar my stomach hurt once; I don't know what from. I had a terrible pain. But I needed to dance anyway. You could not say you were sick. It's not like today where you don't come to rehearsal if your stomach hurts. Perform, perform! However you feel, just go! You'll make it, you'll make it! And if you die there, you die! But go!
>
> You know, Lifar had the kind of name that people would go to see. They didn't care what he did. When we went to the United States and Canada, I did the pas de deux from LES SYLPHIDES and the SYLPHIDES male variation. Lifar danced his "Prometheus" as well as

the "Blue Bird" variation from the ballet we now call THE SLEEPING BEAUTY. That's a terrible role. It is so difficult. Now, when people dance it, they cut half of the variation to make it easier.

I saw Balanchine when we were there. I did not like what he had done to me when he said good-bye in Paris, leaving me to starve, but for me it was no longer necessary to suffer over these things. It was good that Tamara Toumanova left Les Ballets 1933. I don't think that the plan to bring us to America would have worked out because they didn't have any money.

Balanchine was sick when I saw him. He had only one working lung, you see. Dimitriev proposed right away that I stay with them in America, but there was nothing there. Nothing was happening. I would stay for what?

The idea they had was that Toumanova and I would come to America, Balanchine would open a studio and we would teach. But even if he wanted me, you know what? He didn't have any money! "We'll give you a house or an apartment and you can cook there." Again, big story, no money! I was tired of this. It made me happy that I was separate from Balanchine and dancing with Lifar.

Lincoln Kirstein and Balanchine later had lots of problems with Dimitriev. He held the money, and wanted to become the director. I heard Kirstein and Balanchine borrowed $400,000—at least this is the number in my head—to pay Dimitriev off and get him out of there because they couldn't stand him any more. I don't know who told me this story. It was Kirstein's idea that he was the director. They finally got rid of Dimitriev because he was an impossible man.

Years later, when Balanchine died, he had all sorts of money left. I started thinking, "Why did Balanchine have so much money?" They told me Balanchine had $600,000 in the bank.

Where did he get all this? Nobody suspects this—only me. Here is what I think—that when he died Dimitriev left all his money to Balanchine. Balanchine did not care about money. Always when we went some place, Balanchine never paid for anything. Like Lifar. How

> much was he making? I don't have the slightest idea. Money did not exist for him.

At this juncture, with Jasinski in Lifar's company, money didn't exist for Lifar, either. Literally. Critics were cruel. Funds dwindled devastatingly. As he wrote in his autobiography, "My dear friend Barbara Hutton, who had sponsored my journey. . . let me down. So I [was] obliged to hire an orchestra at my own expense and pay the salaries of all the dancers. To meet these expenses I had to sell to the Hartford museum a whole collection of modern pictures that I had obtained with the Diaghilev estate and which were at that moment on exhibition in New York."

Lincoln Kirstein's friend Chick Austin of the Wadsworth Atheneum was elated. It was a major coup. For a mere $10,000 the Atheneum obtained this priceless collection and Lifar was able to bring his dancers back to Paris. An astonished onlooker described Lifar's euphoria at collecting the proceeds at the bank: "In one bound, after a pretty *entrechat,* Lifar was atop the counter by one of those leaps so famous in *Le Spectre de la Rose.* With half drawn revolvers the guards stared in amazement as Lifar flourished his check and bowed." If Jasinski knew that he was in the same precarious situation in New York with Lifar as he had been with Kniasev in Monte Carlo, he never mentioned it.

> I left Balanchine in America. Lifar's company returned to Paris on 9 December, and when we arrived Lifar said, "Jasha, what are you going to do?" "I don't know. I don't have a job here." "If you want, I can take you into the Paris Opera." I didn't really want to do that; people said it was hard there. And opera ballet was boring. I wanted to stay out, but I was going to do anything that was necessary to dance. I wanted to wait a couple of days and see what happened.
>
> Instinct, you know. I had instinct.

## Chapter 10

# Back to de Basil

*My greatest good fortune.*

THEN THE VERY NEXT DAY, 10 December, somebody knocked on my door. I opened the door and recognized the secretary from the de Basil company. "Mr. Jasinski. Colonel de Basil wants to see you. Will you come?" He didn't say anything else. When I went the next day, I signed a contract for five years! I was dancing again for de Basil!

Nine December I arrived in Paris from New York. Ten December the man knocked on the door. Eleven December I signed the contract. Twelve December I left France and went to England to join the company. Right away I was on another boat, once again on my way to America. You know, this was unbelievable.

I had worked here and I had worked there, and eventually I found I didn't lose anything. When James asked me to stay with Les Ballets 1933 it was probably good I didn't stay. If I had stayed there I would never have gone back to de Basil. Even though I had a hard time when Balanchine left me with no money, Serge Lifar took care of me and invited me to go to America. But my greatest good fortune was when Colonel de Basil asked me back. I could never ask for myself. It was not my way. Once I left, it was for life. But de Basil called me. With de Basil, I got my salary again and was able to send money to my family in Poland.

It turned out that de Basil and I became very good friends. De Basil liked me because I was never any trouble for the company. I was only interested in dancing. I was never mixed up with company intrigue. I had learned my lesson with Zailich in Poland. I just danced, and that was that. I was merry. I would talk, but I never let myself get too close to the other dancers, and I found out that that way was good.

I was so happy to be back but you know, a lot of people were unhappy because they now needed to share their roles. I had left the company as a soloist and came back as a premier danseur. Some dancers had already taken over my roles in SYLPHIDES, SWAN LAKE, AURORA'S WEDDING, COTILLON, CONCURRENCE. De Basil and Grigoriev decided who would dance what. De Basil had a Russian feeling; he could look at a dancer and say, "He should do this part." I was not worried about my roles because I knew they would give them to me. In America we performed in a hundred towns. You would dance a role here, and in two weeks you would dance a role there. Everyone had a chance.

Unlike most of the dancers, I was still traveling on a Polish passport. I had to go to the consulate and get a new visa each year. That was my problem. I was always afraid of Zailich, of being forced into the Polish army, of being trapped in Poland. I always took my contract when I went to the consulate to show I had a job.

Others didn't have this problem. They could go any place they wanted. The best passport was the one from Denmark. The American passport was good. Also good were the Nansen passports for the Russians. After the Revolution, the Russians came to France but were not French citizens so they were given Nansen passports. They had no country, but they had no problem traveling, either.

The crossing to the United States took four or five days. I was sick every time we crossed the Atlantic; the boat always rolled side to side. They had to tie my trunk to my bed. People fell and broke their arms and legs. There were only two people in the whole company who could eat. Everybody else was sick.

I liked traveling, but not on the sea. I didn't eat for four days. I just stayed in my cabin and didn't go anyplace. They brought me some crackers or a piece of bread to chew on. Then when I finally got off the boat I walked funny, like rolling. But after one day I was all right.

With de Basil, we always stayed at the Wellington Hotel on 7th Avenue. The whole company stayed there. We had special rates—a dollar a day—but no bath in the room. The bath was down the hall, but that didn't make any difference. It was free! All the boys wanted to stay all day and night in the shower because it was free. In Europe you had to pay ten francs. You might take only one shower a month. You washed from a sink. But in New York, free! The shower was pumping all day!

I was crazy about New York. I had never seen anything like it. An enormous number of people were on the streets day and night. New York never stopped. That was the biggest surprise. To see so many people rushing. You could not get into the subway. There were too many people.

New York was so fantastic. We couldn't believe what it was like. Showers, food, anything you wanted. Breakfast—fifteen cents. Coffee a nickel. We would go to cafeterias where it was cheap. Oatmeal, ten cents. Eggs, fifty cents. Oh, it was unbelievable!

I stayed in New York for one month dancing on Broadway, even though Broadway was not really the place for ballet. We did LES SYLPHIDES, PETROUCHKA, and PRINCE IGOR—the same program every day. We opened in December at the St. James Theatre on 44th Street and when I danced the "Poet" in LES SYLPHIDES, the audience whistled me! They whistled because they saw a man in tights. When I came to do my variation they applauded—big applause—but they also whistled. I was afraid they were going to throw tomatoes! It was very strange for Americans to see a man in tights. Now people can wear anything, but then I could never go on stage without white shorts over the tights. Tights were considered shocking.

CHAPTER 11

# DE BASIL AND BLUM: THE BEGINNING OF THE END

*Poof! They sent me back to Monte Carlo.*

WHILE DE BASIL was accumulating American accolades for his company, his partner, René Blum, was gnashing his teeth in Monte Carlo. Where was his resident company? Where were the dancers who were supposed to augment his operas, dance at the anniversary gala, rehearse in his Monaco hall until the ballet season opened in spring? The company was the "Ballets Russes de Monte-Carlo" in name only. It was changing direction, leaving Blum behind.

De Basil had learned that there was a public hunger for a major ballet company and he was anxious to explore every option and opportunity at home and abroad. The company lingered in lucrative America while its Monte Carlo obligation went unmet. In this exploratory effort, de Basil was aided by impresario Sol Hurok, who added performance after performance in city after city, even splitting the company for optimum exposure.

Poor Blum. Somehow he had to present a ballet season—but with what resident company? The opera season came and went. De Basil remained in America.

Both Blum and de Basil were resourceful. The Monte Carlo gap was filled with European directors and dancers. Bronislava Nijinska's Théâtre de la Danse was hired for the opera season, and for the ballet season de Basil sent a handful

SOL HUROK

Hurok as he appeared in the Original Ballet Russe program, 1940–1941.

Photo by M. Goldberg, Hollywood.

of stars to Monte Carlo to augment her company. It was the beginning of the end of the de Basil/Blum association, a classic example of too little, too late, but the collaboration would limp on another year before the relationship was severed.

> At this time, de Basil really had two companies. One was in Monte Carlo under Nijinska and one was in the United States. De Basil asked Nijinska, "Who of my dancers would you like to have for your company?" "You give me Jasinski. I want Jasinski." I had been only a couple of months in America, and, poof! They sent me back to Monte Carlo.
>
> I said I would go because Nijinska had done so much for me. I remembered when she asked those boys to take care of me. It was thanks to them, Serge Unger and Eugene Lapitsky, that I had danced in so many places after Rubinstein. But to me it was terrible. All my

life I had wanted to be in America. Now I must go back to Europe! Still, Nijinska had brought me out of Poland. I owed her.

I didn't make any money in Monte Carlo. You made money in America, not Europe, but I couldn't tell Nijinska I didn't want to go. Instead I said, "Oh, I will be really happy to come," even though it was not very good for me.

Jasinski, Danilova, Léon Woizikowski, and some others returned to Monte Carlo, and then Boris Kniasev showed up.

We performed in Monte Carlo in April 1934. We did BOLERO but it was not the same BOLERO Nijinska had done six years before for Ida Rubinstein when I first came from Poland. She changed it. She also gave LES COMÉDIENS JALOUX where I was a juggler and someone had to teach me to juggle. I juggled three plates while climbing a ladder. We also did ETUDE—very classic, very stylish—and LES BICHES, as well as VARIATIONS, which was not very successful. They were all new to me.

The members of the cobbled-together company worked valiantly, learning new ballets, challenged by new choreography, putting their well-trained best feet forward. While the effort to keep Monte Carlo happy continued, rumors of the de Basil/Blum rift circulated surreptitiously. Such rumors could only cause anxiety for a young man once again at home in a company he loved and now threatened with still more uncertainty as de Basil's triumphant American tour concluded.

After the season, the two companies came together again and there were too many dancers! My God! It was terrible! Everybody hated everybody because all they could think was "What is going to happen with my parts?" There were three people dancing my parts already. It was a very odd situation. But it worked out, because de Basil released some of the dancers. He couldn't take all these people.

SONO OSATO

Osato as she appeared in the Original Ballet Russe program, 1940–1941.

Photo by Battles, London.

Among those he kept was a new recruit, a talented and provocatively exotic young Asian-American girl, Sono Osato, who had joined the company in Philadelphia. Not yet fifteen at the time of their meeting, Sono would become the twenty-seven-year-old Jasha's first serious relationship.

It was a love that almost missed connection due to an uncharacteristically upset Jasinski. On 12 June 1934, he wrote a letter announcing his resignation from the Ballets Russes. This time he was careful to document his reasons. One lawsuit during the Balanchine debacle had been quite enough.

The reason for his resignation? He was dancing corps de ballet roles during company performances at the Théâtre des Champs-Elysées, although he had been rehired by de Basil as a principal.

The letter was neatly typed and very respectful. "J'ai l'honneur vous informer que j'ai decidé de reprendre ma liberté. . . " ("I have the honor of informing you that I have decided to retake my liberty. . .") This must have been one of those instances where de Basil "talked with you and explained things to you, explained the situation," because Jasinski was to remain with de Basil for another thirteen years, steadfastly refusing all other offers of employment. Besides, there was this new and beautiful girl. . .

> We opened in London in the summer of 1934 after tours to Barcelona and Paris. I remember I was very happy. This company was really unbelievable. I found out that even poor people in England went to the theatre. They would stay all night to get gallery seats. We would finish a performance and already outside would be people in chairs waiting to get tickets for the next one. I would wait this way in Poland to get bread to eat and here they were waiting to see the ballet! I couldn't believe it.

If Jasinski was happy with the London tour, René Blum was not. In a masterly, if Machiavellian, move, de Basil had deliberately dropped prominent reference to either Monte Carlo or his erstwhile partner by the time he reached London. His company now danced as "Ballets Russes de Col. W. de Basil." Lawyers and paperwork loomed. The breach was irreconcilable.

By now Jasinski was firmly ensconced in the company of his choice, a beautiful girl had entered his life, and the future seemed full of promise. Still, the young man longed to see his family again. Too many years had passed since the train to Paris had carried him from his homeland. The time seemed right. There was a brief break after the London tour. But every penny he now made was spent on sheer survival. How could he manage to pay for a quick trip home?

Perhaps it was the memory of Balanchine's company in London. Perhaps it was sheer moxie. But something gave Jasinski the courage to contact Edward James, the wealthy benefactor of Les Ballets 1933, who had created a company for love of his wife and had lost both wife and company when Jasinski left to follow Balanchine's American dream.

West Dean, the ancestral home of Edward James, is located a short distance from Chichester, England. Built of somber gray stone and set in vivid green hills white-speckled with sheep, this imposing structure contains James' private papers and photographs. The father of Edward James, William James, made his fortune from American lumber, rail, and copper interests, and the remnants of that fortune fund the upkeep of this estate today.

In a West Dean library dark with polished wood and hushed with a sense of history are several boxes and books relating to Les Ballets 1933. Tucked into one of these among photographs, receipts, and miscellaneous notes, are three letters signed "Czeslaw," written in French in an elegant hand. Many years earlier Jasinski had spoken of borrowing ticket money from James so he could make a visit home to Poland, and here are found the actual requests, outliving writer and benefactor.

> CAMBRIDGE HOTEL
> 12 MONTAGUE STREET
> RUSSELL SQUARE
> 30 JULY 1934
>
> Dear Mr. James:
> I should love to see you, but I do not know where you are.
> So I decided to write you a letter in which I ask you something

which is not agreeable for me and perhaps not for you, but life is difficult, you will not be cross with me that I dare to ask you for help if you can. I hope you can. I ask you to lend me £50, and I shall be grateful. I will return £5 each month. I need this money to travel to Varsovie [Warsaw]. I should like to see my mother. Because I had a letter from my mother. She wants to see me before I leave for America. You understand, I have not seen my mother for six years because of money. You are the only one who can lend me some. I ask you once more to do this to make me happy. I shall never forget you doing this. Thank you a hundred times.

Yours sincerely,
Czeslaw Jasinski

When there was no immediate response, Jasinski picked up pen again and wrote a second time.

7 AUGUST 1934

Dear Mr. James:

As I have had no reply from you I do not lose hope and write to you again once more. . . . this is my last chance. Lend me only £25. I assure you that I will return it, you can be quite sure of that. . . . You have five days to reply, please. . . . It's not difficult for you, is it, Mr. James.

No, it was not difficult, and Jasinski's pleas were heard. The box contains another missive, this from Edward James himself, where James wrote of Jasinski's "excellent dancing technique" and "sweet character. . . . I never heard anybody speak a word of him that was not of praise and affection."

The money was sent. The way home was paved.

LONDON, 11 AUGUST 1934

Dear Mr. James,

Thank you very much for your cheque—what a joy and surprise for me, you cannot imagine.

How pleased I was that I can rest peacefully during the holiday like the others.

Thank you a hundred times for your kindness and good heart.

Yours sincerely,

Czeslaw Jasinski

In this acknowledgement, Jasha included a spare sketch of a flower, rendered with surprising delicacy. This was another latent talent. Throughout his life, Jasinski would draw and paint with pleasure, a quiet relaxation from the rigors of his profession.

> I liked Edward James and I saw him from time to time. I was grateful to him because I borrowed £20 from him to go and visit my mother in Poland. Travel was very free before the war. You just needed a visa. If I was going to visit Poland I needed a Belgian visa and one from Germany. They didn't cost much money. He was very happy when I said I needed this money to see my mother and mentioned that he no longer had a mother.
>
> I went to Poland with this £20 and changed it to a lot of zlotys.
>
> When I came home I asked my mother, "What would you like to have in your life?" I wanted to send her to someplace she could rest, but she said, "If you move me from here, what is going to happen? Who is going to cook for the family?"
>
> Then I said, "What do you desire?"
>
> "I would like to have a new couch."
>
> One of the springs where she slept hurt her back. When I was in the Warsaw Opera Ballet I had a friend whose father made furniture. We were very close friends and he was very sorry when I left. I went to

his father and told him, “All right, we will make a deal.” And he didn’t charge me much. My mother always said, “Oh, I sleep so well after you give me this present!”

In all, I made two trips home to see my family, one in 1934 and one later. It is thanks to Mr. James that I made the first trip.

CHAPTER 12

# Manic Massine

*Music playing, Massine screaming.*

In fall 1934 de Basil's Ballets Russes started its American tour at the opening of the Palacio de las Bellas Artes in Mexico City. This was a new theatre, but was already sinking into the lake bed that underlies part of Mexico City. "In those days," Jasha recalled, "men walked the streets with guns. All of Mexico had guns." The company also toured to Canada.

> I liked Canada. The people were polite, and they liked ballet. One day when I was coming back from the stage in Montreal the girls from the audience said, "Oh, he's cute. He's cute." I didn't speak good English and I asked somebody, what is this "cute"? I was running from them! Always when we came backstage there were hundreds of them waiting for us to sign programs.
>
> When we came to America they worked us all hours of the day and night. They could call you anytime. If they called you at three o'clock in the morning you had to come. Massine, especially, called.
>
> One time Sol Hurok, our sponsor, came and said we could stay two weeks or a month more in America if we made one new ballet. We would have a second season in Chicago and a closing season in New York too.

LÉONIDE MASSINE

Photo by Maurice Seymour courtesy of Ron Seymour. Private Collection.

Massine agreed to create a new ballet, JARDIN PUBLIC, in order to make the American tour longer. We would finish each performance and the whole company would change to practice clothes and start rehearsing again on this new ballet. Say we finished our performance at eleven at night. We would then rehearse in the theatre until the manager came to say, "I must close the theatre. It is already one o'clock. This is impossible!" Then Massine would say, "All right. Jasha, Tamara, Rachel, come on. Let's go to the hotel lobby." We would start rehearsing there. And Massine would pour me some gin to pick me up so I could learn my part as the "Statue."

Our pianist, Rachel Chapman, was so fantastic. She would play so loud. Music playing, Massine screaming. Then the telephones from the different rooms would call downstairs. "What is this noise? We cannot sleep!" Rachel played so loud the hotel manager would come to say, "What is this here? What is this?" And Massine would say, "We are rehearsing." "No! Go away! Closing. No more. Out!" And the manager would chase us out.

We would rehearse until three or four o'clock in the morning. Imagine! The performance was at eight o'clock in the evening, and we would already have rehearsed two hours before, starting at six. We rehearsed before the performance, gave the performance, rehearsed after the performance, then moved to the lobby.

Massine was a man who really could work all day and night. He never tired. He was the strongest human I ever saw, like a horse. He could work from the morning and never stop, just go and go.

He always choreographed his own part on someone else. When he and Tamara Toumanova were the "Poor Couple" in JARDIN PUBLIC, he would choreograph his part on me and then I would turn around and teach his part to him. He would learn my style, copy my movements, but still make it different. Sometimes, he would do it his way and I would do it my way and he would like what I did. Then I would teach him how I did it. He told me that one day he would give me this part in a matinee but he never did. I made a little bit of scandal over this and went to complain but he always danced this part. He didn't want to give it up.

But, oh, Massine was a fantastic dancer! He was one of ballet's greatest stars when we came to the United States. He was a powerful, strong man on the stage. People went crazy. They screamed and jumped up when he danced LE BEAU DANUBE. And the Spanish ballet, LE TRICORNE—strong! So strong!

Massine became a big star here in this country. BEAU DANUBE was murder. You would almost die in this when the curtain came down. At the end of each performance Massine almost collapsed. I thought to myself, "My God. How this man punishes himself!" It was so much work! He danced the pas de deux with the "Street Dancer" and then he danced with the "Eldest Daughter." One dance would finish and then he would start another right away. It was very hard work. I found out later when I danced his part that it was the most difficult ballet. I don't know why he made so much work for himself.

It didn't bother me to follow him later in this role. I was never "jealousy." He gave his style; I gave my style. But I watched Massine, you see. I made movements my way, but I used Massine's sharpness. Strong movements, head, torso, everything. I saw how he danced. In Russia and Poland people danced this style.

I remember a little story about how Massine lost $600 in Mexico City. He always came to the theatre and did his own warm-up exercise. He would take his money from his pocket and put it on the floor. Mexico City was like Europe, old-fashioned, with lights under the stage and a conductor's hooded window. One day Massine turned around and saw hands come through this window, snatch the money and disappear. And you know, he started screaming like hell. He did not want to dance. He said, "I will not dance until I get this money." He was maybe a little bit hysterical, screaming like a woman. I heard that Hurok had to pay him $600 to take the place of the money that was stolen. Otherwise he would not dance.

You know where I hid my salary? In my dance belt, under my tights! Later on, I became smarter, and I put it in a bank.

Another thing about Massine: he liked very much to work with people who could remember steps. He was not interested in you if you were slow in learning. He became very impatient. You could see he was very unhappy if you slowed down his work. He would get angry sometimes and raise his voice. It depended on who you represented in the company. If you were corps de ballet he would scream at you. If you were soloist or first dancer, he was more careful.

When Massine choreographed, he put combinations down by numbers and showed you this, this, and this. "All right, that will be combination number one." He worked in pieces. This is what mixed me up and mixed many people up. He did a piece and said, "This is number seven." Then there would be another combination, number five. Then he would try to put them together. The first combination would become the sixth, the second one the fourth, and so on. This was very hard.

But you know, Tamara Grigorieva remembered. He would say, "All right. Number three," and she just said, "Oh yes, this!" I have known two others with this memory, Yurek Lazowski, and, later, Freddie Franklin. I remembered Massine's combinations, but not the numbers. Lazowski had a good memory, better than mine. He saw and he remembered. He could pull everybody's parts from some of the Fokine ballets, like PETROUCHKA, from his memory. Franklin was like this, too. But not I.

It was interesting working with the different choreographers during my career. Massine prepared. He had a little book where he put his notes. He would give our Polish pianist, Rachel, the music and she would count all the phrases. That makes it so easy if someone can count the music. For Massine, she was very important. But Balanchine never needed a pianist. He just looked at the music because he was himself a pianist. Sometimes he would show us the step, then go back to the piano. Back and forth, back and forth. Later, when I began to choreograph, I had to count the music myself. Balanchine never did. He just came, listened to the music, and read the score. He would choreograph without preparing first and then he would change it if you couldn't quite catch on. He came and created all the steps on you according to what you could do. Nijinska also read the conductor's score. I think when she came, she already had the idea of what she wanted to choreograph on you.

While Jasinski was rehearsing night and day, de Basil's great gamble was paying off. America was enthralled by his Ballets Russes. Why cool his company's heels in the tiny principality of Monaco when a vast continent awaited them? He cast his die. All that remained was the severance from Blum.

CHAPTER 13

# A Gypsy Once More

*We were never sure where we were going next.*

WE KNEW IN APRIL OF 1935 when we went to Monte Carlo that it would be our last season there. I considered Monte Carlo my European home. It was so beautiful there in the winter. Even when we worked it was like part of our vacation. My friend Yurek Lazowski auditioned for the company about this time and they took him. I had met Lazowski the first time on a street in Paris. I didn't remember him and he stopped me on the street and said, "Pan"—you know, in French it is "Monsieur," but for Polish people, it is "Pan"— "Pan, you don't remember me, but I am Lazowski." He was two or three years younger than I and also came from the Warsaw Opera Ballet school. He remembered seeing me dance at my graduation.

Friendships are funny things, especially in the volatile world of ballet. Often they are fleeting, superficial. As Jasinski put it, "I was merry. I would talk, but I never let myself get too close to the other dancers, and I found that that way was good." But these two Polish expatriates were to sustain each other in times of financial and emotional stress throughout their lives, and when Jasinski's son was born years later, it was Lazowski who stood as godfather to the boy.

Boris Kochno, my friend from the Balanchine days, also was back with the company. He had left de Basil to go with Balanchine in 1933, and then he, too, went back to the Colonel.

I liked Kochno because he was such a very interesting man. He was so knowledgeable. Besides this, he spoke such good French. He was Russian, you know. English I don't think he spoke so good.

After Monte Carlo we went from being a resident company to a touring company. We never knew where we were going next. I think it was better that way. It was better that the director did not tell us. It is not like the United States now where you can have any job. At that time there was only one major ballet company and a hundred people wanted to be in that company. Wherever they told us to go we went. We had a leader and we followed that leader. Otherwise we would worry that we could lose our job.

In June of 1935 we went to London for the Silver Jubilee of King George V. It was very special; they decorated Covent Garden with flowers. There were so many people there that the streets were blockaded. This was the time of the American woman, Wallis Simpson. When King George's son later became King Edward VIII, he left his throne to marry this Wallis and it caused a big scandal. Some people thought this was the end of England. I just thought of it as a change in English history.

London felt like home. As always, Jasinski stayed in a boardinghouse not far from the Royal Opera House at Covent Garden, passing the British Museum each time he walked to the theatre.

We needed to economize our salary so we chose a boardinghouse that was very cheap. We paid about £2 for this pension. A cold wind from an open window was always blowing in the bath, and we had a problem there with the meals because they served dinner at six and we had already left for the theatre. Later we moved to an even cheaper pension where we had only breakfast and lunch. Sometimes after the performance we would go to an Italian restaurant where other dancers went, but often we simply had no food. We were tired after performance and I didn't like to eat too much too late because I wouldn't sleep well.

Nijinska rejoined the company when we were in London. This time, she was hired by Colonel de Basil to choreograph LES CENT BAISERS for the company because the English banker, Baron d'Erlanger, had composed its music and provided the money to put it on the stage. Jean Hugo, the great-grandson of the author Victor Hugo, designed the sets and Madame Karinska created the costumes.

Nijinska choreographed LES CENT BAISERS very quickly. I remember that she wore gloves while she worked and always held a cigarette in a long holder. We boys constantly picked up her cigarette from the floor and put it back in the holder.

I could never understand why she was so hard on her husband in front of the whole company. "Do this and this." It looked to me like he liked her, though. He liked a woman to take care of him. She was demanding on everybody. You needed to do what she wanted.

When Rubinstein wanted to give more money to us in those days, Nijinska said not to give to the artists because they would stay and drink the bottle. That was true for some people. I didn't drink but some of the older dancers would always have a bottle of wine. It was very hard to see them become drunk. Diaghilev and all the Polish boys drank all the time.

Once the Diaghilev company was finished Balanchine took a couple of Diaghilev dancers into the Cochran Review in London and after each rehearsal the dancers would go drink. Balanchine told me this himself. The next day he would have rehearsal and all the English people were ready to roll, but all the Diaghilev dancers were drunk or had headaches. "Oh, I cannot work!" The next time he cast a ballet he didn't take anyone Russian. "Oh, you see how Balanchine treats us! He takes the English people, he doesn't take the Russians!" They were mad. They hang dogs on him!

"They hang dogs on him!" was certainly one of Jasha's more colorful colloquialisms. "I was never jealousy" and "do love in the forest" make one smile, but "they hang dogs on him" has a certain panache all its own. Its sense is clear, although its derivation is not. Jasha spoke five languages at least, some fluently, some haltingly, and could understand several more. Regardless of translation, the image of George Balanchine with dogs hanging from him gives one pause.

> I was the "Flower Gardener" in LES CENT BAISERS. Nijinska gave me a very hard variation. One day I couldn't dance and Grigoriev, the regisseur, asked, "Who knows this part?" Robert Bell said, "I know, I know." In performance he'd start a double tour en l'air, go up and fall down to the right, finishing in the wings. Then he would rush back on stage, jump up into the air and fall down again. And again. I remember Lazowski was hysterical when Robert did this. The whole company was dancing and all the corps de ballet was laughing. They were not supposed to laugh, but it was so funny!
>
> Irina Baronova was the principal in CENT BAISERS. She was very popular in England because she was young and very good. She never complained about her partner. Alexandra Danilova was just starting to get a good name. She was very good, too, but with Danilova you needed to be prepared for anything. When you danced with her you could never relax. You were always standing at attention more than with anyone else. It was possible that she would mess up. Then you needed to watch out. She would sometimes go in a different direction than you had rehearsed.
>
> Toumanova always blamed the partner. Most of the ballerinas were like this. One day they did it this way, another that way. But not Baronova. With most of the ballerinas, if the turn was not good, they said it was the partner's fault. We partners knew whose fault it was. If we had a pas de deux we practiced constantly with the ballerinas. But partners are not mechanical. If we do it always the same way it's no good either. The ballerinas didn't want to work that much, but they wanted a big success, so we would make them practice more.

We opened LES CENT BAISERS in July 1935 and after the performance d'Erlanger took everybody to an expensive restaurant in a hotel and we all received checks. I got £10 or £15 because I danced a solo. It was in an envelope under my plate. Lichine got £25 because he was dancing a principal role and Baronova also got £25. It was a lot of money. This was in addition to our salaries. D'Erlanger gave this to us personally.

LES CENT BAISERS was a big success, but when Baronova left the company later, it was dropped from the repertoire. Baronova always danced the lead. Once she left the company the ballet left, too.

Around this time I called Mr. James and he came to the theatre to see the performance. When I gave him £20 he said, "What is this?" "Mr. James, don't you remember? I borrowed £20 from you last year to go see my mother and now I am returning it. Thank you." "Jasha, hundreds of people borrow money from me and nobody ever pays. I cannot accept your money. You are one of the few honest people in my life."

The young dancer was, indeed, scrupulously honest, but where he could, he pinched every penny. He pooled resources. He was careful with each cent and sou. As a result he now had a small stash to spend on the sweetness of life. He and Sono Osato were a devoted pair. Their happiness would last four short years, but while it lasted it was both deep and intense. Young, in love, with rare vacation time at hand, the summer break began to take on a pattern.

I went to the south of France to Sainte-Maxime to a nice pension named Rosa for my holidays with my friends. We would swim and sun and go back and sleep and eat and rest. The first two weeks we were always tired. I slept all the time. I was exhausted after working all year. I didn't even do a barre, but after two weeks I would start to be stronger and stronger and feel better. We would rent bicycles for a month for not much money. We were not far from Saint-Tropez. I remember, because I made the trip on the bicycle. Saint-Tropez was very artistic. All the artists and painters came there. You walked down the street and they tried to sell you paintings. Oh, it was beautiful!

One year we even rented a big villa near Saint-Aygulf with lots of rooms and we hired a cook. We boys would go to the market and bring home a duck and clean it. Feathers would fly all around the garden of the whole villa. Then the cook prepared the meals and the girls helped clean up. All day long we swam and bicycled.

After our vacations we would go back to Paris and begin to rehearse. We would be so sore we could not walk for three or four days because the bicycle used different muscles from ballet.

Then we would go back to America, to the Metropolitan Opera House. We had absolutely a different audience from before when we had danced at the St. James. These were uptown rich people. On Broadway they had whistled all the way through my variation, but when we moved to the Met our reputation really went up.

LES PRÉSAGES and CHOREARTIUM were two ballets that everybody talked about. This type of ballet was absolutely new. They were Massine ballets danced to symphonic music. To me the symphonic ballet was a great revelation because there was no story.

*Les Présages* was an immensely influential step forward in the development of twentieth-century dance. Traditionalists fought it bitterly, and Kochno, when later writing of its unwelcome impact, wryly called it "la bombe."

The whole orchestra fought against symphonic ballets because no one had ever danced to a symphony before. Massine was kind of modern at this time. We had lots of problems when we came to this country with PRÉSAGES. They thought we shouldn't use this ballet. Before this ballet, every composer used to make up the story and write the music for a scenario. But this time, Massine made a ballet symphony. He opened the door for everyone.

PRÉSAGES was danced to the Fifth Symphony of Tchaikovsky. Some of the costumes were not very nice, but what choice did we have? They were designed by André Masson, the great painter, but only Baronova's costume was good.

When we came to dance CHOREARTIUM in Philadelphia, they asked this very famous Polish-American conductor, Leopold Stokowski, to conduct the orchestra. After the first day, there was a big scandal because Massine had changed the tempo to suit the dancers. Stokowski played it like it was for the symphony. The boys couldn't make their double turns in the air and fell down because Stokowski changed their tempos. There were lots of problems.

A critic went to Baronova and asked, "Are you comfortable dancing with Stokowski?" and she said, "No. It is more comfortable when our own conductors conduct because it was not the right tempo." The next day the critic wrote about Stokowski and called his piece "Scandal!" Sol Hurok had to come to fix things. "What is this? From now on, no more dancers talking with critics!" After all, Stokowski was a very famous conductor. But you know, that critic made a stupid remark. He should never have written "Scandal!"

Today we can change the tempo and nobody cares. Balanchine followed Massine with many symphonies for his choreography, but it was Massine who actually opened the door for symphonic ballets.

CHAPTER 14

# The Vagabond Life

*I have four asses!*

IT TOOK A MONTH TO PREPARE THE SEASON'S program and then the year's tour would begin. When we crossed to the United States we would have two or three days to recover from the boat and then we would perform.

I liked de Basil's Ballets Russes company so much. Everything was there. Rich repertoire, enormous knowledge, great artists, great dancers. Back and forth from Europe to America. This is how we lived. For five years we repeated this pattern—six months in the United States, six months in Europe. New York in the fall, one hundred cities every year, then back to Europe and finally a holiday. I enjoyed the tours, but most of all I liked living in the United States.

Whenever we were in New York we stayed at the Wellington. It was my home. When I was on tour I would leave my trunk there and take just my suitcases. Or I would have two trunks—one to leave in the hotel and one to take with the company. That would be for the big cities. For the little cities I had only one suitcase. Otherwise it would be too hard.

I needed to have lots of shirts. Every two or three days I would find a Chinese laundry to wash the shirts.

And I carried lots of ballet shoes in the trunk. You could not carry too many shoes.

I used my touring trunk as a kind of closet. I put personal programs, books, anything like this in my other trunk at the Wellington. If you are used to it you don't know any different. I tell you what. As a dancer I felt free. I had no responsibility.

I feel sorry for dancers today sometimes. I was a free man! The Hotel Wellington was my home. I came to the hotel to rest, I went to a restaurant to eat, I'd go to the performance, come back, and I did not have any responsibility. I'd go to lie on my bed and it was already clean. Take a shower, go to bed, leave the bed like it was in the morning, come back and it was fixed. It was a beautiful life. I enjoyed traveling. Always, anyplace I went. It didn't matter, good place or bad, I enjoyed it.

We toured one hundred cities. We stayed in some cities, like Chicago, for one or two weeks. We also played the schools. Snow or not, people were there. In New York we were usually one week at the beginning and one week at the end. I always enjoyed this tremendously. Now, if you tell young dancers to go on tour, they cry. But I loved to go. Our tours became so successful that before we arrived they were already sold out. When we finished a performance they signed us for the next time. Big excitement. It was, to me, adventure! Nobody enjoys this anymore. We took our company, Tulsa Ballet Theatre, for a two-week tour and we had so many problems. "Oh, it's so hard!" With people from Europe who were starving to death and now have the opportunity to eat and eat, it is different. It was so wonderful for us to be in America.

I was so interested in everything. New country, new life, new adventure. I was always sorry that I couldn't see the country well when we were traveling by train in the night. In later years, when I was traveling in the car, I went through the whole United States. How I enjoyed this! I saw the United States by car and by bus. Buses were interesting because you could see more.

The train had its advantages. Sometimes in the morning if I was tired, I would sleep. Any place I could put my head I would sleep. We were awfully exhausted. We rehearsed any place we could find. Sometimes Massine had a new ballet and he would catch us anywhere he could. We would even rehearse on the train. When it was moving it made me sick.

Sometimes the train would stand in a single city for two or three days. If it did, I liked to sleep there because this way I didn't have to pay for a hotel. There were other places to sleep, too. Sometimes we would go to the movies—very cheap. We would pay and stay three or four hours. Or sometimes we would go back to the train and sleep, or people would take one room in a hotel and six people would stay there. Or, if we didn't have rehearsal, we would go to the theatre and stay there. But for me, I liked best to go the movies, a double feature. Then there was lots of time to sleep!

I played cards on the train after performances with the stage hands. One time they said, "What do you have?" and I said, "I have four asses." They fell down on the floor, they were laughing so hard. In Europe we say "asses" for "aces." I thought they would die laughing.

Traveling on the train, we would have dinner at midday. It was very hard because from noon on there would be a big line and the company would occupy all the places. The whole ballet was traveling, a hundred people—dancers, orchestra, stagehands. You would have to wait more than an hour before they finished eating. To us, the food on the train was expensive. You could get a good dinner at a restaurant for 75 cents, but it was $1.25 on the train. More expensive, but very good.

We liked breakfast—eggs, porridge, oatmeal. And we liked the milk! The milk in Europe was not that good, you know, because they mixed it with water. Here in America they gave you good milk. In Texas they gave you half cream and half milk. We drank glasses of it. We were crazy for it! We had never seen anything like it. Rich Texas milk and cream! They have good cows there!

One thing the company never had to worry about: the theatres were always sold out. The troupe was a sensation. It brought to the stage a vigorous Russian ballet that America had never seen before.

It was when we were in Boston that something started to hurt in my foot. That's when I learned I had somehow chipped my bones. The chipped bones were like stones which destroyed the healthy bones inside my ankle. I could not do a plié. In LES SYLPHIDES, when I had to land on one leg in arabesque, the moment came when it hurt so bad that I couldn't dance any more. I went to the doctor and he said that I had two choices: I could quit dancing and find another profession or I could have an operation. The company released me from certain dances in the last performances, and then they left me alone in Boston and went back to Europe.

The operation in a clinic took care of my problem. They had to cut through the bones to make them smooth. The company didn't pay for this operation; that was up to me. I must give credit to one man, a balletomane, who paid for this operation. I stayed in the hospital nine days, and for two weeks after that I walked on crutches.

There I was, alone in Boston, and I couldn't speak good English. Before leaving town, this man had made arrangements for a hotel for me to recover in and had paid for everything, but I didn't understand because my English was so poor, so I ended going back to the cheap hotel where the Ballet had stayed. You know, I always promised myself that I would some day help the people who helped me in my life, invite them to dinner, repay them somehow, but this man died and I lost my chance.

When I was finally able, I took the train to New York and went to the office of Sol Hurok on Fifth Avenue. Hurok was born in Russia, so everybody in his office spoke Russian.

He became a famous impresario here because there is so much opportunity in America. They bought me a boat ticket and two or three days later I left the United States and went back to Paris. The company was already performing in London, but I had no reason to go there because I couldn't yet dance, so in Paris I bought a third class train ticket and went overnight to the south of France to my old pension, La Rosa. It was a nice little place with a garden—just rooms, no hot water, nothing but a little pitcher to wash my hands and face before I went down to eat. I'd have lunch and a little wine about two o'clock, then I'd rest a little, go to the beach, and perhaps take a bicycle ride. I found that it was easier to ride a bicycle than walk because of my foot. I stayed there a month or six weeks.

I had always made economy so I was able to pay for it. After my American and English tours I always put some money away—in Barclays Bank in London or at Chase National in New York. I never put any money in Paris! We were scared to leave money in France because the franc was always unstable. The English pound and the American dollar had the power. I would deposit my savings in New York or London and return to Europe.

When the company finally came back to Paris, Jasinski rejoined it, but still could not dance. He performed some walk-on parts and was paid enough to buy food. In all, the injury required nearly six months to heal. "I wasn't afraid," Jasha said, "when I was left behind in America—there is such hospitality there. They feed you. I didn't have to worry about money. I was more afraid to stay in Paris. I'd been there so often without money. Life was very hard in Europe."

To me it was very exciting and interesting to see how they lived in America. Everybody lived good. They went to hotels. They went to restaurants. Restaurants! I was only in a fine restaurant two or three times in my life in Europe. It cost too much money.

But you know, even though we had no money, we were big stars in Los Angeles. Once we met Charlie Chaplin and Paulette Goddard. All the Hollywood stars came to visit us on the stage after performance and they made a big party for the whole company. I remember we met the little girl, Shirley Temple, there. I saw her first in the movies and then I saw her there. She was very small and very spoiled. The others told us they needed to act like monkeys in front of her to amuse her because she didn't want to act.

In 1936, the AGMA union stepped forward. They had heard about Massine's rehearsals in the lobby and said that everyone had to join the union, so that's when I joined AGMA. They raised the salary for the corps de ballet. If you were a soloist or a first dancer it was up to you how much you could make so AGMA didn't really help me. But they made certain regulations. If you had a performance you could rehearse two and a half hours on that day. Not before the performance, but in the morning. If you were traveling you could not rehearse at all. This was only for the United States. When you left America you went back to the same old way of doing things.

This is also when I started to pay the American government. We had to pay the income tax in 1936. Before, we paid nothing. But I didn't have to pay much because I didn't make much money.

There was a man who did the income tax for us. He would say, "Why do you spend so much on dinner?" "Because that is what I pay to eat." "Oh, you could eat hamburgers." And I would say, "No hamburgers. I never eat hamburgers." What was this? I needed to eat less to give more money to the government? We paid for the hotel, we paid for cleaning, we paid for everything. We spent a dollar on breakfast and two to three dollars on the hotel each day.

One year, we were on the train to California, and there was a big snowstorm. We were stopped for two days waiting for a plow to come clear the track.

There was big excitement because of this snow bomb. The problem was we were becoming short on food. People were worried about what to eat. Some people worried that they would die. They were running and screaming in a panic. I was not especially worried. "Oh," they would say, "What are we going to have for breakfast?"

I had been so many times without food, I didn't worry about breakfast.

Some from our group went outside to build a big snowman, but at sunset the engineer came out and said, "Please, after five o'clock you need to get inside the train because of wolves. Please do not go outside." And the wolves came to the train. We heard them. We could see them through the windows. They wanted to catch some food. We stayed about two days there and then the big tractor came to clear the snow.

We were already late for our tour in Los Angeles. "Ballets Russes de Monte Carlo is stuck in the snow. . . " You saw the headline everywhere—in the movies, the newsreels, every place. "The ballet came late!" When we finally came to the station they took newsreels and lots of pictures for the papers. There was a big excitement. Tremendous!

Once I caught a bad cold when we were in Los Angeles and the company had to leave me behind. I stayed in a hotel and the hotel doctor came, checked me and gave me aspirin. That was all. It was the flu. I paid him five dollars each visit. He told me the same thing as that doctor in Paris many years before. "I don't know if I can do anything for you. You look like you are going to die." What is this "die"? I knew I wouldn't die. I sent him away.

Across the street from the hotel was a Jewish delicatessen. I went there after I hadn't eaten for three days and they had good chicken soup. I also had some port wine and it hit me so hard that I started to rain! Sweat ran down my face.

The waiter came up to me and asked, "What's wrong with you?"

"I don't know. I had a little port wine and I started to sweat."

Soon I was absolutely soaking wet. I finished my soup and my God! I was wet absolutely. And you know what? In the morning I was a healthy man. The doctor came in the morning and said, "How are you?" And I was dressing already. I said, "I am okay," and I told him about the wine and chicken soup. He couldn't believe it. He said, "I have never heard of anyone doing this." But it was true and I was able to rejoin the company right away.

Years later, secure in the certainty of plentiful food, Jasha would pause to remember certain meals with a special relish—a whole broiled chicken in Paris, plates full of free spaghetti in Rieti, a breakfast feast after a drenched bed in the Netherlands. He smacked his lips over rich Texas milk ("They have good cows there!"). He lauded the life-renewing properties of L.A. chicken soup. If he remembered tours by performance and role, he also remembered them by taste.

CHAPTER 15

# The American Dream

*Our home was the company.*

FINALLY, necessities, and even some luxuries, were affordable. Members of the company lived in first-class hotels at discounted rates. Hotels posted their glamorous guests' names on billboards, and lobbies filled with fans asking to have their programs signed.

You know, the other dancers complained, but I didn't complain. To sign a program wasn't that hard. The tour in the south of France where we slept on benches in the park—now that was hard! Traveling by train all day for hours and hours with the cows in Spain. That was hard! Stopping in every little town so people could get on and off. But in America, it was so fantastic.

I put my money at Chase Bank in New York. The first time I only put in $25. I was very careful about how I spent my money. I wouldn't throw it away. I was not hungry, because you cannot be hungry in America, but instead of going to a good restaurant I went to smaller restaurants. They had the same food and I paid less.

For five years, every month for six months I sent my family $50 from America. My mother hid the money in flowerpots and then she changed it to Polish zlotys, lots of zlotys. She said, "Cenka is spoiling us. No one wants to work now. Cenka sends the money!" But when I went to Europe, I could not do this because we didn't make very much money.

When we first came to America we took lots of American kids into the company. We didn't need them, but we took them and then we had to train them. It was good public relations, but we had lots of problems with them. They didn't want to work hard. We had class from nine to ten in the morning and rehearsal from ten to one. The Americans came to rehearsal whenever they wanted. I must say, the girls were very good. They worked hard always. But one boy made so much trouble. If we had a ten o'clock rehearsal, he would come at eleven. We would say, "Why didn't you come?" And he would say, "Oh, I overslept." This boy was constantly coming late. Class started at nine, rehearsal at ten and he came about eleven.

No one from the company spoke good English at this time, but a few of the dancers from the Diaghilev company knew a little bit. Grigoriev, our regisseur, screamed to one of the Russian guys who could speak English, "You tell this boy that the next time he comes late like this he will be out of the company. Tell him! Tell him!" The Russian guy told the boy, "Mr. Grigoriev says that the next time you come late you will be out." "Well you tell the old man that if he doesn't stop screaming I will go right now!" Then the Russian guy told Grigoriev, "He says he is sorry and that it won't happen again."

All the Europeans in the Ballets Russes were poor. We depended on this job. If we didn't have this job we didn't eat. It was different for the Americans. One day an American kid announced, "Tomorrow I'm going to my parents' house." Why did he need to care? His father simply sent a ticket to him, and he took it and went back home. You cannot work with people like this. They are independent. They don't have to worry. Everything comes so easy to them.

You see, we could not do this because we were dependent upon the ballet for a living. We didn't have any homes; our home was the company. The Americans were assured of everything they needed.

They could quit any time they wanted to. If they needed money, Papa or Mama would send them money. That was a kind of danger.

In the Ballets Russes we Europeans were all friends—Russians, Poles, everyone. I remember, after a few years in the company, I visited my home in Poland and they tried to tell me something bad about the Russians because the Russians were enemies to the Poles. "We hate the Germans. We hate the Russians. The Russians hate us." In the ballet, we didn't have this hatred. We had all nationalities. Everyone was different. When I came home I said, "What are you talking about? Why are you saying bad things? What is wrong with Russia?" My brother started to talk about what they did to the Tzar, that they had cut off heads, but such talk was strange to me. You see, I was always a little bit different person. I was looking different on life. I didn't have any hatred.

I was living with Russians and I liked them. Even though I was Polish I would go to the Russian church wherever I was: Monte Carlo, Paris, London, New York. Everyone did. Church is church. Nobody cared. If you wanted to go to church nobody cared, nobody bothered you, nobody mentioned it. The Russian holy days were celebrated in the company, but we didn't have the day off. We still had to rehearse.

We had lots of traditions in the company. If a cat crossed the street in front of us we had to run ahead and get in front of him, especially when we were going to the theatre. That's Russian. I really was troubled if I was going to the theatre in a taxi and a cat crossed in front of me. On the other hand, I would feel rich all the next year if I had cash in my pocket on New Year's Day. That's Polish. And on New Year's Eve everyone in the company would "snap the dragon," throwing flaming raisins soaked in brandy into our mouths for good luck. That's English.

Before I danced, I touched the wood on the floor and made the sign of the cross before every entrance. If you danced with Tamara Toumanova, Mama Toumanova would go after you and put the sign of the cross a couple of times on you, on Tamarishka, and on the stage.

Mama Toumanova traveled with Tamara all the time. She protected her. She never wanted to leave her for five minutes. She was very firm. They ate together, slept together in the room, went together to the theatre and came back together. Never, never separate.

But Mama Toumanova had so much temperament. Big temper. She spent her time helping Tamara with the costumes, dressing her, and even told her how to dance. De Basil had to pay Tamara more money than the other dancers because she had her mother with her and sometimes her father. He didn't really pay for the mothers, but he gave the daughters a little bit more money because mother and daughter both needed to live on one salary.

Even so, it looks to me that Tamara was happy with her mother. You couldn't approach her because her mother was close all the time around her. You couldn't kiss her because her mother was there.

And yet, Tamara's doctors told her she needed to go someplace for a vacation from her mother because her mother was making her sick. She went someplace for maybe two weeks and then she came back. She didn't want to leave her mother. That's normal, especially since her mother was sick. But Tamara was sick, too.

The father of Irina Baronova was a painter so de Basil paid him a salary. He helped with painting and repairing the scenery. Riabouchinska's mother also traveled with the company, and she coached Tatiana in her roles. She was like a princess, never mixing with the others. She thought they were a lower caste of people because she was higher Russian.

One of the ballets we all performed was UNION PACIFIC. We used the mothers like railroad ties. We would put brown sacks on them and carry them on stage. No one wanted to get Mama Toumanova because she was too heavy. Everyone wanted to take Madame Riabouchinska because she was light and thin. And we put other people in the sacks, too—people who were not cast in the ballet, people who helped prepare the costumes, people who helped with sewing and dressing. Everybody. And we carried them across the stage in the sacks.

In SCHÉHÉRAZADE we boys were painted black or brown. When we danced this ballet in America we were very careful to be polite with the black people and to use a kind of brown paint on stage instead of black. When we finished the ballet we washed each other's backs because we had other ballets to dance.

For me, I needed to wash right away because I danced "Blue Bird" next. We had only a fifteen minute intermission, you see. When the curtain came down, we didn't stay for the bow. We just ran to the water, already hot, that was waiting for us in the dressing room.

We had more problems in the company than companies have now. There was a guy named Edouard Borovansky who always bothered me because of Sono Osato. He was Czechoslovakian, older than I, and I tried to respect him. He liked her, but I was living with her. One day I told him, "If you mention her name again I am going to break your head." "How dare you talk to me like this!" My friend Jan Hoyer said, "Jasha's right. I'll help him break your head." Jan was a tough guy. He would stand behind me.

Sono and I were together and were very strongly in love, but many girls in the company would have affairs with this man or that to try to get the better roles. In Europe, every man had a wife and a mistress. In the European sense it was normal if a girl was sleeping with the director because he could give her good parts or maybe a raise in salary. Maybe they thought that everyone would respect them. They were poor. They wanted to make a better life for themselves.

De Basil fell in love with Morosova, a very cute girl, very young, very flirtatious, and she wanted to dance. He wanted to marry her even though he was already married, and so she got her first parts. Otherwise she would never have danced them. So you would have this one living with that one and this one living with that one. Everybody knew, but nobody talked about it.

Here in America this didn't exist. The United States is a different country. Everyone is independent! They depend on themselves. Here a girl didn't need to sleep with a director because she could go home.

She could get food. She could have a bed and go to sleep. She didn't need to sacrifice herself in order to get parts.

I don't know why, but I always tried to stay out of company intrigues. People would come to me and tell me different things. One girl who was in love with Massine cut her wrists. They took her to the doctor, sewed her up and that was that.

Another one they had to sew was Paul Petroff, one of our dancers. Now about Paul we kept quiet. We didn't want the newspapers to know. It was New Year's Eve. There was a party downstairs in the hotel and the whole company was invited. There was dancing, drinking, food. I saw Paul Petroff dancing with Madame Psota. When she left and went upstairs, Paul followed her. I'm not sure what happened next. Maybe her husband came into the room and caught them. The doctor told me later there were many holes in Paul, like he had been stabbed with scissors. I was surprised. I had thought there was only one stab hole. I think Madame Psota did it because of the many, many stabs. I think she tried to save herself. I don't know, but that is how I think. De Basil knew who did it. And Hurok—he paid the police because we didn't want to have a scandal like this. I heard it cost Hurok $2500 to keep it quiet. When we left the city it was not in the papers. Petroff bled like a bull but survived because he had strong Danish blood. He never said who stabbed him. People called it "Murder in Fifth Position"!

CHAPTER 16

# The World Darkens

*We knew that Hitler was out there.*

ROMAN JASINSKI was a man who had one central, overwhelming passion: ballet. His knowledge of world politics was narrow; his art was his homeland. When revolution and world conflict finally intruded upon his awareness, his astonishment was profound. He never saw it coming, and his instinct was to escape back into his beautiful, safe ballet world and wait out the burgeoning storm.

> After America, our European tour took us to Barcelona. When the company left, a few of us remained in Spain, found a very good place, very cheap, on the sea and decided to take our vacation there. As I remember, there were Papa, Mama, and Tamara Toumanova, Yurek Lazowski, Baronova, me, and some others. I don't remember if Baronova's father was there. Baronova was more free than Toumanova. We could talk to her and sometimes she would have dinner with us. Tamara was always stuck with her mother. She could never be free.
>
> Life was very cheap in Spain. Cheaper than in France. We spent four pesos at our pension for room, food, and wine. I remember we drank lots of vino. It was sweet, very young, and we drank it straight from the bottle.

We had been there about three or four days when a man from the police came and said, "You must leave Spain right away because there is a revolution. All foreigners must leave today. The war is starting." We said, "War? What war?"

The police went every place. Toumanova was up on the beach exercising. We had to find her and leave or we would be stuck. The Spanish were closing the borders. It was terrible. We left that night, just in time. The soldiers guarded us until we got on a train and made it back to Paris. There was lots of panic. People were trying to get out. There was fighting the next day. You know, it was good we left. We were able to go back to the company and after, we went back to London.

For Jasha, the unrest preceding the Spanish Civil War was a minor glitch in an otherwise routine schedule. For him, all things personal and professional focused on "the company." Every thought revolved around his roles, touring, performing, and a few close companions. He seemed unaware of the turmoil in the world at large and surprised by warring personalities within the company that was his home. But ask him about a city, a theatre, or the nearest cheap boarding house and his memories were sharp and specific.

In 1936 I went with the company to Berlin for the first time. I liked it there. Our biggest successes were in Germany. I lived in the same boarding house every time I went. It was attached to the theatre, the Scala, so all I had to do was come down some steps. The Scala was one of those theatres that had an iron curtain for fire protection. If the applause went too long they put it down, opened a door within the curtain, and we went through it one by one to bow.

In 1936 we knew something about the Nazis. The Germans were building for war like crazy but nobody did anything about it. Supposedly it was a big secret.

I remember our conductor, Efrem Kurtz, didn't want to go with us to Germany because he was Jewish. Lichine was also Jewish, but he went. But somehow, if you came with the company, the Nazis didn't bother you. They were there, but not so strong. We didn't pay much attention to them. I think the Germans were the most enthusiastic people for the ballet I knew. We had enormous success in Berlin with long applause after each performance. The audience never wanted to leave the theatre.

Around this time I received a letter from my brother, Leon. He was maybe five or six years older than me and he counted money in a bank. Leon wanted to go on vacation with his girlfriend and asked if I could give him some money. I sent him £5 but soon received the £5 back. On the envelope it was written that Leon had suicided. That is how I learned of his death.

My family wrote that Leon had been in love with some girl and wanted to marry her, but he didn't have any money. She, too, was poor. They went to the north of Poland, to the Baltic Sea. The girl wanted to leave him or something. They never really told me the whole story, but somehow they knew that Leon took a boat out on the water, sat on its edge, filled his pockets with lots of stones and shot himself in his mouth. He fell overboard and because of the stones he never came up. They never found him. My sister went there later and threw lots of flowers on the sea in his memory. Once again I had to work on myself and concentrate on dancing. It is what I always did when there was a sadness in my life.

This is when Massine had problems with de Basil, and de Basil had problems with Massine. De Basil was afraid of losing Massine, and yet he needed to keep him down always. If you let Massine loose, he would sit on your head! De Basil never gave Massine the title of "artistic director," which I thought was very strange. Massine was really a very dangerous man to de Basil because he carried the whole company as choreographer, dancer, and everything, but he was not easy to work with. Soon after our London opening, Massine came to me and said that he was leaving de Basil's Ballets Russes to start a new company with Serge Denham and did I want to join him? He invited many of the boys, and some left, but mostly Massine found male dancers outside the company. He also took Danilova.

I liked the de Basil Ballets Russes and did not want to change. I didn't leave because I was already a principal dancer and you always got more roles when someone left. So when Massine asked me to go with him, I said, "No, thank you. I am going to stay with de Basil because I already left him once. No more!"

From the distance of many decades the shenanigans of rival ballet companies, their lawsuits and countersuits, raids on dancers, choreographers and choreography, their backbiting and backstage espionage, seem almost humorous, but at the time all was deadly serious. Money was tight. Sponsorships were at a premium. The livelihood of dancers, musicians, and the vast backstage support system of a major ballet company depended on solvency, and solvency was a hard-won entity.

Loyalty prevented Jasinski's defection from de Basil, but never blinded him to de Basil's ill treatment of the company's star dancer and choreographer, Massine. Nor did years of coping with Massine's capricious volatility blind Jasinski to the dancer-choreographer's great gifts.

Always touring, always performing, always observing, Jasinski commented on episodes, incidents, and personalities, describing them without judgment or opinion. The Nazis? "We didn't pay too much attention to them." The de Basil-Massine split? "You always got more roles when someone left."

It was as though turmoil roiled and eddied around the rock that was Jasinski, washing conflicting personalities this way and that but never deflecting the man from his appreciation of all. He just went where the company went, did what the company told him to do, communed with an increasingly enthusiastic audience, and danced.

I didn't know what was going to happen to the other company. At that time there were lots of dancers who weren't working. It was not a problem to fill a company. If there were two companies more people would have jobs.

Lichine stayed with de Basil, too, eventually dancing all of Massine's parts. We had already started to work out who would dance what. We didn't worry about Massine leaving. Some people thought that when he left, the company would fall down but it didn't. Most of the dancers stayed with us.

That same summer of 1937 Massine went to court over the symphonic ballets, CHOREARTIUM and LES PRÉSAGES, and some other ballets like LES FEMMES DE BONNE HUMEUR. He said they belonged to him.

Before, when a choreographer made a ballet it belonged to the company. When Massine separated from us he wanted to take these ballets and others. That was why he went to court.

There was a big battle over BEAU DANUBE, which was very popular. Massine thought he owned BEAU DANUBE, that it belonged to him. The judge agreed.

All the symphonies belonged to Colonel de Basil. Massine tried to get SYMPHONIE FANTASTIQUE from us, but could not. I remember dancing Massine's part in the third movement in London after the war. I was sitting, looking up, and I never moved my eye. The next day I had a letter. "You know, you are amazing. You never moved your eyes. I was watching with a lens and you just held still. Amazing that you didn't move your eyelashes." I never thought about this; I just did it.

We came back to America for Massine's farewell tour. It was in every paper. People thought that de Basil and the company would be finished because Massine was not only a great choreographer, but also a great dancer. When we were traveling in the United States he had to perform constantly because the people buying tickets wanted to see him. He always had fantastic success, especially with DANUBE, TRICORNE, and BOUTIQUE FANTASQUE.

After that tour Massine left de Basil for good. He formed a new company with Serge Denham, and took his ballets with him. This company was called "The Ballet Russe de Monte Carlo."

Here lies a point of utter confusion. What had started out as Les Ballets Russes de Monte-Carlo under the direction of René Blum and Col. W. de Basil in 1932 became in New York, in 1933, the Monte Carlo Ballet Russe by merely dropping a couple of "s's." For the next few years those additional "s's" came and went and came and went. René Blum simply went.

When Massine parted ways with the Colonel in 1938, his new roster of dancers was superimposed upon René Blum's existing "Ballets de Monte Carlo." After the Monte Carlo season was over, the new company adopted the name, "Ballet Russe de Monte Carlo." One wonders if the audience realized how many different companies danced under that title, with the addition or subtraction of a couple of "s's."

Whatever the name, whomever the director, Roman Jasinski simply signed his name to the appropriate contract and kept on dancing.

> By our second trip to Germany in 1938 the Nazis already came to your room and went through your suitcases. I know because I came to my room one day and said, "Something is wrong. I never put this on top like this." And the boardinghouse man told me the Nazis went through my suitcases. They took all the papers and books. No one could have any books, not even Polish books. They took everything. They were very careful, very strict.
>
> The last time we toured Germany was most disturbing. We asked the people backstage why the audience wouldn't leave the theatre at the end of the performance. They had already put the iron curtain down and the people were still sitting there. No one wanted to go.
>
> "Why are they doing this?"
>
> "Because this is a safe place. They know when they are in the theatre nothing will happen to them. But if they leave they don't know. They feel so safe, they don't want to leave."
>
> One day a week all the German restaurants collected money for the army. On this day when you paid for your dinner or anything else, everything would go to the army. The restaurants had no choice.

SCENERY BY CHRISTIAN BÉRARD FOR *SYMPHONIE FANTASTIQUE*

Program, Original Ballet Russe 1940–1941.

Our Berlin season lasted for one month. One day the director came while we were in rehearsal and said, "Everybody in the street. By order of Hitler." We had to go outside. If the director didn't do this, maybe the next day he would be killed. We had to go and watch the planes, the bombers—big ones, small ones, thousands—a black sky. And we looked. But you know, none of us even questioned this. I didn't feel scared. I was impressed by the straight formation. I didn't think about what it meant.

I remember the next day I went across the street to a restaurant and I couldn't get back across after my meal. I had rehearsal and I couldn't get across because the army was showing its tanks. "My God, I have rehearsal." I wanted to run between the tanks. They stopped me

> and it was half an hour before I could find a place to just go, so I was late for my rehearsal.
>
> Hitler came to a performance once. We waited until 11:00 P.M. to start because he had a speech someplace, and when he spoke no one could do anything but listen. Nothing! His voice was heard in the theatre when he was speaking. And you know, we asked some of the stagehands how they could talk and play cards during the talks. "You don't listen to Hitler?" Somebody could have killed them.
>
> We didn't look through the curtain to see him, but we knew that Hitler was out there. We saw Dr. Goebbels because he brought flowers to Riabouchinska.
>
> Dr. Goebbels was a very good friend of the Ballets Russes. He walked like a soldier and always brought the ballerina flowers on the stage. He loved ballet and was always a big help to us. He gave special orders to be careful of the Ballet. We didn't know then what he was really like.

When they left Nazi Germany, the company continued its European tour. The dancers had experienced the Nazis first hand—their regimentation, their restrictions, all the panoply and threat of war. The world they knew was collapsing around them but with discipline and determination they focused forward on performing—always performing.

The famous "Ballet Wars" of London pitted performances of de Basil's Russian Ballet against Massine's and Serge Denham's Ballet Russe de Monte Carlo. The companies took possession of theatres within hailing distance of each other. There was great excitement in the press. Frenzied fans raced up and down the street at intermission to catch glimpses of each opposing company. But as far as Jasinski was concerned, all the hoopla had no effect on the dancers. He dismissed the excitement with a shrug."We dancers were too busy. We were dancing every day. It was the directors' problem." Actually, it was all great for business. The opposing directors would meet for drinks after performance to compare notes and box office numbers. Ballet was the rage of the season, but as usual, there was jostling behind the scenes.

> De Basil told the company that he was leaving for awhile and that the company would now be English. We had to sign new contracts under the name "Educational Ballets, Ltd." Meanwhile, the company planned to go to Australia with Victor Dandré, the husband of Anna Pavlova, instead of de Basil. Gerry Sevastianov, de Basil's secretary, took over as director.

For Jasinski, the true disappointment of 1938 had little to do with dancing. The long-planned American tour was scuttled when Sol Hurok, impresario for a whole succession of rival ballet companies, chose to send Denham's ballet to America over Educational Ballets, Ltd. For five long years Jasinski had counted the days until he would receive his coveted United States citizenship, his goal since childhood. He had to make just one more trip within the allotted time period and his dream would become reality.

> I was supposed to become an American citizen in 1938. It was my dream always. From Europe, everyone wanted to stay in America. I paid an American lawyer $200 to prepare my papers. I didn't know we were going to Australia and my papers were ready. If I could enter America just one more time I could become an American citizen. But I didn't come, so I lost my chance and the American lawyer threw the papers out. The company went to Australia instead.

CHAPTER 17

# Down Under

*Oh! It was beautiful there!*

The blow to Jasinski was softened by the success of the hastily substituted tour to Australia. He rapidly came to love the country, and Australia reciprocated in full. It also gave him a chance to continue to send part of his pay to Poland.

I was the only one who ever sent anything home. I knew my family's lives were hard. My sister, Janka, came to visit me in France before I left for Australia. She came for my sake, but she really wanted to go with us. We went from Marseille to the Red Sea. We were able to rehearse on the boat on the Red Sea because it was like glass. Hot, hot, hot! It was good for our muscles and we had a salt water swimming pool to soak in. We liked life on the boat when the weather was quiet. The voyage took thirty-four days. From London to New York was only four days, but this was thirty-four days! We became like a family on the boat. We knew everyone. "Good morning, good morning!" We stopped in Bombay and on the island of Ceylon, and were able to get off the ship. We would sleep on the boat you see, but we could leave to see things for the day and come back in the evening before going on.

I remember that Bombay in India shocked me. I started to walk on the street and people were lying on the sidewalk. India was terrible at this time. "Why are they lying like this?" "They are working people. These people know nothing else. They are born on the street and they die on the street."

Michel Fokine went with us to Australia to rehearse PAGANINI, which later premiered in London. I was very pleased. I had first heard about him at my school. He once came to Poland to stage LES SYLPHIDES and SCHÉHÉRAZADE. I also knew of him from the other dancers. The first time I met Fokine was in 1935 when he rehearsed SCHÉHÉRAZADE. Later he made a new ballet for us, LE COQ D'OR—a big success. Fokine had a great name. It was as though you had the greatest opportunity of your life to work with him. Every dancer gave his heart and soul in rehearsal. But he was also a very nervous man. He screamed at us like a dog with its teeth bared if we didn't dance full out or made a mistake.

You felt as a dancer that if you made a mistake you were guilty. We felt differently about these things in Europe. Here in the United States if a dancer makes a mistake he is angry with the director. Very mad. It is a different psychology. But for us, Fokine was the choreographer, we were the dancers. He was higher than we were. Anything he asked us to do, we did, and that was all. That was the way we did things in Europe.

We already had Fokine's ballets in our repertoire, like LES SYLPHIDES. SYLPHIDES was choreographed much earlier by Fokine and everybody tried to restage it. When Fokine came to us we showed him our SYLPHIDES which had been restaged by Léon Woizikowski. "No, no!" he screamed, and he started changing everything. When it came to my variation, I put my leg in a certain way and he jumped, held his head, and shouted, "No! Please don't ever do this!" And he changed it. "Who showed you this? I never did this!" Later, when I talked with Léon Woizikowski, he said that he would swear in front of God that Fokine had taught Nijinsky this way in Diaghilev's Ballets Russes.

As a ballet, LES SYLPHIDES was different—very soft and plastic. Not especially expressive. Technically, it was not difficult, but it was a different style. Fokine had a special technique for this. You repeated each step two or three times.

MICHEL FOKINE

Fokine as he appeared in the Original Ballet Russe program, 1940–1941.

Photo by Howard Coster.

Fokine always did pirouettes and double turns to the left. Always before performance, after performance, after class I worked on my turns to the left because I could turn to the right well, but to the left I fell sideways. Fokine was left-handed, which is why he liked to turn that way. I needed to build special muscles so I could turn to the left.

What was fortunate was that Fokine coached me personally in LES SYLPHIDES. He showed me the steps. Sometimes when you choreograph you show the steps and the dancer doesn't do it exactly like you showed it, but you like it. That's what happened in SYLPHIDES with me. Later Fokine said, "No one has ever danced it like Jasinski does. It is classic: beautiful soft arms and a different approach to the mazurka." In SYLPHIDES the mazurka is classical, not character. Most dancers hit the floor with the heel like a peasant, but I was very classical, very delicate. Fokine told me, "Jasinski, if you ever teach anyone I want you to teach it exactly the way you dance it. If you don't, I will turn over in my grave." Years later, that's the way I taught it to my company. The closest thing I know to Fokine's true SYLPHIDES now is my wife Moussia's SYLPHIDES. She knows because she really worked with Fokine. She danced every female role—the corps de ballet, every part. And she has the style. This is what is missing with most companies now. Balanchine didn't know much about SYLPHIDES and he let Woizikowski teach him. It's different.

SYLPHIDES was one of my greatest roles. It was not a very strong role for a man, but it was beautiful.

As a review in one of Jasinski's scrapbooks put it, "Roman Jasinsky. . . has the rare ability to blend harmoniously into the ballet without seeming effeminate. His Mazurka. . . was executed with the true artistry which excludes any obvious, flashy display of technique."

We stayed in Melbourne eight weeks, giving a new program every week. There were three pieces on each program and I frequently danced the "Blue Bird" pas de deux.

This was when Yurek Shabelevsky left the company. He was in love with Irina Baronova who was married to Gerry Sevastianov, de Basil's secretary. Before, Shabelevsky didn't know what it was to be in love. I know because I talked with him. He would be in love with some girl and the next day he wouldn't recognize her. But he really fell in love very strong with Baronova. They fought over her, Sevastianov and Shabelevsky, and Yurek told me one of them would have to leave the company. The next day Baronova told him that she was leaving Sevastianov and that she would go with Yurek on the boat back to the United States.

I came on the boat to be with him for awhile. He was nervous as he waited for her, but she never came. There was a performance that night and she was dancing. I thought to myself, "This is crazy. She will never come. She has a performance tonight. How could she miss the performance? How could she leave?"

Then Shabelevsky made up his mind. "I am leaving the company." I knew that he was in love with her, but I didn't know there would be a problem like this. Later, I received a letter from the boat—almost crying—that said he was ready to commit suicide. But he didn't. He went to the United States and time passed. Later, I saw him again in South America. He danced with us and he had a wife and child. After the big scandal, Baronova was probably glad that he left.

The Australian city Jasinski loved most was Sydney. "Oh! It was beautiful there! Wonderful weather! Sunny weather! And the people were very nice." Jasinski liked the Australians. And the Australians liked Roman Jasinski, too.

In Sydney, I met a mechanic who taught me how to drive. He would come to the theatre to teach me, picking me up about five o'clock when the shops were closing. He taught me how to shift gears. I sweated so much after driving one hour, like I had danced three ballets! We went many different places. I thought it was so beautiful in Australia! Sometimes we would go to the mountains. Then he said,

"You're ready to go get your license." I was scared to death. It was very cheap to drive in Australia. Ten Australian shillings would pay for a car for the whole week. It would be a little car, English. All the boys rented cars.

When I was in Australia the girls in the theatre gallery in Melbourne liked me and gave me an Australian sheepdog. His name was Neptune. But you know, you could not take a dog out of the country. There was a six month quarantine. I had some friends with a big farm in Australia and I gave them this dog. In the beginning we wrote letters and they told me this was the best dog they had ever had on the farm, but I never saw my dog again.

One very old lady, close to eighty, came to the ballet and wanted to meet with me and Paul Petroff. Paul tried to pretend he was interested in her, in love with her, but he took me along for protection. She was one of the richest women in Australia and gave him beautiful presents. Many times she took us in her Rolls Royce and sometimes she had the chauffeur prepare food and drinks for a picnic.

Some of the dancers wanted to stay in Australia and raise sheep and I had a chance to join them. My friends were serious to stay there, but I was not. You need to learn to take care of sheep. It is very hard to raise them because they can have lots of problems.

The company went to New Zealand, too. The pensions there were not very pleasant. We never knew when we would finish rehearsal, but if we came late to the pension, the kitchen would be closed. All the pensions were the same. We would ask them to leave us something and they would leave a bit of cold fish, or a little something for sandwiches. Nothing more.

Once or twice we finished the performance and then rode a bus for a couple of hours to go to soak in the water of some geysers. After you soaked you were like a new person. You were full of strength. They called the mineral in this water radium; it really gave you power. All the people in the world came there. It felt good to go in the water but you couldn't swim there because it was too hot. Very hot! Almost boiling! You would just go and soak the muscles after dancing. Fantastic! The only problem was you needed to drive two hours to get there. We wouldn't get home until three or four o'clock in the morning.

One time two dancers, Jan Hoyer and Edouard Borovansky, found a rope and a big hoop in the ocean. They wanted to see what was in it and when they pulled it in they couldn't believe what they had. The hoop had swallowed lots of fish. They threw the hoop back in the water and suddenly, pow! More fish. Two of them were kingfish! Huge! It took Hoyer and Borovansky three or four hours to bring them in. Their hands were bloody from the rope, even though they were very strong boys with tremendous power. They brought the fish to the theatre and hung them in one of the dressing rooms. Blood was running everywhere. In just one day, the hook was empty because everybody in the company took a piece. My pension cooked mine for us in oil, and oh! It was so good!

In one town in New Zealand, there were no cars, only bicycles. Maybe it was harder to get a car than getting everybody a bicycle. The whole company had bicycles and rode them to the theatre.

I always liked to get a massage once a week. One guy who gave me a massage in New Zealand was very nice. After the massage he said, "My wife has made lunch. Would you like to eat with us?" Oh! You have never eaten any food like this. Dried fish. You know, she cooked it for many hours using milk and potatoes. Oh! Excellent! This fish was salty, but she first soaked it for a couple of days to get the salt out. It was very good! When I asked, "How much do I owe you?" the guy said, "Nothing. It was a great pleasure to give you a massage."

Now he was being treated like Serge Lifar!

PROTÉE.

Jasinski in the title role of the Lichine ballet

Photo by Baron, London. Private collection.

III

# The War Years

1939–1947

CHAPTER 18

# INTERMEZZO

*I didn't know what was going to happen next.*

THE IDYLL ENDED AT LAST, and the company returned to London for the 1939 season lasting from 12 June to 29 July. This time it flew solo under the name of Covent Garden Russian Ballet, without the excitement of rival "ballet wars" because Denham's company was elsewhere in Europe.

After London, I was invited by an American friend, Henry Clifford, to go to his chalet in Switzerland. Clifford was the director of a museum in Philadelphia and an important man. He was also an artistic advisor to the Ballets Russes. He had helped David Lichine with his choreography in the past, telling him stories that would make good ballets.

Alexandra Danilova was with us at the chalet for a while, along with Paul Petroff, David Lichine, Tatiana Riabouchinska, and Sono Osato. We were invited to spend the month of August. We flew to Basel in Switzerland and then the Cliffords took us in their car to their beautiful chalet in the mountains.

We had another Berlin season coming the fifteenth or sixteenth of September, so while I was with the Cliffords I wrote a letter to my family, telling them that it was just a few hours from Switzerland to Poland and that I would come visit them. I received a telegram from my brother Feliks that said, "Don't come! We are going to have war!"

I was so far in the mountains I didn't know about the war. Nothing. I had no idea, even after seeing all the tanks and planes in Berlin. I had been in Switzerland one month, living in the mountains. I didn't read about it and I never thought about it. I was just going to Poland for a few days at the beginning of September and then I was going to go back to Berlin to dance. I had the visa and everything. I rushed to Vevey and bought some papers. As I read them I thought, "It doesn't look so good." Feliks was right. The war started on the third of September.

Maybe I had heard a little bit before, that the Nazis had said the Sudetenland belonged to Germany and that the Germans had occupied Czechoslovakia. I never paid attention.

Everybody left Switzerland. Sono was an American. I tried to send her back home but she wouldn't go. She said, "No, I can't leave you." Mr. Clifford wanted us to stay in their chalet, but I thought, no. I was lucky because somebody, maybe Henry Clifford, told me, "You'd better get your money as quickly as possible. The English will close their bank." I had £50 in Barclays Bank. I sent a telegram to Barclays and they sent me Swiss money. And then two or three days later they closed the bank. All currency was stopped. And that's how we could stay and live there. Everybody else left.

Danilova was an American citizen already, and David Lichine and Riabouchinska had their American papers, so they could all leave Europe. Paul Petroff was Danish and the Danes could go wherever they wanted. I went to Vevey and found a little pension with a room and food for not much money, but I could stay in Switzerland for only one month. Then I needed to travel to Bern, live a day in a hotel and present my permit for a stamp. With the stamp I could stay one month more. Each month I had to go to Bern, stay in a hotel and leave the passport so that they could extend it. Then back to Vevey.

I didn't know what was going to happen. The Nazis had invaded Poland, I was stuck in Switzerland with a Polish passport, my permit to work in France had run out, and my visa was good only for Germany. The Cliffords didn't want to leave me there. They tried to arrange some kind of papers to make me a chauffeur so I could get into the United States, but in the end they couldn't do it.

They were calling for volunteers to come to the Polish consulate, but I didn't go. I found out that the Poles had many soldiers but the soldiers didn't have weapons. They were going to Poland, but they didn't have anything to fight with. They were using arms from the last war. I was worried about what was going to happen. I sent a telegram to Colonel de Basil and he said just to wait. I didn't think about anything because it was such a big mess. The whole corps de ballet was split into different countries. There was only one place to go and that was America. That was my goal.

At this time I didn't have any connection there. I was dreaming since I was a little boy to come to America but in this situation, with fighting here, fighting there, what could I do? Henry Clifford gave me a big hope that maybe when they got back to America, they could work it out and I could come, but I didn't hear from them because I had already left the mountains.

The Colonel wrote, "Wait. . . wait. . . wait . . .We will write and tell you what has happened." It was constantly like this. I received many communications from de Basil. "Jasha, sit quiet and I will let you know when we are ready for you to come."

Meantime, fifteen or sixteen dancers were taking their holidays in Germany, waiting for the season to open. They came two weeks before the season because they already had visas and Germany had good museums, a beautiful zoo, and you could take the train to Hamburg or visit another city. When the war started Goebbels gave an order that gave safe passage to the dancers back to Paris. We had Polish, Czechoslovakian, French, Italian, Danish. He let all of them out of Germany. Nobody touched them.

One good dancer, Léon Woizikowski, went to Poland and was stuck there. Woizikowski was a terrific character dancer. My God he was fantastic! Very talented. Extremely musical. He was caught during the war in Warsaw and sent to a concentration camp. He survived, but it was a terrible time.

You know, I was surprised by the Germans. They loved ballet so much and were so very enthusiastic. People are people, you know. There are bad people everywhere. I love Russian people, too, but there are bad ones. I didn't have any hatred for the German people, but I was upset about all these things.

To fill the hours when we were in Vevey, Sono and I went on trips to cathedrals and all kinds of historical places and museums nearby. We went to Lausanne. We went to the ski resorts. I didn't ski, but I liked to watch the people there. I also painted in Vevey, but I was painting the canvases over and over for the economy. I painted mostly nature. I did some of them outside, but mostly copies from old paintings. It was there that I painted my copy of the Black Madonna that I have in my house even now.

I had many sleepless nights. I heard about the bombs dropping on Warsaw and I was absolutely sure that they would kill my family. I was sure that everyone in my family was dead. The reports said that many thousands were killed.

Imagine the anxiety of all those dancers scattered and stranded throughout Europe. Multiply that concern by those in charge of the Ballets Russes who were trying their best to round up and safely corral their lost sheep.

Among Jasha's effects is a letter in French from de Basil in London, dated 14 October 1939. It suggests that Sono and Jasha leave Vevey and escape through Italy to Australia. Two weeks later that message is countermanded in another letter, this time in English, from the company headquarters in Paris, and they are told instead to "await quitly [sic] in Vevey. . . . The boat on which the Company is sailing will not enter in Naples or in any other port of France or Italy. . . . arranging necessary permission to leave for Jasha . . .".

Oddly, while the messages came from de Basil's office, Jasha saw de Basil only as a conduit. He credited his final rescue to Lifar alone.

> It was very funny how many times Serge Lifar showed up in my life when I most needed him. Lifar contacted me through the office of Colonel de Basil. De Basil and Lifar were both in Paris. They worked together.
>
> Lifar had a connection at the consulate. He had already telegraphed a general about me, and then wired me that I must get a visa from this general. The next day I took the train from Vevey and went to the consulate.
>
> My Lord! There was this big line around the building—three hundred people were there. It was winter, snowing and cold. I didn't have anything to warm me because I had been on summer vacation and had all summer clothes. I had only brought one jacket; that's all. So I came to the consulate and I saw this line. Sono said, "Let's go inside." We went inside and showed the secretary my telegram to get my visa. "Wait a minute." He took it and came back. "Passeporte, s'il vous plaît." I gave it to him, he stamped it and we went back to Vevey. It was that quick! That night we left for Paris!
>
> As soon as we were in Paris we heard the sirens. The German planes were coming. There was a loud knock on the hotel door. "Alert! Alert!" We had to run across the street with our coats over our pajamas because our hotel didn't have an underground shelter. We stayed there for an hour and then the siren came on again and everybody went back to the hotel.
>
> Lifar rescued lots of dancers. Massine was already an American citizen so he just went back to America, but some of his dancers were stranded in Europe. Massine left them behind. Some were in Holland and some were in Belgium. Lifar helped collect all the dancers. He also got them out of the army. Most of the dancers stuck in Europe went with us. Our company got bigger and bigger. That's why we had seventy people. Even Lifar went to Australia.

I was in Paris for only three days. I went right away to the office of the company. They said, "You are here! We are going to go to London. And from London we will take the boat and go again to Australia." We were supposed to go to Australia anyway after Berlin. It was good luck that we had Australia ahead.

16 Rue de Gramont, the Paris office of de Basil's Ballets Russes, is now just another faceless, featureless, nondescript building. There is no hint, no aura, that once it was the command center for a galaxy of stars—dancers, composers, designers—and the vast support system that makes an international ballet company possible. One stands on the street, looks up, and sees . . . nothing special. Its days of glory and glamour are gone, its lifeline long cut.

The boat to London came from Le Havre and when it crossed the channel I was terribly sick. We arrived in London in the evening and it was absolutely dark on the street. A blackout. We took a taxi and went to the same pension I had lived in for years, but we only stayed there a couple of days. There were no sirens while I was in London but it was absolutely dark. The English were fantastic. The discipline was tremendous. It was different from Paris where policemen were screaming, "Close the lights! Lights! Lights!"

CHAPTER 19

# A Star in His Own Right

*I was ready to dance.*

THEY TOLD US IN LONDON, "Tomorrow we are going on the boat." That night they took us to the boat in the dark, but when I got up in the morning the boat was still standing in the port. They said, "Tomorrow." But nobody really knew. They kept the departure date secret because of the war. Everyone was afraid of German submarines. There were two thousand people on the boat because there were so many Australians going home, but for us with the Ballet, we didn't need to worry. Once we were on the boat the food was free!

In all, we were thirty-four days on the boat. Once, after traveling at twelve or fourteen knots, two German submarines were spotted following us. The passengers didn't know that we were being followed. The boat went up to twenty-four knots, zigging and zagging, and they couldn't catch us. They could only go six. We learned of this the next day in the boat paper when we went to breakfast.

We stopped at Port Said before we went through the Suez Canal. There was an air raid at the fortress when we came from the Mediterranean. German planes came and we just sat there in the boat. They only passed us by because it was dark. There was already a captain's order that after six in the evening we couldn't go on the deck or smoke a cigarette. Nothing. There were double doors to the outside. If you opened one door there was another to open. That's why the ship stayed dark.

But it is a funny thing. I don't think the ballet people felt this danger. Ballet people are so sure of themselves. Even in Germany they recognized us so well. Ballet, ballet, ballet. We felt a little protected. Even the submarines—we think they didn't know the Ballet was there when they were following us! A couple of years later, when we were in Argentina, Germans from a submarine came on our boat and the submarine captain said, "Who is on the boat?" The captain said, "The Ballet Russe dancers!" That made it all right.

David Lichine rehearsed the principals for GRADUATION BALL on the ship to Australia. Everybody was there, the whole company. When Lichine created the "Drummer's" solo for himself on the boat, I learned it. Later, when he left, the "Drummer" became one of my most popular roles.

It must have been quite a sight: keen-eyed sailors alertly watching for U-boats, the ship surging forward under a blazing sun, dancers doing what dancers do on a deck that simulated a stage. The other passengers, less isolated from reality, may have suffered agonies of anxiety on that thirty-four-day trip, but the dancers? They danced. "We felt a little protected."

The Colonel was with us on this tour. Everybody had dropped the lawsuits. De Basil was a very smart man and this was his chance to come back to Australia as our leader.

The company was now called Colonel W. de Basil's Ballet Company or, in some articles, "Colonel W. de Basil's Russian Ballet Company from Royal Opera, Covent Garden." Elegant as the titles were, they were thoroughly matched by the elegant season. The company was the repository of the best dancers, sets, costumes, and choreography available during those war-torn years, and the Australians greeted the Colonel and his crew with joy.

Ballerinas were suddenly elevated to the status of today's Hollywood stars. Their domestic skills, fingernail colors, hats, and hobbies were highlighted in newspapers reeling from grim war news. What a salve to the collective angst of Australia—the escapism and elegance of the Ballet! And amidst the uproar, Roman Jasinski, now a mature artist, came to the fore, his skills honed to their highest peak, his artistry impeccable. Australia fell upon him with something akin to adoration.

> Our second tour to Australia, 1939-1940, was the greatest success because of the enormous repertoire, the scenery, all the big ballets. Before, the Ballet did not have this big repertoire; it was a smaller company. The second time we took sets and costumes for everything because we could not leave them in Europe because of the war.
>
> We stayed as long as we could in Australia. We spent three months here, three months there. We had seventy dancers, a big company. We had to have a painter for scenery. We had to have costumers, a man and a woman. And Colonel de Basil had two wives—at least, he had one former wife, Nina Leonidova, and one he wanted to have, Olga Morosova. He needed to get both of them out of Europe. He was a good guy. He took everyone who was interested in going. He added people to the company and cut our salaries so everyone could be paid. He cut, cut, cut. Sometimes we had just enough money to pay our hotel. I remember I had a contract where I was supposed to get twenty Australian pounds weekly, but I got only ten pounds—half. And then eight pounds and later seven pounds.
>
> But it was good luck that we had Australia. I had great success in South America later, but this was the greatest. Maybe it was my age. I was young, and stronger, more experienced than before. Everything.
>
> Anatole Oboukhov went to Australia with us to give company classes. I liked him very much. He was a very good teacher and also a good friend. He made jokes about Colonel de Basil because de Basil had promised him a salary, but when he came to Australia there was no salary. Oboukhov had a wife—well, not a wife, but like a wife, Vera

Nemtchinova. She was dancing with the company although she was already older. Colonel de Basil promised Oboukhov that she would dance some of the parts but then he gave them to Baronova. That made a problem between them.

This large company, rife with estrogen and testosterone, created a good many "problems." As with Oboukhov, as with de Basil, there were always love affairs, liaisons and peripatetic pairings. Dancers were thrown into close proximity, and attractions ebbed and flowed. Jasinski himself, termed by one correspondent the "best-looking man in the company," was in a long-term devoted relationship with Sono Osato and was neither judgmental nor fascinated by the personal foibles of his friends, but they did impact the company and from time to time he mentioned them.

One day Riabouchinska left Lichine and went with Lazowski. She had cats, and Lichine called her and told her that the cats were crying for her. She went back home. The cats missed her!

There was a Dr. Anderson who was in love with one of our dancers. He was gaga. He may have been married, this guy, but he was absolutely in love with her. He gave parties on account of her, with lots of drinking and eating. Everybody was invited, the whole company, all seventy people. Except the stagehands. They never invited stagehands.

Dr. Anderson made many films of the company, but I don't think he ever made a film of my ballets. I am sick! I was always filming other people, but I don't have any films of when I danced.

It was in Australia that I had a fight with the regisseur, Serge Grigoriev. First of all, he was Russian and he didn't like Polish people—mainly because his wife, Lubov Tchernicheva, always paid a lot of attention to Polish men. He was really in love with his wife. He was not really "jealousy," but he hated Polish men because they made love to his wife. She was a very sexy woman. Grigoriev didn't need to be jealous of me because I was with Sono. Besides, Tchernicheva was not my type. In the end we became good friends, but basically, he didn't like Poles.

We brought lots of dancers to Australia who did nothing—just stood in the wings. Meanwhile, Grigoriev tried to put me in every ballet. I already had so many ballets that I didn't see any reason why I should do small parts when I had all these big parts. I lost my temper one day. I screamed at him, then I threw things down and left the company because I didn't want to dance this ballet. It was a solo, but there were so many people standing there doing nothing. "Oh," he said, "You are doing so well!" "Yes, but these others are doing well, too, and they have no parts." Then de Basil came to me, to ask me to come back to the company. Then Lichine came, because some of his ballets needed to be danced and they didn't have anyone to dance them. Eventually, I came back. I was gone just one or two days.

I didn't talk to Grigoriev for awhile. Afterward, we became good friends again. He changed his attitude toward me. He liked me and I liked him, but Sono hated him because she was on my side and knew what he was doing wasn't right. Later, he loved Moussia, my wife. He was crazy about her and took care of her like a father. But that was later when we were in South America. This was the first time that I ever had an argument with him. He was surprised that I screamed at him. I just lost my temper, which was unusual for me. As a ballet master, he screamed at us, but he needed to scream to pull the dancers together. He was an older man so we respected him.

I had one part in LES PRÉSAGES that I wanted to get rid of, the part of "Fate." I went to de Basil and told him that Igor Schwezov could be fantastic in this part. He was a very tall man, imposing, and as "Fate" you had to stand up with your arms out to separate the people in love. I had a hard time convincing de Basil. He said, "But you are doing the part so well. Why do you want to give it up?" Still, I taught Schwezov this part the whole time we were in Australia and eventually, he got to do it. Schwezov was an unusually strong man, but when he came on the stage as "Fate" he looked like elastic. He was probably nervous, but he was very bad. De Basil was so mad at me the next day! I was sitting on the street having breakfast and he said, "Did you see what you did last night? Schwezov was terrible! Terrible!" "I don't know what it was. He'll be all right." "No! No! Never again!"

His reviews were bad, too. De Basil left and I saw Igor coming. He was angry and said, "De Basil has already come and made problems. It's your fault. You got me into this!" I said, "I thought that you would be good in this role. It would be different if you had danced SYLPHIDES."

Without knowing it, I had insulted him badly. It turned out that dancing SYLPHIDES was his greatest ambition in life. He thought that he was a great classical dancer. I had wanted to do another part in PRÉSAGES, the part with Baronova, and later I got to do it.

In all this time I had heard nothing from my family. I didn't know what had happened to them. I was worried, but I couldn't help them. We didn't pay a lot of attention to the Australian newspapers. We would get *Time Magazine* or something but we really knew very little about the war. Still, when we were in Australia we did a Polish Relief performance. The program cover was designed by Lazowski. He painted constantly and was a good painter, better than I.

This Midnight Gala Concert in Aid of Polish Relief took place 12 March 1940 following the farewell evening performance of Colonel de Basil's company in Sydney. Polish company members Lazowski, Jasinski, Ladre, and Matouchak organized the concert. All the artists gave their services free and the Theatre Royal was provided without charge. The English, French, and Polish national anthems preceded the program, and proceeds were sent to Polish Relief in Great Britain and France.

For his professional choreographic debut, Jasinski choreographed *Etude,* a pas de deux with Osato to music by Chopin.

This was my first time to choreograph professionally. Whenever the music played I put in another new step. Afterwards, Fokine gave me this good advice: "Don't put too many steps in one dance," because I put in too many steps, all of them different.

Jasinski followed this simple advice faithfully in his future works, but if this first effort was flawed, the critic of *The Sydney Morning Herald* found it "outstanding" and went on to praise Jasinsky's brief number as "admirably devised to show Osato's graceful line and his own finished classical style." Later in the evening, Jasinski danced a variation from *Raymonda* arranged for him by Oboukhov. In all, seventeen pieces were performed for the audience, each contributing to the cause.

While this particular gala focused on Polish Relief, other Ballet galas benefited other causes. Recipients included the Red Cross, the Royal Melbourne and Children's Hospitals, among others. De Basil's dancers may have lived in their insular, artistic little worlds but the war always hung on the fringes of their minds, ignored by preference until their own artistry could aid in its effort.

> By now the Colonel gave me many roles because I was ready to dance. Once in Australia there was a ballet they gave to a few people, LES DIEUX MENDIANTS, but nobody could do it. It was a Lichine ballet. Actually it was the ballet that Balanchine had staged for Diaghilev as THE GODS GO A-BEGGING, but we had the costumes and scenery and so they gave it to Lichine to stage. The director came to me and I said, "No, I don't want to do this ballet. You asked everybody else and now you come to me. Nobody wants to do this because it is very hard." But I was a very good friend of Lichine and he said, "Jasha, do it for me." "I will do it for you, but not for anybody else." So I did it. It was hard, but I could do it because I had more technique.

Apparently his "more technique" made the difference. An anonymous newspaper clipping culled from Jasinski's personal scrapbook proclaimed *Les Dieux mendiants* as "amusing. Riabouchinska and Jasinsky were at their best in that little pastoral, making the final scene where the divinities throw off their rags and appear in their classic grace a moment of jewel-like loveliness."

Jasha's fans concurred. ". . . the sheer joyous rapture and ecstasy of your dancing in 'The Gods Go A-begging' roused my deepest admiration." "I think you excelled everyone else in your performance of 'Les Dieux mendiants.' "

LES DIEUX MENDIANTS
Roman Jasinski as the "Shepherd" in Lichine's *Les Dieux mendiants* (The Gods Go A-begging).

Photo by Spencer Shier, Melbourne. Pl courtesy Jerome Robbins Dance Division, York Public Library for the Performing Ar Lenox and Tilden Foundations.

> I liked Lichine very much as a dancer and I learned from him. That's why I was always watching him. When he left I knew all of his dancing and I took many of his parts—PRODIGAL SON, the "Drummer" in GRADUATION BALL, LES DIEUX MENDIANTS, and others.

It had been twelve years since the two young men, Czeslaw Jasinski and David Lichtenstein (Lichine), had first met to paw at the ankles of Ida Rubinstein. Their friendship was firm, their mutual admiration sincere. And now Jasinski could dance his friend's choreography, adjusting it to match his own body, technique, temperament, and interpretation.

That was Jasinski. Never too proud to observe the strengths of others. Always learning. Always appreciative. Combining instinct and shrewdness, he gave new insights to older roles. Dance critics took note in review after review.

*Les Dieux mendiants:* "[The] accenting of [Jasinsky's] big allegro dance was as perfect a bit of art as even Colonel de Basil's company can show."

*Protée:* ". . . Roman Jasinsky, a signal success in the name role. . . ."

"Blue Bird": ". . . the house thundered its applause." [Jasinsky's] ". . . pure classical style and flawless grace made this a highlight in an evening which touched a very high standard all round."

> One of my biggest triumphs in Australia was "Blue Bird" in LE MARIAGE D'AURORE, from SLEEPING BEAUTY. It was very difficult technically because it is very short and you do lots of jumps. It is all jumping high with beats in the air, purely classical, demanding perfect, clean technique.

"Blue Bird" struck a chord not only with the critics, but with the fans themselves. Jasinski tucked away a number of fan letters from this period. They were amazingly alike. "I have never seen the Blue Bird danced so beautifully as last night." ". . . the finest [Blue Bird] ever seen in Australia."

My greatest triumph, though, was ICARE, choreographed by Lifar. It was a Greek story. I was successful in this role because I told myself that this story was real. I forgot I was Jasinski and believed I was just "Icare," a young man with the ambition to fly with wax wings. I really worked out every step. I believed in what I was doing.

Lifar was suddenly called back to Paris. He told the Colonel that he would leave ICARE with the Company only on one condition, that I would dance this ballet. But de Basil said, "No!" He didn't agree with this. "Maybe there is somebody else." "No. The only one who can dance this ballet is Jasinski. Nobody else. No other dancer in the company." And he left me this ballet.

It was a classical ballet, technically very strong. It took about fifteen minutes and I was all the time on the stage. It was so hard I was dying at the end of it! I think my debut was in Melbourne because Lifar did it in Sydney before he left.

Indeed, Jasinski's "Icare" was "the surprise of the season" according to many reviews. Article after article echoed an anonymous review in *The Sun* of Monday, 15 July 1940. "The outstanding thing about Saturday's presentation was the splendid performance of Roman Jasinsky, as Icare. When it was first done here, Lifar took the leading part in his own creation, and did it very badly, so that it almost moved one to mirth instead of admiration. Jasinsky did make us appreciate what it was all about, and gave a most virile and intelligent interpretation. [He] "enlarged the scope of the ballet by converting it from an anecdote about ancient days into an allegory of the human spirit's struggle to invent and aspire in the face of manifold dangers and discouragements."

No doubt Jasinski's "interpretation" drew upon his own past struggle "to invent and aspire in the face of manifold dangers and discouragements." Whatever its secret, *Icare* impacted its audience. The words "magnificent," "brilliant," "triumph" followed each performance as Jasinski danced the story of the eager Greek youth whose father gave him wings for soaring, only to see him plunge to his death when he flew too near the sun.

ICARE

Jasinski was highly acclaimed as the young man who flew too close to the sun.

Photograph by Hugh P. Hall; nla.pic-vn4173901, National Library of Australia.

They made the costumes there in Australia with two wings to help me in my practice. It looked like the wings helped me to fly as I made big circles around the stage, opening the wings each time. It was all timing, you know, with twelve big jumps around the stage. I remember feeling afraid when my father first lifted my arm and I said, "No!" And then he lifted the other arm and I said, "No!" And then he lifted me up and I said, "Ahhh." I really believed that I would fly. Then I left the stage when I started to fly. In the story I flew so high that I touched the sun and the sun melted the wax which held the wing to my arm. The wing came down first, then there was the sound of a big drum and when I fell down I had just one wing. I danced with this wing as I was dying.

And fly he did—straight into twenty curtain calls! *Icare* was an astounding, recurrent success, performance after performance, its enthusiastic reception belying its earlier easy dismissal when choreographer Lifar danced the lead.

> Antal Dorati did the music for this ballet, and his idea was to use percussions and a wind machine. Lifar didn't bring the score with him when he came from Paris. Maybe de Basil didn't ask him to dance it until he was in Australia. After Australia, something happened to the score. It was gone. When we went to South America later, to Buenos Aires, I knew the music so I took a stick and played it for our conductor and wrote everything down on paper. Then the conductor orchestrated it with harp, violin, drums, and they added the machine to make the wind.

To remember and recreate such an unusual score with its oddly matched instruments was a feat of memory and tenacity. It was worth it. *Icare* continued to be a favored ballet and Jasinski performed it often, with enthusiastic acclaim, long after Australia was behind him.

Another great triumph for Jasinski during the Australia tour was Lichine's *Prodigal Son.*

> I liked to dance in story ballets. I liked them more than just plain dance. I liked to express myself with the ballet—feeling or crying or tragical. When I danced I didn't talk to anyone when I came into the theatre. I just came, sat in my dressing room quietly, made my makeup, warmed myself and dressed. I prepared myself. If I had to do two ballets, I had to change my feelings. The hardest thing was after PRODIGAL SON. This ballet had everything. I really didn't want to dance anything before or after. I really had to concentrate on this part and put myself in this role. PRODIGAL SON and ICARE were two ballets that strongly affected me.

There were other challenges as well. He called his hugely successful *Spectre de la Rose* "murder" because of its seemingly unending jumps. "You jumped and jumped and got a pain in your stomach." As for his acclaimed "Drummer" solo in *Graduation Ball,* "It was a great dance, a very successful number, but it was just a number. I liked to dance it but it was not like PRODIGAL SON."

Ballets that he seldom mentioned touched others to the core. "I am always enchanted by your art in 'Francesca da Rimini.'" "You are the only man I have ever seen in 'Sylphides' who really expresses the poetry of the music."

FRANCESCA DA RIMINI

Jasinski as "Lancelot" in David Lichine's *Francesca da Rimini.*

Photo by Maurice Seymour, courtesy of Ron Seymour. Archives, Tulsa Ballet.

LES SYLPHIDES

Roman Jasiński with Tamara Toumanova in Fokine's *Les Sylphides.*

Photograph by Hugh P. Hall; nla.pic-vn4180305, National Library of Australia.

Roman Jasinski was now a star. Fans begged for photographs. They stood in long lines in the hope of seeing him pass by. "Your work seems to have a quality which few others possess, the spark of genius which makes a really great dancer."

Today's dancer-athletes perform to a different standard. Turns and jumps are technically astounding, but they sometimes override yesterday's artistry. The "feeling" which once made Jasinski a star is out of sync with the modern mechanics of dance, but in his time and place Jasinski touched heartstrings. Unfortunately, his purse strings were sometimes touched, too.

> When we were in Australia de Basil had to go to New York to make a new contract with Hurok but he didn't have any money for

the trip. So he asked the company for money. He even tried to borrow from Grigoriev. He said, "If I don't have money, Hurok can press me to sign a contract I don't like. When I have money in the pocket, I can talk differently with Hurok." He asked Lichine but Lichine didn't have any money, either. De Basil asked, "Then who does have money?" Lichine said, "Jasinski."

And he was right. I had in the Chase National in New York $2,500 in an account. When I left my home my father gave me good advice: "Count on yourself and not on your friends. Don't borrow any money; don't give any money." I always tried to live by his advice. Then, when everybody was without money I had money because I was very careful. It is true I was making more money, but if my family survived the war, I wanted to support them. De Basil said, "Jasha, nobody has money but you. I need $500. I need this money for New York." I was afraid to give him my bankbook but our secretary signed that he could only take $500 from this book.

Everybody was mad! Whew! Lazowski said, "What you did was stupid. You will never get this money back." But when de Basil arrived in New York he signed the contract and Hurok gave him $10,000 right away.

Later, when the whole company got to New York, Lazowski said, "Why don't you go and ask the Colonel about your bankbook?" So I went to Colonel de Basil and said, "May I have my bankbook back?"

"What book? Oh yes. You know, Jasha, I never touched one penny from this book. I will get you this book." De Basil had never used my bankbook but if he kept the book he would keep me in the company. He also liked to keep the dancers' passports for the same reason. Two or three days passed and I asked him again.

"I don't have it. I will get you this book later."

"Yes, but I need it now. I need to take some money."

"You need money? For what do you need money? I'll give you some money tomorrow." And tomorrow passed and the next tomorrow and the next tomorrow. . . Lazowski told me I had better go to Chase National and tell them that I lost this book. Later, de Basil said, "I still have your book, Jasha. Don't worry."

"Colonel de Basil, that's all right. I have another one. I told them at the bank I lost that one. You can throw that book away."

He was not very happy, but everybody else congratulated me. I really needed the money.

At last it was time to go. However much he loved it, Australia was still just one more stop on the road of a traveling company.

At the end of Australia it didn't matter if we were happy or sad to leave. When the directors told us it was time to go we never asked why. We just left. Now dancers want to know everything. One week before you go you must put the time they are leaving on the bulletin board. Why? If you belong to the company you are leaving! And if you change the schedule they want to know why you are changing it. In the early days they never tried to mix up the dancers with this. We just went.

CHAPTER 20

# Dark Days

*I was a very unhappy man.*

I COULD SEE SOMETHING WAS HAPPENING WITH Sono. It was a hard time for me. I had been very happy with Sono for almost five years. She had joined the company in 1934 and not much later we began to be together. We were very strongly in love, both of us. Sono didn't have much chance in classical ballet because she didn't like to dance on pointe. I don't know how far she could have gone. She was doing some big parts, but she was planning on something else.

Sono was a very open person and if she didn't like something she would tell you. She was also a mysterious person. In the end her mother came between us. She wanted Sono to leave the ballet. I proposed to marry her many times, but her mother was not so anxious for her to marry. Her mother had bigger plans. She liked me all right, but thought Sono should change from the ballet and be in a movie or on Broadway. At this time, Sono was very original, being Japanese and American. Maybe the war spoiled lots of things because she was part Japanese. I know her father was put in a detention camp during the war.

I understood Sono's decision to leave the ballet, even though it meant that I suffered. I would never try to stop somebody else's progress because of my own selfishness. Sono didn't like de Basil and maybe she thought she had gone as far as she could in the de Basil company. Eventually, she did a lot on Broadway and I think she was in some movies. We separated very good friends. We liked each other, and now when we meet we are very friendly. Maybe we separated at the right time. I don't know.

It was a very hard time, but I worked on myself. I could never afford to ruin my life. I needed to get myself under control. Sure, I was a very unhappy man—there was no doubt. But I explained to myself, "That's the way it is and you need to find something else."

The company, now called the Original Ballet Russe, hit the continental shores in Los Angeles 7 October 1940, and after a Los Angeles tour, performed in Minneapolis and Chicago on the way to New York. Here Jasinski and George Balanchine once more made contact, with the mutual cordiality that marked the rest of their lives.

We invited Balanchine to a rehearsal of his COTILLON because it was in our repertoire and we wanted to know if it was still correct. After all, Balanchine had choreographed it in 1932 and it was now 1940, eight years later. Balanchine sat there and looked and looked and finally said, "You know, I don't remember this ballet." COTILLON was a great success when the company began, but maybe he didn't want to fool around with it. He didn't need de Basil in his life anymore so he didn't care.

I was always glad to see Balanchine again. I always liked him, even after what happened in Monte Carlo. It didn't make any difference. He liked to work with me and I liked to work with him. He said he could create anything he wanted with me. You know, they said Balanchine never did any good ballets on the de Basil company in New York. He said, "I don't have the dancers. The one dancer who could do it is Jasinski. I could create on him." I think it was my technical ability, because I knew every kind of dance. It was easy to

Souvenir booklet for the Original Ballet Russe,

1940–41 Season, Sixth American Tour

adapt to his choreography. If he used Russian steps and turned them upside down, it was easy for me because of the connection with all my education. I had needed to learn all the dances during my studies. It is one thing to learn the step, but the approach to the step is also important. When Balanchine did something a little bit different, I could catch his meaning and put it into my body.

Whatever the personal dislike between de Basil and Balanchine, they did have one further collaboration at this time, *Balustrade,* reuniting Jasinski, Toumanova, Tchelitchev, Stravinsky, and Balanchine for the first time since Les Ballets 1933. It turned out to be a short-lived, enigmatic work quickly dismissed by Jasinski and most of its audience, but its lead ballerina, Tamara Toumanova, looked upon its choreography as a maturation of Balanchine's earlier themes in *Cotillon,* in which she had starred as a young girl. Perhaps the awkward 1940 rehearsal of the 1932 ballet sparked a chord, a memory, which matured into the later work.

De Basil asked Balanchine to create this ballet, BALUSTRADE. If de Basil could take advantage of someone he would take it; it didn't matter if he liked them or didn't like them, but Balanchine hated de Basil. He really couldn't stand him because of when Massine came to the de Basil company all those years ago.

The music for BALUSTRADE was by Stravinsky who had become a very good friend to Balanchine. I liked Tchelitchev's designs; he had his own style and made his designs sort of mysterious. BALUSTRADE would probably be received better now. Always when Balanchine choreographed he made all kinds of sexy movements. Now it would look normal, but back then most people didn't like it. It was not a very successful ballet. I think we gave only one or two performances.

On 22 January 1941, *Balustrade* premiered at the 51st Street Theatre with Jasinski, Toumanova, Leskova, and Paul Petroff in the leading roles and music composed and conducted by Igor Stravinsky.

Film fragments in the Dance Collection of the New York Public Library are achingly unsatisfactory. The overall impression is of black and white with a few splashes of color. Toumanova, dressed in black, fades into a dark background, her movements vague, her lines indistinct. Jasinski and Paul Petroff, in a ménage à trois with Toumanova, seem contorted as they pull her this way and that. Was it too "sexy"? Certainly there are some strange slitherings among the three principals, accented by hip thrusts and pretzel-like pairings.

A large chorus winds around in characteristic Balanchine lines and two girls flank Toumanova in unexpected ways, but the fragments are so brief it is difficult to determine what was good—or bad—about the ballet. There is a sense that it might have been far more interesting than critics of the day acknowledged, but it is just too difficult to determine based on its tonal darks on dark.

What we do know is that it was a huge disappointment to impresario Sol Hurok who funded it. Hurok lost a considerable amount of money on the piece and his own recollections of the effort are discreetly scathing. "As is so often the case with Balanchine, [*Balustrade*] had neither story nor theme nor idea; it was simply an abstraction in which Balanchine set out to exploit to the fullest the brittle technical prowess of Tamara Toumanova. . . . Unfortunately, despite all the costs, which I paid, it had, all told, one consecutive performance."

Setting aside the *Balustrade* debacle, it was during this period that critic Edwin Denby wrote: "Among the men [of the Original Ballet Russe] is a dancer for whom I feel a particular affection, Jasinski, the most modest and most poetic of the stars. The flexibility of his upper spine. . . shows you how elastic ballet dancing can be, against the military rigidity many people think the back of a male classicist should be confined to; and his arms are correct enough, and free. He shows you that the batterie of the feet can be a game instead of a test, and that at some brief moments you can hold your shoulders too high and still be right. I wish I could see him in the Spectre [de la Rose], the touchstone of unaffected lyricism." Yes, the company was once again in New York, but the old ease and familiarity were gone. War raged in Europe. Anxiety gripped the American nation. The company resumed its tour, but without Osato, Denisova, and eventually Toumanova. Baronova, under a separate contract with Hurok, was sent to step into Toumanova's roles when the company went on to Mexico City.

I went to Mexico City with the company, although it was hard when Sono stayed behind. Two lovely French girls were running after me, but I decided to stay alone.

The next stop on the itinerary proved to be an unexpectedly long one. It was in Cuba that the bottom dropped out of the Original Ballet Russe. The contract signed between Sol Hurok and de Basil included a clause which stated that every performance must take place as scheduled with its full complement of dancers. Unfortunately, some dancers disputed their meager pay and "struck" the company. This was unprecedented! A strike in a ballet company! Retrospective rumors and later admissions by Baronova blamed Sevastianov, who was already

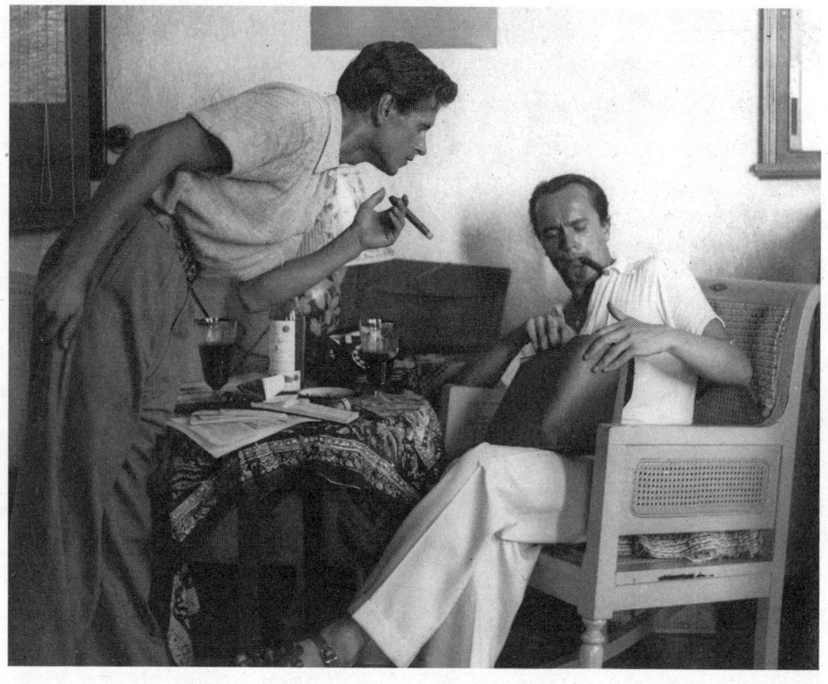

DISCUSSING THE STRIKE

Jasinski and Yurek Lazowski endure the strike with fine Cuban cigars.

Private collection.

GUILTY IN BLACK AND WHITE

Guilty directors versus stranded dancers. Painting attributed to Roman Jasinksi. Private collection.

on Hurok's payroll, for instigating the strike. Others said that Hurok was looking for a way to sponsor a new company, Ballet Theatre, instead of de Basil's and this provided him with an out. As an end result, the strike was held, the contract was voided by Hurok, and the Colonel's most loyal dancers were stranded in Cuba.

> It was sabotage! Hurok was very close friends with Baronova's husband, Sevastianov. The company was supposed to give a performance in Havana, Cuba, but there were fifteen or twenty people on strike. Sevastianov was working with them. We came to the performance and there were people missing. We dressed and from one ballet we jumped to another because we knew all the parts. At the end of the performance Hurok came to de Basil and said, "Colonel de Basil, I have a contract with you that fifty dancers are supposed to dance on the stage. There were only thirty-five." "But the strike!" "I don't care. This voids the contract." After this the company was finished and everybody was without a job.

According to grievances listed by those artists unhappy with the company, the strike was caused by de Basil's habit of cutting dancers' salaries when money was tight. Perhaps. But it is also true that Hurok became manager of Ballet Theatre immediately after the strike, and that his friends, former de Basil employees Sevastianov and a reluctant Baronova, joined him right away. Sabotage or not, it led to yet more hardships for those company members remaining loyal to Colonel de Basil's Original Ballet Russe.

> Sol Hurok dropped our company. He did it on purpose to break the contract with de Basil. Meanwhile, Hurok took the tour he had arranged for us and gave it to Ballet Theatre. We were stranded in Cuba for six months.
>
> When the company broke apart we were living in a very good hotel, the Hotel Presidente. Since we didn't know how long we were going to stay in Cuba, I moved to a pension on the beach in Varadero that only cost two dollars a day for food and a room. It was very cheap, very simple, nothing luxurious. I lived there for two weeks. I liked Cuba and I was enjoying this. Other dancers also lived in very cheap pensions or together in one room of a hotel. We ate the same food, beans and chicken, every day.
>
> Then Lazowski came from Havana and said, "Jasha, listen, we are in trouble and need some help from you. The Hotel Presidente threw us out because we cannot pay and they kept our trunks. We don't have anything—no money and no place to eat. Maybe we can find a good apartment together." Lazowski was my good friend and Paul Petroff also asked me. So I went back to Havana and we took an apartment together. It was a big apartment, luxurious, with four or five rooms, a kitchen, and a big flat roof. It was so hot that we took our mattresses on top of the roof and the mosquitoes couldn't bite us there because the roof was too high. Everybody said, "All right. We owe you the money." I think I paid $140 monthly for this. They said to keep a record of what they owed me and they would split it. I was there, and Petroff, Grisha Alexandrov, Lazowski, and Leskova. Four men and one

REHEARSING IN CUBA

Private collection.

girl. We all lived there several months and you know, no one ever paid me back this money that I spent.

My money went very fast. I went to the market and bought the food but every day somebody had to cook. The days were easy; we just had sandwiches, but dinner was a bigger meal. About six o'clock they'd cook, I'd cook, we'd all cook together. My mother had taught me to cook. I was always sniffing in my mother's kitchen and I became a good cook. The best cook was Paul Petroff. He would buy the whole leg of lamb and make a fantastic stew. The girl, Tatiana Leskova, could cook nothing, she was terrible, but the two French girls, the Moulin sisters, also came. That was okay; they were French and could cook. We would invite them to eat if they would cook. We did better than the others because we cooked for ourselves.

So actually, I supported five or six people. It was in our contract with de Basil that if we were stranded he would pay our passage home. I had counted on de Basil, but de Basil said, "I don't have any money."

CUBAN REVERIE

Private collection.

When the Colonel left to look for work for the company he said to Grigoriev, "If anybody gets work, try to help them with the costumes." First Lazowski and I tried to make a little company. The Cuban ballerina Alicia Alonso and her husband helped us and we gave performances in Cuban schools. They didn't pay much, but they gave us a bus and we made a company of about ten people. I danced I don't know how many performances of "Blue Bird," and other pas de deux and variations. It was a great success but it was very hard and the work was not steady. I put $450 of my New York money into this business. After a month's work I had to pay the dancers and the pianist, and then I had to buy food for the apartment. Madame Alonso gave us her theatre to rehearse in, but we still had to pay the pianist.

Then Madame Alonso called me and Lazowski and said, "There are about thirty-five people from your company. Why can't you give a performance in the theatre?" She was going to pay us a good salary for the whole company. We could even take back the people who had been on strike.

We told Grigoriev that we had this proposition from Madame Alonso to perform *Francesca da Rimini* and *Paganini* and he said, "You are going too far! You want to run the whole company now! I need to call Colonel de Basil!" I screamed at him and he screamed at me. He was so surprised when I hit my fist on the table. We had worked all those months with the kids there in Cuba while Grigoriev sat with his son, Vova, and did nothing. And when we told him about the performances he screamed, "Oh, you are going too far! Vova! Vova!" And he called his son. "We need to do something! They are going too far! We need to stop them!" He didn't like it that we had found this job instead of him. It was a job for the whole company. We had worked months and months all day long and then he told us that we were doing the wrong thing!

When Colonel de Basil heard this he flew right away to Cuba, called Lazowski and me, and said, "This is fantastic! Sit down here and talk with me." I told him the story and he talked with Madame Alonso.

ENTER MOUSSIA LARKINA

Moscelyne Larkin.

Photo by Maurice Seymour courtesy of Ron Seymour. Archives@Tulsa Ballet.

But I said, "Wait a minute. I've already put in $450. Who is going to pay me this money?" Madame Alonso said, "Jasha, wait. I will put some extra chairs in the theatre and all the money will be paid back." So then we gave the performance. Grigoriev knew he was wrong, and he and I were on good terms after that.

De Basil brought Fortune Gallo, the opera impresario, from the United States to see the performance. Gallo liked the company and signed a contract and that is how we finally came back to New York. This Fortune Gallo really saved de Basil, and Lazowski and I really saved de Basil's company. Thanks to us de Basil got the company out of Cuba, and thanks to Gallo we went to New York and Washington, D.C.

And that's when Moussia joined the company.

CHAPTER 21

# Uh! Oh! Bad Eye!

*I looked on her and I liked her.*

Moussia. Tiny, strong-willed, exuberant Moussia. She could not have entered his life at a better time. Jasinski was an established principal; she was a brand new, wide-eyed, inexperienced corps de ballet girl. War was upon the world. Funds were tight everywhere. Artists danced wherever they could. It could have been a sad, lonely, frustrating time for Jasinski after the loss of Sono, but the vivacity, enthusiasm, joie de vivre of a young, naive girl from Oklahoma brought a new sparkle to his life and changed his future, almost at first meeting. Of course he didn't know it. But she did!

Blessed with an exquisitely beautiful face and form, the dark hair and eyes of her American Indian-Welsh papa and the fiery ambition of her Russian mama, Edna Moscelyne Larkin was born in 1925 in Miami, Oklahoma. Almost from birth she was a force to contend with.

By the age of fifteen and a half, after studying in New York with a host of extraordinary teachers, the adventuresome young ballet student heard of the Original Ballet Russe auditions and cut school to attend. Logic told her she was too young and inexperienced to audition, but curiosity and daring won out. So there she was, before the piercing eyes of the famous Colonel de Basil, as he put each hopeful neophyte through her paces.

"Walk like a happy girl. Good! Now, cry!" The audition was as much about emoting as dancing and the young Moscelyne was a match for its demands. De Basil and his associates were impressed with her budding beauty, expressiveness, and promise, and by audition's end, this little American Indian–Russian girl from Oklahoma found herself a fledgling member of the prestigious Original Ballet Russe. It was the start of a career, a stage name ("Moussia Larkina"), and, always far more important to Moussia, a lifelasting love affair.

Not long after joining the company, this lowest of the low on the scale of ballet hierarchy first saw principal dancer Roman Jasinski. He was bronzed to perfection from his months in Cuba, handsome, charming—and nearly twenty years her senior. Ever after she called him her "Greek god," and in her diary she drew a big heart, wrote "Roman Jasinski" inside, and around it wrote "pitty-pat, pitty-pat, pitty-pat!" Below she inscribed, "If I can do this, I can do anything." The pursuit began.

In contrast to Moussia's teenaged raptures, Jasha merely "looked on her"-albeit with considerable interest.

> I first saw Moussia in New York. Her mother was there but she went home to Oklahoma when we started the tour. In Washington, D.C., I saw Moussia again. I looked on her and I liked her from the beginning. She was coming from her dressing room. Lazowski was there and he said, "Uh, oh. Bad eye!" He knew me well! This was at a rehearsal. I think she was wearing a short black tunic and pink tights. The corps de ballet was all the same. With de Basil, girls had to wear black tunics. Boys wore black tights. Only the soloists and principals could be different.

It didn't take long for the sparks to fly. He was "Greek-god" handsome; she was young, delightful, and impressionable; and best of all, her mother had already gone home to Oklahoma.This might be a time to digress a bit to introduce "Mama." Eva Matlagova's story is every bit as colorful and picaresque as Jasha's. Born into rural poverty in the Carpathian Mountains on the Russian/Polish border, Eva (Yevka) Matlagova walked shoeless in the snows as a child, burying her feet in warm, fresh cow dung to keep them from freezing.

A priest linked her family with a childless couple in Lvov, and for three or four years she was given a taste of "society" and its manners, until slanderous tongues hinted that Eva was her foster mother's love child. Poor Eva! From exposure to fine ballet and opera, dancing and singing in her church, social engagements and balls, she found herself abruptly sent back home to live once more the life of a peasant.

By then, however, she was an enthusiastic exponent of the "Russification Movement," a grassroots effort to remove Polish, Austrian, and Roman Catholic elements from the Russian/Greek Orthodox culture. In Lvov, Eva had developed into a skilled reactionary under her foster parents' guidance and encouragement, and once back in her home, she went from village to village with a group of like-minded youths, singing and dancing in patriotic pageants and tweaking the noses of frustrated authorities.

Finally, those authorities had had enough and began to search out Russification ringleaders. Twice they came seeking Eva at home, but, as luck would have it, she was away. Her foster parents in Lvov were not so lucky. Many years later Eva learned that they had been executed for their efforts in the movement. Escape to America saved Eva, but catapulted her into a challenging new culture.

Her first shock in America came when an émigré brother burned the clothes she had worn on the trip and doused her head with turpentine to wash out the louse eggs. Her first English lesson taught her to say, "I want job." Her first American job was washing dishes for three dollars a week. Nonetheless, Eva Matlagova was blessed with a capacity for hard work, a sparkling vivacity, and a sharp, incisive mind. Sustained by her singing and dancing lessons from Lvov, she won a place in a Russian vaudeville company and began to tour her adopted country.

At a stop in Oklahoma, a young man of Welsh and American Indian descent took one look at the laughing little dancer and utterly lost his heart. In time they wed and had two children, and Eva became a ballet teacher of unusual excellence. Her gifted daughter Moussia, trained by "Mama" and polished by summers in New York, inherited the laughing charm and intense ambition of her mother. In Moussia's performing years her effervescent sparkle was paramount, but as the years passed she was to feel more and more "a thousand hands pulling me back," an inheritance from her reticent papa's Indian blood. The combination of personalities made for a fascinating human being, but nothing of this native introspection was visible at that first audition before de Basil. There Moussia was pure Russian, radiant with the instinct to emote, to dance, to perform. It wasn't long before the neophyte and the prince began a wary, shy, pas de deux.

> The company danced on a barge at the Watergate in August of 1941. Then we toured Montreal and Toronto under another impresario, and began our big tour with Gallo. The next month Gallo appeared in Detroit, said the company was finished, and cancelled our West Coast tour. I remember Moussia cried!

Once again, tensions, disagreements, and antipathies between the man with the pocketbook and the man at the ballet's helm brought plans to a shuddering halt. Left in the lurch—again—members of the company were sent back to New York to await an uncertain future.

> We went back to New York where the whole company stayed at the Park Central Hotel. We paid for our rooms day by day ourselves and just kept rehearsing without knowing what was going to happen. We didn't look for other jobs. And then suddenly an impresario came in with contracts to go to Mexico.
>
> After we arrived in Mexico City I was surprised to see Edward James again. I saw him sitting in a restaurant and went to say hello. He asked me what I was doing and I told him I was in the Ballet Russe. The man had lots of money. After all, he had been director of Les Ballets 1933. For him, this had been something new and I think he had enjoyed it. And then it was over and I think he was kind of disappointed. He had been bitter in the beginning, but somehow for him, it was also enjoyment.
>
> We danced in Mexico for nearly a month—January 1942—and then Riabouchinska and Lichine left the company to go back to New York. This is when I took over Lichine's roles in the company.

CHAPTER 22

# South American Saga

*To me, it was fantastic.*

AS FAR AS WE KNEW we were just going to dance in Mexico and then we were going to go back to the United States. We didn't know then that we were going on to South America. Moussia was only sixteen but she was happy to find herself going straight to South America. There were seventy-two people in the company. De Basil traveled with us in South America; we never really knew where we were going but we had confidence in him.

Lots of managers didn't want to pay after performances. It was a problem to get this money. So de Basil began to collect the money before each performance. Sometimes we would give a free educational program for the children and the government would give us buses which made the trips less expensive for us.

Life in South America was easier than in Paris. I knew we were going to eat; I only worried when there wasn't any food at all. The Indians would cook corn, sweet like sugar, and we would eat the corn on the bus. De Basil would pay for everyone.

I remember that in La Plata they had the most beautiful market I ever saw. They had fruit, all kinds of meat. In between each kind of cut there were flowers and leaves. The way they decorated! I just walked and walked and looked at these things. They made designs with fruit and meat and flowers. It was so fantastic. Leg of lamb. One pound filet mignon, 25 cents American! The meat was out of this world.

They paid us a little something while we were traveling. The train would stop and we would go to eat. We ate pigs and chickens and I think we ate buzzards a couple of times. It tasted like chicken.

In a way, South America was like Europe—rich and poor and nothing in between. But I already knew this kind of life. For me it was normal; for the Americans it was different. After a performance they would say, "I want this. I want that." And they could not get it. I didn't even try to get it because I knew that it was a different life here. In the beginning the Americans had a little trouble, but eventually, they adjusted and when they came back to America they said, "Oh, in this country we can get anything we want!"

Most of the time de Basil traveled with us. We'd finish a performance and then find out where we were going the next day.

Sometimes we would fly. We didn't fly much because there were not many planes. The planes were very small but we flew from one place to another and then the plane would go back and pick up more people. It didn't worry us; we were used to being scared!

We also traveled by boat. The first time I ate frogs' legs was on a boat. We were shocked to see them! But I tried them and thought, "It's just like chicken." I loved them and had them many times after that.

One time on a boat we had cows living on the deck right above us. Every time they did their business the roof leaked, and we had to move the bed out of the way.

Each day one cow would disappear. The butcher would come, kill it and open its stomach. The sailors would catch the blood in glasses and drink it. Then they cut the cow into pieces and cooked it, but you know, it was tough. It was fresh meat. And after all this, when they threw the rest into the sea, you could see the sharks following the boat. The sea was full of sharks. One day the captain gave all the people rifles because there were so many sharks around the boat.

We also traveled by train in South America. The trains were so slow that we would jump off and walk along the side for exercise. When we arrived in the next town I would jump from the train and Moussia would push the bags out the window to me. It was first come, first served at the good hotels.

We had so much time in South America. We didn't perform every day. We would come and rehearse, maybe one week or two weeks, give performances for maybe one week, then stop and rehearse another week. On our week off we did nothing—just class and rehearsal every day—as well as tour the city.

It was in South America that Roman Jasinski added a new title to his repertoire—that of arm-wrestling champion. After opening in a new town, a table would be brought onto the stage, and the contest was on. Jasinski became famous for never losing, even when pitted against burly stagehands. Each year they would await the return of the Original Ballet Russe, when the word would go out that Jasinski was back and ready to defend his title. He rarely lost. His secret? He used the muscles in his legs to plant himself solidly in the chair, and then just waited for the much larger—but untrained—stagehands to tire. He left South America with the undisputed title of arm-wrestling champion.

This was different from our tours in the United States. Nothing was ready in South America. Nothing was prepared. When you came to a city you needed to work things out. You could never arrive there and then dance right away. You needed two or three days to find the technical people, the stage, the lighting, and everything. Sometimes you would have to look for an orchestra. You would go to every bar to find the musicians and then you would have to teach them what to play. De Basil told us not to expect much from these musicians. We had four violins with the company, and William McDermott joined us when we needed a pianist. Willy played for PAGANINI and some of the other ballets. Sometimes the other musicians didn't know what they were playing, but we still danced.

It was an interesting life in South America. You didn't worry about anything. The war was in Europe and I thought it was fantastic to be anywhere that was out of the war. We could read the paper and find out what was going on. We would buy one paper and pass it around. We ate plenty and had a good life. I was worried about my family, but you know, I was so far away. We knew what was happening, but what could we do?

I always thought that South America was an adventure. We were there for almost five years and it was interesting always.

CHASTENED AND DESTITUTE, THE PRODIGAL SON RETURNS.

Photo by Thorlichen, Buenos Aires. Private collection.

L'APRÈS-MIDI D'UN FAUNE

Roman Jasinski with Tania Stepanova in Nijinsky's *Afternoon of a Faun*.

Photo by Thorlichen, Buenos Aires. Courtesy Archives, Tulsa Ballet.

And what of the romance? A beautiful French girl had early marked Jasinski for her own, but before the company left the U.S., Jasha had turned his attention to the lovely teenager from Oklahoma. That glance at the Watergate came just in time and eventually led to a forty-seven-year marriage that lasted until death did them part.

How did she do it?

If corps member Moussia heard that principal dancer Jasha had dinner plans for the evening, she would "happen" to be at the very same restaurant at the very next table. She followed him wherever he went, worshipping from afar. He didn't have a chance! Flattered and enchanted, it didn't take long for the Greek god to descend from Mount Olympus. Mama in Oklahoma became alarmed. In her mind, her brilliant, beautiful, gifted daughter deserved no less than a prince. A real prince. Not one with the stage for a palace. Despite the difficulties of wartime travel, "Mama" made plans to intervene.

A letter came from Moussia assuring Mama that there was no cause to fear. Mama was calmed. All was well. Temporarily.

> Every year we went back to the same cities for another season. We never knew, really, where we were going.
>
> I think that it was in Bolivia that one girl got polio. It was Thérèse Moulin, the sister of Geneviève. It happened on the boat back to Buenos Aires where we were going to dance at the Teatro Colón. She was paralyzed. It was terrible.
>
> The company was still traveling and we were afraid they would keep us there for months in quarantine. You know what they did? They lowered a chair from a bridge, picked her up from the boat and flew her to Buenos Aires while we stopped at some other place. Colonel de Basil had some friends who let her come and stay with them in Buenos Aires. She remained paralyzed and after the war she returned to Paris.
>
> It was in Buenos Aires that I danced Balanchine's MOZART VIOLIN CONCERTO. Balanchine was working for the Teatro Colón company at this time and the members of their company and ours liked each other

very much. One of the Colón male dancers was injured and the Colón said they wanted to put somebody else in this ballet, but Balanchine said, "No, there is only one person who can dance this part and that is Jasinski." Then he had to call Colonel de Basil and ask de Basil's permission for me to go there. De Basil asked me if I wanted to do this and I said yes. This ballet belonged to the Colón and not to the Ballet Russe.

I liked the Mozart ballet. It's funny how things are in life. I brought this ballet to Tulsa forty years later. At the Colón I danced with an older ballerina, very strong, who danced all three parts. I danced with her the second and third movements. Someone else danced with her in the first movement.

The Teatro Colón was very interesting. It had a round place for rehearsal, an underground rotunda with no air to circulate so it was very hard to breathe. It had no air conditioning and there were no windows. That's where we rehearsed.

It had been a couple of years since I had seen Balanchine. Again he tried to take me away from de Basil. "Jasha, why do you stay here?" But I was already with Moussia. I was in love and told him no. I had already left de Basil once and I didn't want to leave him again. "But Jasha, here at the Colón you can stay until the end of your life." And I said, "Yes, Georgi Melitonovich, but to me, if you go there you die there. There is no excitement."

It was like in the ballet in Warsaw. You started there as a little one and worked there until you were forty-five, and then you were out. So I said, "No, I don't want to leave Colonel de Basil. He doesn't have anyone who can dance the big roles in the company. There is no one to take my parts. I cannot do this." Balanchine said, "You need to think about yourself." But I said that my conscience would bother me.

I didn't want to stay at the Colón. All my life it was my hope to go to the United States; I had always loved America. I had already decided to make my life here in America and I never changed my mind. People wanted me to stay in Australia and Buenos Aires, but

PHOTO OF THE YOUNG MOUSSIA INSCRIBED

"LOVE, FROM YOUR DANCING DAUGHTER"

Courtesy Archives, Tulsa Ballet.

I didn't want to. Buenos Aires was strict, like Poland. I wanted to be free. In the company you were free. Besides, I liked traveling. We went on tour every place. To me it was fantastic. Very exciting! Adventure!

I liked the people in South America. They were nice, close to Europeans. I liked Buenos Aires because I had lots of friends there. And Rio—I think Rio de Janeiro was my favorite. It is a beautiful place. Also Chile. Every year we went back and back and back for another season: Montevideo, São Paulo, Rio, Buenos Aires, La Plata, Rosario, Lima, Santiago. But I never planned to stay in South America.

It's a funny thing about "fame." You feel that you are so great for a moment but when you leave the theatre you feel nothing. You go to the hotel and you feel lonesome. There is a big change when you are leaving the stage. I remember in Buenos Aires that Colonel de Basil invited me to dinner with a lady. She was so happy. She said, "My God! I can't believe that I just saw you in the theatre and now I am sitting with you so close!" This lady loved her husband, but she worshipped my artist. We went to a nightclub after the performance and I danced with her. She couldn't believe that this was the same man she had seen on the stage.

I had an understanding of the people who meet the stars. I came from Poland and dancers are very respected there. People were very proud to be with a dancer. It was a very great honor. They'd say, "Oh! I was with him!" Or, "Oh! I met him!" But in France this didn't exist. In France they didn't respect the ballet world. Oh, they respected Serge Lifar. If you asked "Who is the president of France?" they wouldn't know, but if you asked "Who is Serge Lifar?" they would tell you. England is another fantastic country that never forgot you. Even after ten or fifteen years.

The United States is different. They remember you when you are dancing but when you are finished they forget. It is very sad but it is true. You don't exist any more. In Buenos Aires they recognized me. But here in America, it is very sad. You die.

There was one time years later though, when a very nice thing

HONEYMOON, DECEMBER 1943

Private collection.

happened. I had just come from Europe and stopped in New York to see Baryshnikov in GISELLE. I couldn't even get a ticket. All were sold out. A man from England overheard me at the box office and he had a ticket. He was an admirer of mine and gave me his ticket. "You don't know me, but I admired you when you were dancing. I always watched you from the gallery." That's how I saw Baryshnikov, because of this man.

You know, though, I had one experience in South America where that recognition was not so good. I was dancing PRODIGAL SON and a big name critic wrote a headline, "Roman Jasinski and Ballet Russe." Colonel de Basil was very upset. He called me the next day. "No, no! No 'Roman Jasinski and Ballet Russe!' It should be 'Ballet Russe and Roman Jasinski!'" It was wrong what the critic did, even if I was doing a good job. He was excited about the performance but the Ballet should have come first.

Jasinski's life of lonely stardom was coming to an end. Midway through the South American tour Moscelyne Larkin's mother received the word she had long dreaded. On Christmas Eve in Buenos Aires, her beloved daughter Moussia had finally married her "Greek god." She was eighteen, Czeslaw Roman Jasinski twice her years. They were wed by a judge and surrounded by special friends from their company family. Colonel de Basil gave the bride away. When the Polish-born groom didn't understand the Spanish for "Do you take this young girl to be your lawfully wedded wife?" best man Marian Ladre nervously leaped in with "He does, he does, he does!"

I married Moussia in Buenos Aires. It was 24 December 1943. I had very good friends there and they made a party for the whole company all night with a beautiful Christmas tree and lots of food. We were free because it was Christmas and the theatre was closed. They don't celebrate Christmas like we do here in the United States. It is hot there, summertime.

The South America idyll continued, going round and round the continent by bus, train, plane, and boat. But now Moussia and Jasha were husband and wife. The rest of the tour was an extended honeymoon.

When the war finally ended we had been in South America for almost five years. At last we were coming back to Mexico.

It was New Year's Eve and a bus brought us close to the river between Guatemala and Mexico. It was night. When the bus stopped because the grass was too high for driving, we carried our heavy suitcases through this grass. There could be anything there, snakes, anything. We just followed the lead men. A couple of men had knives and they cut the grass ahead of us.

When we came to the river they told us, "Get in the boat, please. No talking. Sit quietly. There are lots of alligators. They can attack the boat." And so we just sat and did not talk. The boat was pulled by ropes from the other side, very quietly, very smoothly. One boat came and took two or three back and then another group came. This was not a ferry; a ferry could have taken more people. This was a little boat. And then when two or three got out they went back and got others. Forward and back, forward and back. We followed their movements with flashlights.

When we got to the other side of the river we had to go to the train. We put the suitcases on top of big carts with bulls instead of horses to pull them, then we followed them, walking for maybe two or three miles to the train until we came to the station.

This was New Year's Eve. The Mexicans were drunk, shooting their guns and screaming like crazy. The bars were full of them. They would come outside and shoot their weapons. We waited for the train in Mexico and it finally came and got us. We didn't celebrate New Year's much that year. I was worried about the alligators and the drunk Mexicans, and how to get away from this place, but nobody was hurt, everyone was fine.

When the company finally made it to Mexico City, who should be in the audience but the Marquis de Cuevas, a Chilean-born ballet lover of great enthusiasm and wealth. He had once formed his own short-lived ballet company—yet another artistic triumph and financial failure—and in Mexico City he gave some thought to investing in de Basil's Ballet Russe. Sol Hurok talked him out of it.

The dancers struggled on, returning to Rio via Havana. It was in Havana that the friendships Jasha had formed when stranded during the ballet strike came to his rescue again. Moussia needed surgery on her leg. In a performance in Chile she had burst through a red curtain in *Graduation Ball* and a curtain weight had struck her heavily in the shin. Infection had set in, and for months everything was tried—draining the wound, cutting holes in the bone, and finally unprotected radiation. Nothing worked. She continued to dance, but the pain was daunting. On that last trip to Havana, Alicia Alonso stepped in and insisted that her doctor treat the injury. A local anesthetic was applied and decades later Moussia recalled hearing the scalpel attack the bone as the doctor scraped away. Natalie Claire, her dearest friend and fellow dancer, stayed with her all night, waving legions of mosquitoes away from the bloody bandages. It was a grueling interlude, but it saved her leg, if not her life, and her gratitude to Alicia Alonso was intense and heartfelt.

The company was coming back to Rio, but the "they" was soon to be different. Once again, impresario Sol Hurok was arranging things and the company changed accordingly. Hurok sent new dancers to de Basil and they were given solo and principal roles that before had belonged exclusively to the de Basil family. This did no good to the veterans' esprit de corps and it did little good to the company itself. Styles were different. Personalities clashed. The cohesiveness of nearly five years' proximity was rent apart.

In Rio, on top of all the other traumas, the company was stranded by a general transportation strike. That settled, the dancers faced a rugged eleven-day boat passage to New York, arriving at the end of September, two days before their New York opening. Sea legs and performing legs are two different things, and the latter suffered intensely from the former.

CHAPTER 23

# Tattered Shadow

*All the beauty seemed gone.*

NEARLY FIVE YEARS IN SOUTH AMERICA may have honed Jasinski's sense of adventure, but the lack of balletic competition and the unsettled life of peripatetic dancers sapped, for a time, Original Ballet Russe technique and sharpness.

In fall 1946 Colonel de Basil's Original Ballet Russe was "back." Unfortunately, New York audiences anticipated an instant replay of its glory days. The reality was that tired, weak-kneed, incohesive dancers could hardly begin to match their former glory. Perhaps that was why Hurok was so vitriolic when the company returned, unrehearsed and unprepared, and danced at the Met. He could find nothing to praise. He decried their tarnished technique, their limited repertoire, their shabby sets, their threadbare costumes. Reviews were lukewarm. Some cast members defected. The Original Ballet Russe suffered both from extant American competition and its own renowned reputation. The resulting slide in public opinion was the more galling given the contrast to the success and adulation of the South American tour.

> When we were in South America, Hurok had sent lots of people to join the company—people like George Skibine, Rosella Hightower, and Marjorie Tallchief.

He got them from other companies because he wanted to make us stronger. We were all exhausted.

The Original Ballet Russe was no longer the only game in town. During its South American hiatus, Massine's "Ballet Russe de Monte Carlo" had come to the United States with great hoopla, and Ballet Theatre had debuted and charged ahead. Once de Basil was back, dancers whizzed back and forth between companies with dizzying speed. The ballet dollar was stretched to the nth and competition between companies, choreographers, and dancers was rife. Through it all, Hurok lamented the thousands upon thousands of dollars lost to presentations of differing ballet troupes.

When we came from South America to New York I went to take class with Balanchine. Some of his dancers worked in a cafeteria because he couldn't pay them. They would come for a rehearsal after they finished working. It was very hard for everybody.

Balanchine told me, "Jasha, I would like to take you into the company, but you would perform only once a year." And I said, "Oh, no." With de Basil we were performing every day. Balanchine might do just one performance each year in New York which in my opinion is why Maria Tallchief was not so happy there. She didn't like to perform like this, although she was his wife. That is why she danced so many guest appearances with the Ballet Russe de Monte Carlo. She had to have something to do.

Balanchine had had a problem when he opened the school back in the 1930s. He found that American dancers had no expression because their lives had been easy. They had been given everything. They were strong technicians but they did not seem to develop as artists. That is what he told me.

In Europe, people knew suffering. They knew hunger. They had had a different kind of life. And they developed an expressiveness, showing how they felt. Some of Balanchine's dancers were missing this. They were cool. It took many years to develop them.

I think Balanchine expressed emotions more in his early choreography. In his earlier ballets with stories the dancers had to express themselves. In America he tried to teach dancers to dance with expression, to act, but it was too hard, so he set abstract steps on the dancers. Emotions weren't really necessary. Instead he moved the dancer fast on the stage. His classes changed, too, after he came to America. He was always looking for speed.

Balanchine also found out that the girls here are so beautiful they don't need stories. He just put them in tights and they looked great! The Diaghilev company women didn't have the body. Americans have beautiful legs. The whole body is nice. They are beautiful girls.

Then too, without story ballets he didn't have to buy scenery, which was good because he didn't have any money. He was kind of a free man. He could do what he wanted. I always had the feeling that he wanted to choreograph with nobody bothering him. He decided to do his style and didn't care about scenery and costumes. When he came to New York he changed everything. He was smart when he saw he could do this. Balanchine made a tremendous revolution.

Classes with Balanchine honed Jasinski's tired technique, a loving wife danced at his side, the stimulus and joy of New York was around him, and yet, there was a recurrent emptiness.

One day I heard on the radio that my sisters were looking for me. This was just after we came back from South America. My sisters went to the Red Cross in Poland and gave my name, so here in America the Red Cross was looking for me. My sisters had survived! They were in Warsaw. I needed to find my family. I wrote them a letter. Oh, the terrible things that I learned…When the bombardment of 1939 started in Warsaw, the Germans came with four hundred planes. They threw bombs at every house without looking at a target. They just threw them and people died. Only five percent of the buildings were left. Can you imagine the fire? Ninety-five percent were down!

My mother died during the bombardment of 1939. Each time the planes came she had to run down under the houses to the bomb shelter. During one bombardment my mother died on the steps before she was able to get to the shelter when the building above her exploded.

I had thought that maybe one or two people in my family might have survived, but even my two brothers, Stefan and Feliks, were still living at the end of the war. It was a miracle!

During the bombardment my sisters were running from Warsaw when the Germans picked them up. They were sent to different concentration camps. The Germans froze Janka's legs with ice. They made an experiment to see how much pain she could suffer, standing her in frozen water for hours and hours until her legs were swollen for life. Afterwards, she could still walk, but very painfully, very slowly. The point is, she survived!

Stefania was caught in another place. She worked in a concentration camp preparing bandages for the army.

My brothers Stefan and Feliks were also picked up. They were sent to Germany to work in factories somewhere close to Poland.

My sisters only found each other after the war. Janka went back to Warsaw and then went looking for Stefania and brought her back. Janka's husband, the army doctor, had been killed at the beginning of the war.

With the rediscovery of his remaining family, a grieving yet relieved Jasinski resumed his role as supporter and supplier for his siblings. Clothing and cash were contributed annually and he kept in touch throughout the remainder of his life until he outlived them all.

Stefania was a very sick girl all of her life. She had asthma and died a couple of years after the war. We had been very close, Stefania and I, throughout our growing-up years. My brother Feliks died in 1960 or so. Stefan married, but died a few years after Feliks. Feliks and Stefan both lived until they were in their sixties. Janka was the last of my Polish family to go.

Several decades after the war, Jasha made several pilgrimages to Poland to introduce friends and family to his homeland. On his second trip he, his wife, and son saw first-hand the manipulation of history by Poland's Communist regime.

> On my first trip back to Poland, Moussia, my friends, and I went to a big salt mine, Wieliczka, in Poland. It is about thirty-five floors down beneath the ground. The guide there said, "This place was very famous. There were two thousand Jewish people working here. Day and night they had to work. They could not stop. And when the war was lost, Hitler gave orders to kill them all. Two thousand of them! And they were very smart, educated people. The Germans killed every one of them."
>
> One young German was on the tour. He became very angry. He didn't know what Hitler did. The army didn't know a lot of this. The killing of Jews had been kept secret from them. The soldiers on the front didn't know. It was absolutely two separate wars—Hitler against the Jews and Hitler against the world. The German people couldn't believe it. I knew at the time that the Germans would lose. I knew that Hitler would never win this war. I was sure.
>
> A year after that trip I took my son Roman there to the same place but this time there was a woman guide. She came to the same place and said nothing about the Jews who were killed. I said, "Did you forget something about the Jewish people?" And she said, "There were no Jewish people here." "There must have been, because I was here just last year and the man told me that this was the place." We came to the end of the tour and someone touched my shoulder. It was the woman. "Pan, you are right. It was like this. But I have been ordered never to tell about this. The Communist government told me I could never mention this."

Warsaw's "Old Town" has been lovingly rebuilt, its medieval streets and buildings painstakingly recreated after the massive destruction from the bombardment. Meticulous paintings by the eighteenth-century nephew and namesake of the painter Canaletto were invaluable guides to its reconstruction, for the younger Canaletto had lived in Warsaw for thirteen years, consigning minute architectural details to numerous canvases. These canvases gave the reconstruction experts exact guidelines to follow.

Houses are painted with charming patterns, wonderful wrought-iron signs are suspended from the eaves of shops, a fine lion's head fountain pumps water for the populace. All seem delightfully new. All carefully echo the medieval Warsaw that was.

And yet—interspersed among the bland modern canvases sold on street corners are canvases painted in bold, angry, primary slashes, their images grotesque and distorted. The war has not been forgotten. Cannot be forgotten. The paintings are a reminder that this picture-postcard-pretty fragment of a city has been rebuilt upon the ashes and bones of absolute horror.

Six million Poles were murdered throughout Poland during the war. Three million were Jews, mostly from Warsaw. Poles never knew when a Nazi death squad would swoop down on casual passers-by, line them up and shoot them. One can find red and white flags all over Warsaw commemorating martyrs caught in a time and event beyond reason.

Jasha took his family to visit the rebuilt Warsaw Opera House, the scene of so much of his youth. A few of the original pillars survive, pock-marked with bullet holes. After the war, the Opera became a symbol of Polish unity and revival. Desperate though they were for housing in Warsaw, citizens nonetheless banded together and spent fifteen years rebuilding the Opera, Jasha's sister Janka among them. Such a symbol kept them going, even in the face of their new nemesis, communism.

There were so many memories here. Jasha's early ballet schooling, his humiliation with Zailich, his graduation as first in his class, the letter from Nijinska. All were bound together in this building pocked with bullet holes.

Just as Warsaw had to rebuild its pre-war past, the Jasinskis of 1947 had to look to their future. The Original Ballet Russe had lost intensity and sharpness during its grueling hand-to-mouth existence during the war years, and a new company, Ballet Theatre, had become the darling of American balletomanes.

Impresario Sol Hurok sponsored the Colonel one more time, and then saw him depart for Europe with great relief. The Original Ballet Russe was on hard times. Europe was on hard times. The Jasinskis together had some hard facts to face.

> After New York the company went back to London, Paris, and Belgium. My crazy friend Boris Kniasev worked with us in London when we came in 1947. He did some ballets for us. One ballet was THE SILVER BIRCH. It was almost the same as the BERIOSKA I did with him so many years before.

INTERLUDE IN A PARIS CAFÉ

Roman Jasinski, Moscelyne Larkin, Renée Jeanmaire, and Vladimir Skouratoff.

Photo by the London News Agency. Courtesy Archives, Tulsa Ballet.

In London, I was walking with one of the English guys there and I said, "They told me about the bombardment," and he said, "Come over here." He opened a door to a house and inside there was nothing. Only the sides were standing. Everything was burned inside.

It was a dead time in London. They gave you a ration book to buy food. You had to give the book to the hotel if you wanted fish in the morning. From your ration book you got one pound of chocolate for a month. One pound of sugar. Tea and coffee. I saw this in Europe and I didn't want to stay there. There was so much to worry about in Europe. Why go back to this miserable life?

I was ready to come back to America. I had the permit that I could live in the United States for one year but I was afraid that time would run out. I was married to Moussia and I didn't want to work anymore in Europe.

Paris was not the same as before. In Paris the people were different after the war. All the beauty seemed gone; the people were very hard. There was nothing to eat, no food. The French people became cool toward foreigners. The French were mad with Polish people because they said we started the war with Germany, but all we did was resist invasion.

Lots of people opened hamburger carts on the streets of Paris or sold sausages. When you go to France, you want to enjoy their cuisine. Before the war you could go to any restaurant, even a cheap restaurant, and they always had good food although there was very little of it. They gave you a little piece of meat or chicken and little vegetables. You would pay five or seven or ten francs and you would get lots of different foods. Now there was a tremendous change in Paris.

At the time he made these statements, Jasinski was thinking of the Paris he had known before, its foods, its culture, its beauty. The loss to the world was far greater than he first realized, for it included the sacrifice of many thousands of men, women, and children shipped off by the Nazis to extermination camps. Their murders epitomized a double loss of culture and kindness.

Tucked away at the side of the Seine, on the Île de la Cité, is a solemn monument accessible through a gated corridor. It is the "Mémorial des Martyrs et de la Déportation." Two hundred thousand French souls left quays such as this on long, agonizing routes that most often led to death. Only a few returned. In this tiny corner of land heaviness lies in the very air, belying the traffic on the avenue nearby, where twenty-first–century Paris sweeps heedlessly by.

One man, in particular, is called to mind as one stands at the quay. René Blum of Monte Carlo was among those deported, never to return. By Nazi standards he had three strikes against him: he was a Jew, an intellectual, and the brother of Socialist leader and former French Premier, Léon Blum.

He was also, by all accounts, a "gentle, cultured intellectual. . . a genuine artist." His failure in his dealings with de Basil stemmed from an instinct to avoid confrontation, and yet when friends urged him to flee Paris or promised him refuge in other countries, he refused. He was a Frenchman and belonged with his country!

For nine and a half months, he and his fellow intellectuals bolstered each others' spirits as they were moved ever closer to extermination. Lengthy confinements were succeeded by the final, fatal move to Auschwitz.

Blum's death accomplished nothing, but those in the dance world who survived never forgot the man he was, the gentleman he was, and the legacy of his bravery.

> Brussels was the last performance we did with the company. We could have stayed in Europe but I was afraid about my permit to come back to America. I didn't want to lose this. They reorganized the company again and took even more people, even some Belgians, because lots of people had left.
>
> I had an English friend working in the company and he told me that the company was finished and to go back to America right away. I told him that's what I planned. The company had too many people in England and then we started losing them. It was not only this, but you see, there were no engagements. There was nothing to do. You couldn't work in Europe; it was impossible.

At this point in my life I had one purpose: to get to America. Working in Europe was not the future. I was not so young and I thought I had better start to think about the future.

So after all these years with de Basil, Moussia and I decided to leave. The company, as I knew it, was finished. I was scared to death that if anything happened I'd be stuck in Europe. I was still traveling on my Polish passport. I wanted to come back to America.

The last time I saw de Basil was the time I told him we were leaving. The Colonel came to our apartment in Paris to have a meeting. He asked who wanted to stay and I told him about our decision. De Basil said, "Oh. This is not possible! Why don't you wait? We'll do this and this." Moussia and some of the others were very upset, hysterical almost. He kissed each one good-bye. Everyone cried—a separation after so many years. Colonel de Basil was not very happy that we were leaving, but I was tired and happy to go.

Moussia and I came back to America in December of 1947. We came into New York and the city was snowbound. The cars were half under the snow. There were no taxis, nothing. No one could drive.

When we arrived we had our big trunks with us. My friend Yurek Lazowski came to the pier with a big sled and we pulled our trunks all the way to 57th Street where he and his family had an apartment. It was very quiet, very hushed.

Yurek had been waiting for us at the pier. He grabbed us and said, "Come!" I really didn't want to. I'd rather have gone to a hotel. But Lazowski was without work and was having a hard time so Moussia and I stayed with him and his family. One of his daughters was already born. I paid for food and tried to help them this way. We had been very close friends for a very long time.

When I was living in Lazowski's apartment I took classes constantly at the American School with Balanchine. He had his company by then and it had started to grow.

So there they were. Unemployed. Living with Lazowski. Making their own decisions now that the paternalistic Colonel was no longer in charge of their lives. Jasha had reached the age of forty; his young wife was nearing twenty-three. The accolades of early successes were behind them and their future was uncertain.

> It was during this time that I began to know Serge Denham. Denham was one of those who had fallen in love with the ballet and knew lots of people with money. It was with Denham that Massine made a rival company, the Ballet Russe de Monte Carlo, when he broke away from de Basil. I remember that Massine wanted me to go to the other company but I didn't want to leave de Basil. My opinion was the de Basil company was the real company.
>
> I had always known that Denham wanted me to come into the Ballet Russe de Monte Carlo. Danilova had brought Denham to my dressing room one time after we came from Australia. Denham wanted to meet me, to see if I would join his company. "Jasinski, any time you want to come into my company, I am prepared. Let me know." But you know, I never asked. I didn't want to. I said no. He said, "Maybe in two or three years or something like that." I said, "Thank you very much, but I already have a contract."
>
> But I liked Serge Denham. He was a very funny man. He liked jokes. He liked the young girls. He liked to invite us to have a drink with him. He was not a boring person. He was always feeling that he was young, you know. Lots of fun.
>
> Denham and de Basil were very different people. Denham always tried to play the very high class, blue-blood Russian. His father was a banker. De Basil came from the army. He was a more simple man. He always made me feel safe, like his company was my family.

Impresario Sol Hurok, who had to work with—and against—both men, had an entirely different take on Denham. De Basil frustrated and infuriated him, but nonetheless possessed "an instinct for the theatre, a serious love for ballet, [and]

PAQUITA

Photo by Maurice Seymour courtesy of Ron Seymour. Private collection.

broad experience" in Hurok's eyes. There was no such appreciation for Denham. Instead, Hurok wrote scathingly that Denham was "a mere tyro at ballet direction, and an amateur at that." His comments on Denham crackled with disdain. For a man who loved ballet as deeply as Hurok did, its backstage machinations and manipulations dimmed the magic it could bring its fans in the audience. Jasha, however, saw the best qualities of both de Basil and Denham and worked amicably and effectively with each in turn.

“THE HAPPIEST DAY OF MY LIFE”

Polish passport and U.S. Certificate of Naturalization for Czeslaw Roman Jasinski, 15 May 1950.

Collection Roman Larkin Jasinski.

# IV

# *Life in America*

1948–1991

CHAPTER 24

# Falling Star

*To be in the company dancing nothing—no!*

DENHAM CAME TO ME IN NEW YORK ONE MORNING and said, “Jasha, I need you to come. Freddie Franklin has hurt his foot and cannot dance this afternoon.” Denham was desperate. Believe me or not, Denham took me into the Ballet Russe de Monte Carlo on the spot to substitute for Freddie because nobody else was there to do this. No one! They had the company but you see, nobody was allowed to dance for Frederic Franklin. He never let anybody else dance his roles. He would never teach them to anyone. So Danilova said to Denham, “You know Jasinski, and Jasinski knows these roles,” so I stepped in. Freddie didn’t need to teach me anything because I already knew the parts and that afternoon I partnered Danilova.

I danced LE BEAU DANUBE, the original version of Massine’s ballet. Nobody else in America besides me and Freddie knew this role. The version Lifar changed for de Basil’s company, LE DANUBE BLEU, was not exactly the same; Lifar had changed some stage directions because of Massine’s lawsuit against de Basil. When they called me to dance the Hussar I started to come and they said, “No! You cannot come from this side. The girls come this way.” Otherwise the dance was mostly the same.

"ALBRECHT" IN GISELLE

Photo by Maurice Seymour courtesy of Ron Seymour. Private collection.

I also danced "Albrecht" in GISELLE when Freddie was injured and lots of other ballets. I didn't know GAÎTÉ PARISIENNNE and had to learn it. Then NIGHT SHADOW. Danilova, and the girls who danced with me, taught me. What they taught me were the steps. Acting, I didn't need to be taught. I could do that myself. Freddie doesn't remember that I danced NIGHT SHADOW because he wasn't there. Then when Freddie came to Montreal and saw me in GISELLE, that was it! "Out, out!" He didn't like the competition.

I had danced all these things and had great experience with them. I was not only a dancer but also an artist. That's why Denham was willing to do anything to keep me in the company. He said, "I feel so wonderful when you are here in this company. I feel secure."

You see, Denham had a problem with Franklin. Franklin would say, "I want this and this," and Denham would have to do it. But this way, with me in the company, Franklin would ask for something and Denham could now say, "Well, let me think. . . you know, I have Jasinski. . . " That's why he wanted to keep me in the company and pay me a salary to do nothing. Just so he could deal with Freddie Franklin! When Freddie Franklin was hurt I danced everything, but when he came back he took over and I had nothing to do. What was I going to do there?

I was probably with the company for half a year because the season had already started when I was called. First I went without Moussia. When Denham asked me if I wanted to stay I said, "No. I want Moussia. I cannot stay without my wife." That's when Moussia joined the company.

From early 1948 to late 1951 Jasha, later joined by Moussia, toured with Denham's Ballet Russe de Monte Carlo. For Moussia, it was a blow to revert to corps de ballet status after being a respected soloist with de Basil, but she understood the pecking order of an established ballet company and, as its newest member, simply bided her time. It wasn't long before she was once more inching her way up the professional ladder into challenging and satisfying roles. She

SERGE DENHAM

Denham as he appeared in a 1959–1960 Ballet Russe de Monte Carlo program.

danced the "Cowgirl" in Agnes de Mille's RODEO, "Zobeide" in SCHÉHÉRAZADE, "Harlequin" in NIGHT SHADOW, the "Glove Seller" in GAÎTÉ PARISIENNE, and many other roles. Dance historian Olga Maynard later wrote of Moussia, "She was remarkable for her tiny physique, sparkling personality and tremendous jump—the greatest, for her size, in the contemporary theatre."

For an extended time, at the suggestion of Agnes de Mille, she danced as prima ballerina of the Radio City Music Hall. Her phenomenal memory for choreographic detail was rewarded when she was invited to become the Radio City ballet company's "Directrice." The excellent money the position would bring was a sore temptation, but it would mean leaving the Ballet Russe. The day she reluctantly returned home with the offer Jasha asked, "Why you cry?" "Jasha, I don't want to do this, but we need the money." The man who had once lived with real hunger simply shrugged and said, "We not need the money." "Need," in Jasinski's terminology, applied only to imminent starvation.

For Jasha, however, the transition to Denham was not so easy. After many years as a principal dancer with de Basil, the restrictions put on his dancing by Frederic Franklin were disheartening—if not galling.

> You know, Freddie was the star and he built this company with Danilova. He was upset with me for dancing his roles. After two months or so, Freddie came back into the company. He was more "jealousy" than I. It's a funny thing, but I was never "jealousy." I had known Freddie Franklin before—we had met, but we had never worked together. He had followed my career and was always remembering stories about me. He remembered all the ballets from Les Ballets 1933.
>
> He was a member of the Sadler's Wells Company, and at one point I had heard that he had auditioned for the de Basil company before Massine left. Massine really worshipped Freddie. Massine liked anyone who could pick up his choreography quickly and was musical. Franklin was perfect for Massine because Massine didn't like to teach anyone too long.
>
> It's strange, but I don't care about this now because I like Freddie. He's a nice guy. Who could have guessed that many years later he would help us in Tulsa with our company? Later in life we worked together very well, both of us. Life is strange.

The mutual respect and friendship that would come had to await the end of both men's major dancing careers. A glance at programs from that period tells its own sad tale. Jasha continued to dance occasional principal roles—the "Prince" in *Swan Lake,* the "Hussar" in *Beau Danube,* the "Baron" in *Gaîté Parisienne*—but his performances were increasingly rare and often relegated to matinees.

GAÎTÉ

A favorite role: the "Glove Seller" in *Gaîté Parisienne.*

Photo by Maurice Seymour courtesy of Ron Seymour. Private colletion.

While his technique was enviable, his charm palpable, his looks princely, more and more Jasinski was overlooked or ignored, and more and more his star drooped. Still, in talking of those days, ballerina Yvonne Chouteau remembers vividly that every time she danced with him, her heart would stop. He was so very handsome.

Programs from this period showed him in his signature solos—the "Drummer" in *Graduation Ball,* the "Poet" in *Les Sylphides,* but he shared those roles with others with increasing frequency. Most disturbing, he was also found in negligible roles—the Shah's brother in *Schéhérazade,* a billiard player in *Gaîté,* a corps de ballet member in *Raymonda Divertissements.* Although still listed as a principal dancer, one program alternately named him "Pasinsky" and "Jazinsky." One could simply blame this on sloppy editing, but it is doubtful anyone would have misspelled Franklin's or Danilova's names without correction or consequences.

Still, the contrast of Jasinski's prestige with Denham versus that with de Basil rankled. Touring with nothing rewarding to dance at day's end led Jasinski to reevaluate his life.

That three-year episode with Denham's main company was always to be more bitter than sweet for Jasha, but it did have one shining moment unrelated to the ballet world.

> After a little more than two years in America I became an American citizen. This date is the most important date of my life: 15 May 1950. I remember the day! I was here in the United States and I flew to El Paso. I went into Mexico and spent the night in a hotel. You had to leave America so the consulate could check on you that you were clean and not involved in anything bad. The next morning I went to the American consulate and my papers were ready. I took them, crossed the bridge and—I was an American! I didn't want to move any more from America. I wanted to stay here. You know, when I crossed the bridge a guy came out and looked at my passport. I was so happy! I was an American citizen! After all those years it took only one day!

The importance of this act cannot be overemphasized. This was Jasinski's lifelong dream. In later years, again and again, he said that the happiest day of his life was 15 May 1950. He had come far from the poverty of his Polish youth. He was world-traveled, culturally sophisticated, multi-lingual, highly respected. But for Czeslaw Roman Jasinski, the most treasured two words in the English language were "American citizen." After years of longing, those words were his.

> Denham kept asking me to stay in the company but I told Denham I wanted to rest. "Let me stay in the company but give me one year off." And he said, "All right." But there was one condition. Any time Denham called me, if he had any trouble in the company, I would have to come at once. Still, he let me go. He wanted me to stay in the company very badly because he liked me so much. I told him, "Yes, any time you need me, I will come back. But to be in the company dancing nothing—no!"

In the winter of 1951, the names Jasinski and Larkin disappeared from the programs of Denham's Ballet Russe. Once again, the pair was "at leisure," a ballet euphemism for "out of work."

> When I left Denham I was absent from a company for nearly one year. I took an apartment in New York with Moussia and we went to the school at the New York City Ballet and took classes every morning with Balanchine.

The two also kept a sharp eye out for opportunity and jumped at every chance to perform. Jasha taught or choreographed upon occasion, but it was Moussia, in the heyday of her energy and effervescence, who found some unique ways to see that food was on the table. For one six-month period, when television was in its infancy, she and a partner danced on a weekly television show hostessed by Fay Emerson. The show was very popular and ballet reached a brand-new audience.

Meanwhile, major defections from Denham's Ballet Russe were on the rise. There was turmoil in the company, due largely to a beautiful Polish dancer, Nina Novak, who had become Denham's professional and personal obsession.

SCHÉHÉRAZADE

Moussia as "Zobeïde" in *Schéhérazade.*

Photo by Maurice Seymour

courtesy of Ron Seymour. Private collection.

Novak's meteoric rise had caused many to question Denham's taste and judgment, but it was not the first time they were questioned. Jasha recalled an incident with Sol Hurok before Novak ever became prominent. "Mr. Hurok offered me and Moussia a tour d'orchestre—just the two of us before an orchestra dancing different pas de deux. He was very nice to me and I was very nice to him but I told him I couldn't go. I told him that I had signed the contract with Denham. He said to us, 'When it rains one gets under the roof. You just went from the rain to the gutter.'"

If that sounds like less than glowing praise for Denham, that is exactly how it was meant. Hurok later mused of Denham, "You are apt to think that restraint and reticence are the only virtues. Until you meet a quiet fellow. . . and then discover his stillness is merely a convenient mask for deceit."

Poor Hurok. He loved ballet, but the ballet companies he presented, led by directors he alternately supported and abhorred, cost him dearly in headache, heartache, and humor. Fortunately for the American balletomane, he kept on trying to find the perfect company, and his efforts led to stellar balletic careers, an increasingly sophisticated ballet audience, and indelible, lifelong memories for those fortunate enough to enjoy the fruits of his tenacious efforts.

There was no softness in Hurok's remarks about Denham, but when it came to a postmortem of de Basil, Hurok was torn between personal frustration and grudging respect. "By one means or another, (de Basil) formed a great ballet company. . . . His methods were, to say the least, unorthodox; he was amazing, fantastic, and. . . . incredible. . . . De Basil was a sharp businessman, a shrewd negotiator, an adroit manager. He was a personality."

> I was in New York when I heard about Colonel de Basil's death in 1951. I think it was in the paper, telegrams too.
>
> De Basil was a different type of leader. If a girl came and said she didn't have any money to pay her bills, he wouldn't want to raise her salary but he would pay the bills himself. Or if she came to say she was cold and didn't have a raincoat on a rainy day, he would buy her a raincoat. But he would not give her the money.

> When I was married, de Basil said he didn't want to give Moussia more money because "Jasha is making a good salary." Moussia said, "But why are you paying so and so more than me?" And he said, "I need to pay her more because she has her mother with her, that's why." After this de Basil came to me and said, "Oh, you make me so much trouble!"
>
> De Basil died a few years after our last meeting. He had already been very sick in South America. The doctor had told him that he needed to stop smoking and stop drinking, but he said, "Why would I want to live if I can't drink and smoke? I would rather die."

It must have been quite a blow. This was the man who took Jasha back after the Balanchine debacle and gave him a second chance.

The de Basil Jasha knew was an argumentative, flawed personality, streaked with intermittent bouts of kindness, who struggled to keep artistic temperaments in check, extol excellence, flummox the unwary—and make a profit. He surrounded himself with sycophants and geniuses, but couldn't always tell the difference between the two. Paternalistic to the core, he strove to keep egos at bay and squeeze the utmost from his artists, and yet he responded like a fond papa when a moment of generosity was called for. He was an oddity.

CHAPTER 25

# Gypsy Prince

*I was very happy, but it was very hard.*

Without de Basil, without Denham, and in lieu of a steady job, the "prince" reverted to his "gypsy" ways. The ballerinas he had known began to branch out with little tours. As a favored partner, Jasinski found himself dancing with old friends! What a difference from his youth. Now he was chosen to shine with the greatest of the greats: Markova, Toumanova, Danilova. He traveled the world once more as a principal dancer, but this time found himself looking longingly for some settled ground, some solidity. It would take time, but his path was now to pull him towards domesticity and that greatest of all blessings, a family, and the chance to put down roots.

> In August of 1952 I was supposed to dance with Alicia Markova in Buenos Aires. We had heard that Eva Peron had died a couple of days before. When our plane landed in Argentina, a man from the government came and said, "We are going to give silent respect for Eva Peron." Everyone followed him to a chapel where we stood in silence. "Thank you. And now you can go through customs."
>
> We were supposed to open the season quickly, but because of Eva Peron we had to move everything back. For one month there could be

no theatre, no orchestra, nothing. Everyone had to go to sleep at 9:00 P.M. If they caught you in your room with the lights on you could go to prison. We couldn't perform and we stayed at the hotel. Each time we went into the elevator, the elevator would stop. "Silence for Eva Peron." And we would stay in the elevator for ten minutes. People were panicking from being trapped together. I think they did this every hour, nationwide. Everything stopped. Automobiles. Everything. They made her like a saint. Her picture, about fifty feet high, was on the avenue where we lived. My friends told me that the government paid people from outside Buenos Aires to lie on their faces in front of her picture. Twenty people would lie before it for one hour. Then another twenty people would come.

I had friends in Buenos Aires who had a party for me. These were the same people who had had a big party when Moussia and I were married, but this time they had to close the windows and curtains so no light or noise could go outside.

Jasinski was greatly loved in South America. A highly respected critic from Lima, Pablo de Madalengoitia, once commented that Jasinski held South America in his hand.

A fan letter dated 30 August 1952, raved, "During 8 years I have been longing for you; no other dancer has been able to give me the deep joy that invades my whole self when I see you dancing.

O dancer of dancers,
Triumphant and Matchless!
O never forgotten
King of the Dance!
Your body is breathing beauty,
Your movements a flaming speech.
You are in my heart forever
The picture of Dance itself . . .

After Buenos Aires, and still unwilling to abandon his long career, Jasinski found himself in yet a new role—maître de ballet (ballet master)—of Denham's newly-formed traveling Concert Company. He was suddenly in the same shoes he had so long observed on the feet of de Basil and Denham, overseeing everything. As ballet master he taught the classes, inspected the theatres, rehearsed the ballets, paid the artists, settled disputes, smoothed ruffled feathers, and on top of everything else, danced.

> I started the Concert Company for Denham in the autumn of 1952. I was happy, but it was very hard. I held an audition in New York. The dancers who came were very young, some of them, but I worked on them. I would pull out their last tooth to get some emotion, some feeling, but we started to work and in the end we had a company.
>
> We rehearsed in New York for about a month or six weeks. In all, we had about fifteen people in the company. I restaged CIRQUE DE DEUX, "Blue Bird," parts of SWAN LAKE, and GAÎTÉ PARISIENNE. Denham signed the contracts and the company was a big success. Denham's secretary, Doris, would write, "Oh, another wonderful review." But we didn't see the reviews on tour because we left every morning to go to the next city.
>
> When I left with the Concert Company the big company still existed, but after a while, it fell apart. I was still working.

Denham focused his attention on the intrigues of the Concert Company. Letters and telegrams preserved in Jasinski's files show a tongue-in-cheek humor that was to sustain and bolster Jasinski through two years of tours. Regarding dueling pianists Denham wrote:

> Feb. 5, 1953
>
> Dear Jasha:
>
> . . . Please try to pacify the nerves and the humors of the involved, emphasizing the fact that the end of the tour is looming and that for such a short remaining time there hardly will be moral justification for a murder.

A week or so later came:

> I hope that peace reigns in all departments and especially that the wood of the two pianos isn't being used as weapons.

During the first year of the Concert Company, Moussia was the secretary while Jasha was the maître de ballet. The marital team effort was most effective. The little Russian–American Indian solemnly wrote out her husband's reports and received the accolade from Denham's secretary that "That Moussia is a terrific secretary—for a ballerina!"

Still, for both of them it was a tiring time.

> I needed to report to Mr. Denham every day after the performance. First thing in the morning I had to go to the post office to send my report special delivery. I was the manager and I paid the salaries. Everything. The worst thing was the money.
>
> I had about $3,000 or $4,000 with me at a time and when I went to the theatre I hid this money every place because I needed to perform. Most of the time I had a coat. I made a hole in one of my sleeves and put all of the money inside of it.
>
> On Saturdays, I paid everyone. I had envelopes and in each one I put their salary. Sometimes I went to the bank to wire the money to Denham. It was necessary for the theatre manager to pay me before each performance.
>
> Along with managing, I also danced! I had SWAN LAKE and after SWAN LAKE I had to dance the "Blue Bird" pas de deux and then GAÎTÉ PARISIENNE. The repertoire was the same every night, only I changed the ballerinas. One of them was Nina Novak.

Yes, that's right. Nina Novak! The beautiful Polish girl who had risen so fast, offended so many, and mesmerized Denham in the process. It was no secret that the Concert Company was formed to showcase Novak; nor was it secret that her fellow ballerinas chafed at their second-tier status.

In a way, this fly in the ointment of contentment was one of Jasha's own creation. It was Jasinski who had earlier learned of Novak's hellish life in the Polish concentration camps, and Jasinski who had recommended her as a dancer to Denham. He felt sorry for his fellow Pole and wanted to help her after her use and abuse by a succession of Nazi captors. It took a woman of unusual will and strength of character to survive those war years with balletic ambitions intact.

What Jasha could not have anticipated was that Novak would rise higher and higher in the company with the patronage of a besotted Denham. Even in the Concert Company, Denham insisted on giving her principal ballerina billing. The infighting that resulted was fierce, but Jasinski could only follow orders. The other ballerinas had very sharp feelings about the usurpation of "their" roles, but Novak held the upper hand. Despite the despotism of the casting couch, Jasinski always felt sorry for the girl. In his eyes, the war horrors she had endured mitigated much of her behavior. Warring ambitions and artistic anxiety aside, the Concert Company included triumphs, trials and occasional funny gaffes.

> One time on this tour we danced at a theatre inside Walla Walla prison. All the prisoners came, just men. It was unusual to dance in a prison. We danced at Los Alamos, too. You know, the town was closed for security reasons, so they always tried to bring in entertainment. When we came there they said, "Oh, we built you the most beautiful theatre." It was a terrible theatre! Terrible dressing room! The bench was high, the mirror was low, but at least the stage was okay.
>
> This is how we toured to small cities that had never seen the ballet. Fifteen people were on the bus, plus two stagehands and an electrician. The tour was a big success but it was also very hard.

Denham was more than satisfied with the success of the tour. He reported in an undated letter: "Here is another appraisal of our adorable bastard, our 'junior' company, our concert company. . . . 'The performance went off with great enthusiasm. . . . Everybody danced with the greatest pleasure, with discipline and honor and . . . top-notch excellence. Bravo, bravo and my congratulations from all my soul.' "

Later in February, Denham wrote Jasinski that Columbia Artists wanted to renew the ballet's contract for another twenty-two weeks, but whimsically added "I doubt very much that we would continue to renew the contract with that very inefficient assistant of mine or his bad Indian dancer." Whatever the whimsy, the Concert Company made a big impact on small-town America. Its own publicity crowed that it was especially created to bring ballet to communities too small for a visit from a major company. A delighted Denham wrote, "Judging from the hundreds of letters we have received. . . the public thirst for entertainment. . . at a cost commensurate with limited budgets and small halls has never been greater."

That it was also created to showcase Novak was understood by all. At the end of the season, a miffed Moussia and exhausted Jasha, both worn out from continual conflict, were happy to put the company behind them and head for a Florida vacation.

> During our vacation, Moussia and I saw that everybody had a car. I saw so many cars! And I said, "You know what? Let's buy a big car!" A friend took me to Daytona Beach and showed me an open car, a 1950 Studebaker, I think. I asked how much was this car. $1200! I told them I had an Australian driver's license but they said, "No, you have to get one here." Moussia didn't drive either. So both of us started to drive. From Daytona Beach we drove with this car back to New York. We fought for who would drive.

One can feel their euphoria and delight through Jasha's comments, but more delight was to come. Little did they know at the time that they were returning to New York with much more than a car.

> When our tour started again, Moussia was expecting our baby! I needed to change some lifts, but Moussia was able to dance for another six months.

*The Community Concert Association*

*Presents*

# THE BALLET RUSSE de MONTE CARLO CONCERT COMPANY

S. J. DENHAM, *Director*

ROMAN JASINSKY

MOSCELYNE LARKIN — ANNA ISTOMINA

FERNANDO SCHAFFENBURG

| | |
|---|---|
| CHRISTINE HENNESSY | KEITH ALLISON |
| NANCIE LEONIE | JOSEPH BUSHEME |
| JOANNA LOUISE | ROBERT HIRST |
| BARBARA MCGINNIS | GLENN OLSON |
| MADA SARGENT | GERALD TEIJELO |
| RACHEL WEBSTER | |

*Maitre de Ballet:* ROMAN JASINSKY

1952 — 1953

## *Program*

I. Swan Lake . . . . . . . . . *Tchaikovsky*

(*Choreography after* LEV IVANOV)

*Intermission*

II. The Blue Bird and The Enchanted Princess . . . *Tchaikovsky*

*Intermission*

III. Cirque de Deux . . . . . . . . . . *Gounod*

(*Choreography by* RUTHANNA BORIS; *Costumes by* ROBERT DAVISON)

*Intermission*

IV. Gaite Parisienne . . . . . . . . . *Offenbach*

(*Choreography, revised version, after* MASSINE)

COMMUNITY CONCERTS Inc., 113 WEST 57TH ST., NEW YORK 19, N.Y.

WARD FRENCH, PRESIDENT — ROBERT FERGUSON, EXEC. VICE PRESIDENT

*a Carnegie Hall*  *In Every Town*

Private collection.

Moscelyne Larkin as the "Young Girl" in *Beau Danube*.

Photo by Maurice Seymour courtesy of Ron Seymour.

Private collection.

JUMPS AND TURNS

Known for her soaring leaps, a radiant Larkin is caught mid-flight.

Photo by Maurice Seymour courtesy of Ron Seymour. Private collection.

For Moussia, dancing during the first six months of pregnancy required much more than changing a few lifts. The challenge to Madame Sophie Pourmel, the wardrobe mistress, was enormous. The bigger the baby, the more creative the costuming. But there were compensations. There is a very famous moment in *Swan Lake* when the Prince tenderly cradles the Swan Queen in his arms and rocks her slowly back and forth. During one performance, Jasha wrapped his arms around his wife and whispered, "Now we are three!" It was a moment they both treasured for the rest of their years.

The 1953-54 tour continued with the usual repertoire of *Swan Lake,* "Blue Bird" pas de deux, *Cirque de Deux,* and *Gaîté Parisienne.*

> Denham had to send me Gertrude Tyven, another ballerina, when Moussia couldn't be lifted any more. The last three months she was in Tulsa with her mother and I had no more secretary! I had to call Denham every day until the end of the tour.

When the Denham tour ended, Jasha's dancing continued, this time with Alicia Markova in Canada and Washington, D.C. The separation was hard on both Jasinskis, but it was time for Moussia to rest and prepare for a whole new role. As the birth neared, Jasha found himself stuck on the East Coast, dancing with one ballerina while waiting to hear from another. The Markova partnership ended just a couple of weeks before the baby was due.

> I needed to make a decision. Tamara Toumanova had offered me a contract, but something about it was not quite ready. If I didn't work with Toumanova I needed to sign a contract to go back to Denham. Toumanova was telling me to wait, but I really could not wait. I sent her a telegram to give me an answer right away because I didn't want to sign the contract with Denham. She sent me a ticket to California and a contract to start rehearsals.
>
> I had wanted to go back to Tulsa before Moussia had the baby but I was waiting in New York on this contract. Moussia's brother called me at the hotel. "Moussia has a little Indian!" We named him Roman Larkin Jasinski. It was 21 February 1954.

To celebrate the birth of the newest Jasinski, Serge Denham prepared a special contract. In it, Roman Larkin Jasinski was accepted, without audition, into the Ballet Russe de Monte Carlo at the tender age of infancy. That he, too, would become a dancer was never doubted by Denham, and Denham, as it turns out, was quite right. Those dancing genes were strong!

I had to drive about eighteen hours a day to get to Moussia and my son. I would get up at six in the morning and drive until almost midnight. It was not like now when we have turnpikes. It was bumper to bumper. It took me about three days but I needed to see my wife and son.

When I came home, Moussia's brother Lloyd was with the baby. Roman was ten days old. When I came in the door, her brother jumped up and did an Indian dance chanting, "Moussia's had a little Indian baby." Then he laughed and said to me, "That's the only dance I'll ever do for you!"

In the years to follow, Jasha would speak of "my son" with pride and delight. Moussia had given him a son and namesake. He now had a family to care and provide for. While his career as a dancer continued unabated, there was a subtle shift in his priorities from premier danseur to family man, and each step away from his family became harder to endure.

From Tulsa I flew to Hollywood to rehearse for a tour. Toumanova was married to a man named Casey Robinson and had a big house there with a built-in studio.

Toumanova and her husband were very separate in their lives. One day I saw a woman going in to see him, a beautiful young girl. "Who is that?" I asked Toumanova. "Oh, that is my husband's secretary." I thought, "Oh boy! And we are leaving the country!" Her husband was going up the stairs and this girl was standing to the side. He went with us to the airport to see us off and I remember thinking that there was something funny there.

And so the tour began, with Tamara Toumanova, her mother, Jasinski, and their pianist.

THE SOUTH AMERICAN YEARS

Photo by Carlos, Rio. Private collection.

We went first to Havana for one performance, and the next performance was somewhere in Central America, then Montevideo, Buenos Aires and São Paulo. Each night, in an hour and a half, we danced pas de deux from SWAN LAKE, DON QUIXOTE, LES SYLPHIDES, and BOLERO. Tamara also danced "Dying Swan."

We'd change costumes while the pianist played something to entertain the audience. It was very hard.

We were getting on a plane in Rio when Toumanova read a telegram and said, "Jasha, I need to go back." I still had a contract with her for another month, so she said, "All right, I will pay," and she paid me for the month.

Later she sent a telegram saying she wasn't coming back; her husband was divorcing her. He gave her the big house and some money, married the secretary, and moved to Mexico City. He was not happy with Toumanova because her mother was a problem. Mama Toumanova was very hard on them. When Toumanova was married Mama didn't let her sleep with her husband. She had to sleep in her mother's room. "Tamarishka needs to dance tomorrow." Her mother had terrific power over her.

Toumanova was absolutely like nun, not to church, but to ballet. She was always very close with her mother, almost never leaving home. She was successful, but she was lonesome. Baronova, Riabouchinska, Toumanova—they had all been close when Tamara was a little girl. The first baby ballerinas were very close. But later her mother kept her away from them. I had friends in the company, but I don't know if she did.

She never married again. She saw herself as "the great ballerina!" She had no children. Her mother probably never let her have any. She started young and she finished young. She was thirty-something when we danced together for the last time.

Mr. Denham sent a telegram asking me to rejoin the Ballet Russe de Monte Carlo, but I didn't want to go back to Denham, so I signed a contract with Danilova for her tour, *Great Moments of the Ballet,* along with Moussia and Michael Maule. I would be the tour manager to

South America, Japan and the Philippines. Denham was very upset, but I was looking forward to ending my career, not starting it.

In South America there were lots of crooks. They would say they would pay us and then they wouldn't. I would say, "My offer is. . . no check, no performance." Once we had the check we would start right away.

Roman was six months old when we went on this tour. We were gone from him several months so we left him with Moussia's mother at first, and then with Moussia's sister-in-law. When we came from Japan, Roman cried, "No! No!" He called his aunt "Mama," and ran away from us. That hurt! "Moussia, we cannot leave our son again. If we go any place he will go with us."

So, when we next toured the United States and Canada, Danilova bought a little bus for five people and I bought another car, a Ford, so we could take Roman with us. It was the hardest period of my life. I was exhausted. In Paris, when I was young and hungry, I would go to sleep to forget my hunger, but here, while I had a full stomach, I would have given a couple of lives to go to sleep! Everything was harder. I was driving. We would come to the hotel in mid-afternoon and a baby sitter would be waiting for us. I was so sleepy from driving I would give half of my life to go to bed but Roman would want to play with me. How can you dance when you are so tired? I would have coffee or something to get me going, and then after the performance I would have to take the baby sitter home. I remember one baby sitter who lived a couple of miles from the city. It was dark and I couldn't find her home. Then I couldn't find my way back. I lost two or three hours when I could have been asleep.

Sometimes, if we traveled more than 250 miles in a day we did not perform that night, but usually, we would get up about 9:00 A.M. and travel about five hours. Then I could sleep, if Roman did not jump on my head. He was around one year and wanted to play. Moussia had to wash the diapers in the hotel. We traveled like this for months through the United States and Canada.

GREAT MOMENTS

Danilova's "Great Moments of the Ballet": Michael Maule, Alexandra Danilova, Roman Jasinski, and Moscelyne Larkin.

Photo by Maurice Seymour courtesy of Ron Seymour. Private collection.

It was very hard, but exciting, too. There were only four people dancing, so each performance was murder. We danced parts from CHOPINIANA, COTILLON, GAÎTÉ PARISIENNE, NUTCRACKER, MADEMOISELLE FIFI, and THE BEAUTIFUL BLUE DANUBE. Michael Maule gave us CARIB PEDDLAR and I danced the "Drummer" solo from GRADUATION BALL.

My favorite part was the "Hussar" in DANUBE. Because I am Polish, I danced the mazurka with a certain movement of my head which was natural for me. In Chicago, I received the most fantastic letter from a Polish actress. It touched me so deeply, this letter. She said I reminded her of Poland when she was young. "I never saw anybody like you. Your whole body. Your head. The way you stood." She wrote so beautifully, like poetry. I almost cried.

We finished the season and then were supposed to go to Africa and Japan with *Great Moments of the Ballet* in April of 1955, but I said, "Thank you very much. I cannot go any more." I asked Danilova to release me from this contract. I did not want to leave Roman any more, so Freddie Franklin took my place.

How ironic. The man whose place he once took with Denham now took Jasinski's place with Danilova. Professional rivalry was behind them and a long-enduring friendship was ahead.

That was the end. I was very happy to have finished my performing life as a premier danseur. I had danced with Balanchine, the Original Ballet Russe and the Ballet Russe de Monte Carlo. For two years I had had the concert company. And I had had the tours with Markova, Toumanova, and Danilova. That was enough.

CHAPTER 26

# A Home of His Own

*To me, it is something like happened in a dream.*

WE CELEBRATED ROMAN'S SECOND BIRTHDAY in Florida. I had had an offer to teach in Phoenix, but all of my life I had worked for other people. Now I wanted to work for myself. I wanted something that belonged to me. I wanted to have my own place, be my own boss. Moussia desperately wanted to come to Tulsa. Always, this was her home. She had memories of how beautiful her life was here and she wanted to live close to her mother.

Before we went to Japan we bought property for a new studio in Tulsa. We started to build in 1954 and opened a year later. Moussia's mother, Eva Matlagova, closed her studio and joined us with her students.

I knew how to design the school because my father was an architect. I knew exactly how large I could make it—two studios, an office, dressing rooms, shower and bathrooms. The whole studio plus the property cost me $45,000.

Miss Eva trained all the students until 1955 when the last tour was over. Then these former stars of the Ballet Russe, filled with knowledge, experience, and hope, eagerly became fulltime teachers and property owners.

We worked up to about four hundred students. For years we took care of everything. We painted the walls, trimmed the bushes, cleaned the mirrors, washed the floors. It was not work, just enjoyment. All my money I put into my studio. What was important—it was my studio!

FATHER AND SON

Jasha and Roman on a beach in Florida.

Courtesy Archives, Tulsa Ballet.

TO CAPEZIO

"To Capezio—We have danced our way around the world in your wonderful shoes. Many thanks—Moscelyne Larkin Roman Jasinski Ballet Russe de Monte Carlo."

Photo by Maurice Seymour courtesy of Ron Seymour. Courtesy Archives, Tulsa Ballet.

The loss to other cities was the gain to Oklahoma, and the artistic state of the State has never been the same. The Jasinskis, as teachers, were an interesting mix. Miss Larkin, known best for her blazing beauty and magnetic stage presence, became a stickler for strict technique with her students. Jasinski, developed as a child under the strictest of teachers and choreographers became the one to push his dancers to "Move, move, move! Don't stand there! Dance!" It was a reversal of roles that developed generations of outstanding young dancers.

> In Europe, you don't have chances like this. Here in the United States you have opportunity. If you work you can slowly make money. In Europe you must work all your life before you are able to buy a house. We could not afford to buy a house there. But here, you come to this country and one of the first things you buy is a house. That's what I did in Tulsa. I borrowed the money and I stood at the first house and thought, "Here I am, standing on a gold mine!"

The "gold mine" was a modest little home with a fenced half-acre backyard. Together they plugged the grass, bought a raised swimming pool from Sears, built a patio and furnished it with tables. And then one sultry summer night they opened their gates and invited in their friends. To their home. To their new roots in Tulsa.

At long last the prince had his very own castle.

Life in Tulsa was different, settled. Jasha even joined a men's business club, reveling in the chance to have male friends on a casual, social, non-competitive basis. It was an association he would treasure for years.

In their new home their energies revolved around their son, their studio, Moussia's mother, their friends. Finally, they were a real, settled family with a business to build. No one appreciated the transition more than Jasha.

Six years later they found the house that was to be theirs for the rest of their time together. Sand in the backyard and hand-slicing Johnson grass were painstakingly replaced with carefully positioned trees and grass. A fireplace clung to an inside corner, providing interior warmth. Walls were hung gaily with memorabilia from around the world. And most important, there was room for their friends—Danilova, Franklin, Lazowski, and their peers—who shared past memories and made the roof ring with nostalgia uttered in half a dozen languages.

Tulsa would be the Jasinskis' home for the rest of their lives, but their impact on the dance world continued unabated. As teachers, they had no regional parallel, yet more was soon asked of them.

"Share what you know," urged a local doctor. "You have all this knowledge, all this background. Why don't you start a civic company?"

That one potent remark birthed a mini-Ballet Russe renaissance in America's forty-sixth state. It turned students into dancers, dancers into artists, and molded a restless quest for excellence into the life-changing discipline that true dancers must achieve.

> The most important thing about the Ballet Russe was that it was so rich in choreography and music and costumes and scenery. The Ballet Russe really enriched our knowledge. After working so much with the Russian people, we adopted their style, their discipline, and their respect. It is very hard to put that discipline into this country. Dancers don't like it when you tell them "discipline." Americans are a free people. We had to teach them to be free through discipline.

Slowly, slowly that foreign discipline began to be absorbed. Classes were strict. Students learned eagerly, but learning can be meaningless without display. "Young talent must have an audience and . . . artists must have a vehicle of self-expression," the Jasinskis were quoted as saying.

In late 1956 a "bonus attraction" to an ongoing "Celebrity Series" was announced in a local newspaper, and a child of the Ballet Russe tradition was born, its tickets on sale at a local shoe store. The premiere performance of Tulsa Civic Ballet took place 15 December 1956, at Temple Israel in midtown Tulsa. With the Jasinskis in leading roles and music provided by an oboist, a harpist, and pianist Rosalie Talbott, students culled from local studios combined to dance "The Snow Country" from *Nutcracker,* Jasinski's own *Mozartiana,* and the second act of *Coppélia* with Miss Larkin as the mischievous "Swanhilda." Nothing the students did in that first fledgling venture was very demanding, but the sheer fact that they were on stage with real professionals raised the performance above that of a simple recital.

Indeed, the premiere's success was so warm, its audience so enthusiastic, its future so enticing, that pianist Rosalie Talbott joined the Jasinskis in signing letters of incorporation in early 1957. The newborn Tulsa Civic Ballet was now incorporated as Ballet Arts, Inc. The Jasinskis had been teaching in Tulsa for only a year or two and already the city's arts horizons were expanding.

Swift upon the heels of their early successes, a charitable group, the Pilot Club, supported the company for almost a decade, while turning ticket sales into dental care for needy children.

In time, a board of directors was created, its "office" in the trunk of the secretary's car. As the dancers improved and their training increased, the little company joined the local orchestra and civic opera to highlight the city's burgeoning cultural scene. From the beginning, the Ballet Russe heritage of the company was stressed, proceeding quickly from that first *Nutcracker* excerpt in 1956 to stalwarts such as *Graduation Ball* and *Choreartium* by the mid-sixties. The patrimony of the company would be apparent to all by the eighties, when staples from Tulsa Ballet Theatre's Ballet Russe repertoire were shown on tour.

PASSING ON THE TRADITION

The Jasinskis in their studio.

Photo courtesy of the Oklahoma Arts Council. Courtesy Archives, Tulsa Ballet.

The Jasinskis had dared the move to Oklahoma, put their savings into their studio, purchased a home, started a company. One would think that enough of a challenge. . . but more was to come in 1957.

In a rare breather from the rigors of teaching, they made a brief escape to New York. A meal at the famous Russian Tea Room brought forth another new vision when *Dance News* editor Anatole Chujoy, who had encouraged their return to Tulsa, scolded them for concentrating too narrowly on their students and tiny company, and ignoring the blockbuster beneath their noses. Oklahoma, he reminded them, was unique for the American Indian heritage of its five renowned ballerinas. It was time to trumpet their triumphs to the world. The concept caught immediate fire. The timing was perfect. Oklahoma was soon to be fifty years old and was looking for ways to make a celebratory splash.

Who could have imagined that the youthful state of Oklahoma could have, would have, produced five ballerinas within the decade of the 1920s, each of whom possessed an American Indian heritage? Moscelyne Larkin and Yvonne Chouteau even shared the bloodlines of a common ancestress, tribal leader Maria Silverheels, although Moussia's heritage was principally Shawnee-Peoria and Yvonne's Shawnee via the Cherokee rolls. The very famous Tallchief sisters, Maria and Marjorie, possessed Osage blood, and the fifth of the group, Rosella Hightower, was part Choctaw.

The end result of the challenge was that four of the five Indian ballerinas danced in Tulsa in the fall of 1957, assisted by local student-dancers termed "a corn-fed corps de ballet" by a critic from London's *Times*. The fifth ballerina, Marjorie Tallchief, was detained in Europe for a scheduled performance and lost the chance to join her sister and peers.

Headlines shouted their enthusiasm and the widespread world image of a state confined to oil wells and dust bowl disasters shuddered in their wake.

*Dance News:* "Oh! What a Beautiful Evening!"

*The Times* (London): "Red Indian Queens of the Dance"; "An Oklahoma Gala."

*The Tulsa Tribune:* "History was made" ". . . a program of sheer beauty."

*Tulsa World:* "No more brilliant or appropriate climax to the state's semi-centennial celebration could possibly have been staged."

The festival had a reprise a decade later with performances in both Oklahoma City and Tulsa when the second Oklahoma Indian Ballerina Festival became a major project of "Showcase '67," sponsored by the Oklahoma Arts and Humanities Council to celebrate Oklahoma's sixtieth anniversary.

This was a far more sophisticated affair that required immense coordination, collaboration, and cooperation between the state's two largest cities. By this time, Yvonne Chouteau and her husband, Miguel Terekhov, had their own studio and civic ballet in the state's capital, Oklahoma City.

FIRST OKLAHOMA INDIAN BALLERINA FESTIVAL, 1957

Clockwise from top: Maria Tallchief, Rosella Hightower, Yvonne Chouteau, and Moscelyne Larkin.

Photo by Bob McCormack, Tulsa. Courtesy Archives, Tulsa Ballet.

SECOND OKLAHOMA INDIAN BALLERINA FESTIVAL, 1967

Moscelyne Larkin, Marjorie Tallchief, Rosella Hightower, and Yvonne Chouteau in *The Four Moons.*

Photo by Bjarne Holm, Tulsa. Courtesy Archives, Tulsa Ballet.

Intense, hours-long meetings were held at a restaurant midway between the two cities. Both civic ballets rehearsed feverishly. The National Foundation on the Arts and the Humanities and The Oklahoma Arts and Humanities Council also helped in the funding, and once again the work paid off. Performances in each city sold out.

In this second festival, Marjorie Tallchief at last took her place on stage, collaborating with her colleagues on *The Four Moons* ballet. Maria had retired, so once again only four of the five ballerinas performed.

*The Four Moons* was an immense undertaking. Indian composer Louis Ballard echoed Native American motifs in his work; the ballerinas danced to his throbbing score accented with native percussive instruments and flutes. A brilliant young Indian artist, Jerome Tiger, created the painting that inspired the work, and the choreography, with the exception of the variation that Rosella Hightower produced, was set by each ballerina's husband. Jasinski choreographed the stately opening movement and Miguel Terekhov, the ballet's impressive finale.

Again the festival was reviewed with excitement in *The Saturday Review, The National Observer, Newsweek, Dance News,* and a host of other publications. It was a tremendous coup for the state and its arts, and a tremendous accomplishment for its instigators. New York dance critic Walter Terry would later write in a personal note, "My beautiful Moussia, what honor you have brought to both your ballet ancestors from abroad and your noble Shawnee heritage in the heartland of your country."

These performances also fostered the development of the Jasinski's fledgling student company. It was to become one of the best-known civic ballets in the country. At a time when regional ballet festivals were raising the standards of ballet nationwide, the Tulsa company received accolade after accolade, year after year, under the tutelage and inspiration of its artistic directors.

> Every year we were a little bit better. Every year we made progress! Markova came as a guest artist and I partnered her. Tickets sold out like pancakes. The English ballerina Margot Fonteyn came also, although, at that time, she was not well-known.

Through contacts with friends from the international ballet world, stellar artists years younger than the Jasinskis performed in Tulsa. The names were legendary: Edward Villella, Patricia McBride, Jacques d'Amboise, Fernando Bujones, Peter Martins, Violette Verdy, Melissa Hayden, and others of equal repute. These stars of a different era came to Tulsa because they could learn so much from their Ballet Russe forebears. All gained as much as they gave and the audience responded with bravos.

Many tasted their first choreography from Lichine or Lifar or Fokine. Cynthia Gregory commented to *The New York Times,* "They always want something new, at the Tulsa Ballet," recalling that her first appearance in Balanchine's *Agon,* her first *Tchaikovsky Pas de Deux,* and her first partnerings with Peter Martins and Adam Lüders occurred—not in a major metroplex—but in Tulsa.

Still, for many years Miss Larkin privately lamented that "Tulsa doesn't know who Roman Jasinski is!" She was right. This modest, unassuming man never spoke of twenty curtain calls in Australia, accolades in South America, the aura surrounding a stellar career. Nor was it generally known that superstars like Danilova, Toumanova, Markova thought of "Jasinski" when planning their personal tours. But if Tulsans were ignorant of his past, they swiftly learned to appreciate his present and to treasure the mature Jasinski for the way he poured his life's knowledge into the youth and audiences of his adopted city.

In 1975, as the company's twentieth anniversary approached, the Ballet Board announced the date for its annual formal dinner. As far as the Jasinskis knew, it was just the normal, pleasant fundraiser and gathering, and it wasn't until they reached the designated hall that they found costumes from their Ballet Russe days had been filched surreptitiously from their attic for use as party decor. This was no ordinary party. It was, instead, a huge outflow of appreciation.

Son Roman flew in from New York. That was the first surprise. A living fir tree stood in the center of the hall, its branches laden with congratulatory telegrams from colleagues all over the world. A paper chain wound around and around the tree, symbolizing the Jasinskis' strong links to colleagues, dancers, and students worldwide.

Danilova wrote: "How bright my memories of our years together!" A former student reminisced: "God gave me a terrible turnout and no extension. You gave

BALLET IN TULSA

Top: Roman Jasinski in *Icare* with the early Tulsa Civic Ballet.

Photo by Woodie Mullen, Tulsa. Courtesy Archives, Tulsa Ballet.

Bottom: Jasinski with guest artist Alicia Markova, *Les Sylphides,* Tulsa, 1959.

Private collection.

me magic in my childhood and made me a balletomane for life." First Lady Betty Ford, herself once a serious dance student, added to the accolades. The audience stood in homage to this pair, thanking them for nearly twenty years of selfless service, and for the beauty and honor they had brought to this city and state. For the next two decades the fir, dubbed the "Memory Tree," thrived in their backyard, a living reminder of their city's esteem.

The company could have continued indefinitely in this civic ballet vein, but three pivotal progressions changed its course: Jasinski developed and expanded his own choreography; local dancers grew in talent and professionalism; and in 1978 the company changed its image and name to the more prestigious Tulsa Ballet Theatre, with the intent of becoming fully professional.

> A few of my dancers were really tremendous—like the baby ballerinas were. These kids, both girls and boys, worked without a penny. Sometimes we would take them and give them some food—sandwiches or something. It reminded me of my days in Egorova's studio when I would dance for food; but of course, these kids weren't starving.
>
> Still, they gave the most of anybody because they were given no money in the beginning. When they got really good, they had to leave Tulsa to dance for a salary. Later when we could pay a little bit, people slowly started coming back to us. My son Roman danced with American Ballet Theatre. We had people in Europe, at Ballet West, New York City Ballet, American Ballet Theatre, all over. But they came back when we could pay them. The way we did this—we stopped paying for an orchestra. We were a ballet company and needed to pay our ballet dancers first.
>
> I also made the choreography. I was always thinking about Balanchine and Massine in my choreography. Balanchine told me, "Listen to the music until it is in your blood." Steps would come to my mind. At night I would dream about the steps and then I would write them down on a book or paper in the dark, but in the morning, I could not read my writing!

FIRST BOYS' CLASS

The first boys' class in the American heartland was taught by Roman Jasinski and sponsored by the Ford Foundation.

Photo by Lee Gillette for the *Tulsa Tribune*. Courtesy Archives, Tulsa Ballet.

You know, I had my feelings, my emotions, but I took more influence from the music than my feelings when I choreographed. To match the beautiful music with the beautiful steps of ballet and to show the dancer's technique at the same time—sometimes it seemed impossible. Sometimes you needed to catch the music by the tail.

I also did things from different periods of my life that had nothing to do with the Ballet Russe. I was a different kind of dancer, you see. I was Polish. When I graduated from the Warsaw Opera Ballet I needed to know every dance: the czardas belonged to the Hungarians; the polonaise to the Poles; the mazurka to the Russians and Poles. All were different and I could draw on them all.

> And I drew from choreographers I knew. Balanchine could invent steps—he was an inspiration to me—and my "Arabian" from NUTCRACKER was very close to Fokine. Only three or four steps but used in harmony.
>
> When I choreographed I was always thinking about Balanchine or Massine or Nijinska. Critics said I had some kind of unconscious connection with Nijinska's choreography, but I would say that I had more with Balanchine than anyone.

Balanchine, Nijinska, Fokine, Massine—all tumbled together in an already fertile mind to produce ballet after ballet. His dancers loved his choreography. In his thick Polish accent he sometimes would confuse his many languages when trying to make a point. "Square. Dance in square!" and when puzzled dancers stared at him at a loss for his meaning, he would sputter, "Moussia! How you say 'square' in English?"

Tulsa Civic Ballet eventually attained "major company" status, the highest category in the National Association of Regional Ballet, and several of Jasinski's choreographies were carefully filmed for the Jerome Robbins Archives at the New York Public Library in New York. Whatever his Nijinska-Fokine-Balanchine-Massine roots, he had a Jasinski spin that was all his creative own.

Jasha was quick to share his creations, too. Bartlesville in northeastern Oklahoma, the Chouteau-Terekhov company in Oklahoma City, Cincinnati Ballet, and others asked eagerly for his works.

While it was exciting and fulfilling to create his own ballets, the works of his heritage also were restaged. *Gaîté Parisienne, Les Sylphides, Giselle, Swan Lake* rolled with Ballet Russe finesse and verve across the Tulsa stage. Ballet legends like Vladimir Dokoudovsky and Frederic Franklin, Jasinski's old nemesis and now dear friend, aided in their re-creation and shared their accolades.

Even more important, great ballets lost to the modern world were painstakingly revived, pulled from living memories with consummate care. Dokoudovsky and the Jasinskis searched brains and records to remember each move in Michael Fokine's *Paganini.* From Buenos Aires came ballerina Esmeralda Agoglia to help Jasinski recall Balanchine's long-lost *Mozart Violin Concerto,* last danced by

Jasinski in 1942. Other revivals included Serge Lifar's *Icare,* Balanchine's "Hand of Fate" from *Cotillon,* and excerpts from Léonide Massine's *Choreartium.* The *New York Times* critic Jack Anderson headlined succinctly, "Sometimes a Revival Is More Rewarding Than a Premiere."

In 1983 Balanchine's "Hand of Fate" pas de deux was revived by the Jasinskis from the 1932 ballet, *Cotillon,* at the Brookings Institute for the Performing Arts in Brooklyn. Jasha had danced *Cotillon* in those early performances, and for fifty-plus years had held the memory. Critics, curious to see Balanchine's fledgling masterwork, approved and applauded its performance, then lingered to watch the rest of Tulsa Ballet Theatre's New York debut. The ambitious undertaking included *The Four Moons, Convolutions* (Jasinski), *The Seasons* (Jasinski), *Gaîté Parisienne* (Massine), and *Rhythmetron* (Arthur Mitchell).

Their praise was heartwarming. "Tulsa did American dance proud. . . ." said *The New York Times.* One year later the same reviewer said that Tulsa Ballet Theatre was "a leading American regional ballet company with a distinctive look and style."

Meanwhile, major contemporary choreographers shared their works with the young company. Dance Theatre of Harlem director Arthur Mitchell told Miss Larkin after the performance of his *Rhythmetron,* "There isn't a company in the country that has the classical movements of your company." Clive Barnes of the *New York Post* summed it up when he exulted, "Tulsa Ballet is one of the best things to be associated with Oklahoma since Rodgers and Hammerstein."

Four years later the New York critics were in the audience again, this time to see another TBT program anchored by Balanchine's lost *Mozart Violin Concerto.* Once again a ballet company from Oklahoma was daring to show its face in New York City, and all of New York's chief critics were there. It was a huge gamble. It became a huge coup.

Yet by this time, no one was really very surprised at the company's success. *Ballet News* critic Walter Terry had earlier assessed company dancers as performing "...not only Ballet Russe-style choreography, but also [bringing] to their roles that eager-to-please exuberance, once a Ballet Russe trademark," and had praised the Jasinskis for raising "ballet standards in the heartland of America to Ballet Russe professional heights."

How did they do it? *Dance Magazine* captured their simple formula in an issue in 1986. They simply passed to their dancers the "pure classical line, gracious port de bras, technical clarity, sensitive dramatic interpretation, and exuberant stage presence that the Jasinskis themselves had learned from the Ballet Russe master teachers and choreographers." What more could be asked of any teacher?

When George Balanchine, father of American ballet, was in his final illness, he held Jasha's hand and said, "A mistake was made. We began together and we should have ended together." It was the ultimate accolade, an acknowledgement and homage from one great artist to another.

CONCERTO IN D

Premiere of *Concerto in D,* 1984: Choreographer Roman Jasinski on stage with Moscelyne Larkin and company.

Photo by Bob McCormack, Tulsa. Courtesy Archives, Tulsa Ballet.

The awards began to flow. Roman Jasinski: 1982 Recipient of the Oklahoma Governor's Arts Award. 1985: Lifetime Achievement Award for both Jasinskis from the Arts and Humanities Council of Tulsa. 1988: Induction of both into the Tulsa Hall of Fame. And eventually, notification that both would receive honorary doctoral degrees from the University of Tulsa.

The greatest personal and professional accolade came in 1988 when they were presented with the *Dance Magazine* Award for their "shining example." Yet, while the awards meant much, Jasha never mentioned them. They were merely peripheral incidents in a life of vision and hard work. The one "award" he put above all others and treasured most deeply was his citizenship in the United States of America, the state of Oklahoma, and the city of Tulsa.

In 1990 Tulsa Ballet Theatre purchased an old elementary school building and consolidated its far-flung offices. Before this, sets were stored in a warehouse, costumes above the Jasinskis' garage and in a home across the street, and rehearsals were conducted at the Jasinski's private studio. A former dancer with the company who was now an architect turned the derelict school building into a state-of-the-art studio with three large rehearsal halls, a costume shop, scene shop, set storage, and office. Tulsa Ballet was now fully professional in terms of site and talent.

> I am most excited about the new home for the ballet. The board has raised a million dollars. The new home will be the power of the company—a place to rehearse. At our studio it's impossible. We need to finish rehearsal in the middle of the afternoon so our students can come in. Then the dancers are free the rest of the day and they are not happy. Now we will be able to rehearse all day while the school carries on separately.

Jasinski had reached the apex of his life. He was an American citizen, a homeowner, a businessman, an artist. Husband, father, citizen, he was loved by his peers and admired by legions. With all of this behind him, he and Moussia relinquished their positions as active artistic directors of Tulsa Ballet Theatre in March 1991, leaving the field open for their son, Roman, to succeed them.

FOUNDERS

Tulsa Ballet Founders reunited: Roman Jasinski, Moscelyne Larkin, and Rosalie Talbott.

Photo by Bob McCormack, Tulsa. Courtesy Archives, Tulsa Ballet.

To me, it is something like happened in a dream. It is unbelievable. It is a miracle what we did. We had plans, but I was always afraid we would not succeed with these plans. But the board of directors came to me and said, "Don't worry. We will work it out." They gave me a kind of courage. I knew when I retired I wanted to have something continue. My whole point is, I don't want something to just stop. When you have your own home you can continue for one hundred years.

I had in my life a certain destination. And I think that everything that happened was right. For the best. Yes. I look over and over these things and I think it was fantastic. I came to paradise in America. I really want to give something of myself to this country, to leave something, to donate, because I have the knowledge of these things that not many people have.

HALL OF FAME

Moscelyne Larkin, Oklahoma Indian Ballerina, upon induction into the Oklahoma Hall of Fame, 1979.

Photo by Bob McCormack, Tulsa.

Courtesy Archives, Tulsa Ballet.

LIKE FATHER, LIKE SON

Roman Larkin Jasinski in Tulsa Ballet Theatre's *Prodigal Son*, 1985.

© Jon B. Petersen, Tulsa.

Courtesy Archives, Tulsa Ballet.

> When I came here I tried to learn about America because it is so different from Europe—different people, different attitude towards everything. All my life I had been fighting to survive. But since I came to this country I didn't need to fight anymore.
>
> In America, you have a chance to become someone! In Europe, if you are born poor, you die poor. Here you have opportunity. It's up to you.
>
> I was given an unusual chance. I have had a good life. . . . Ate lots here.

"Ate lots here." The ultimate accolade. As he spoke these words his eyes began to twinkle, his face split into laughter, and he summed up his whole success in terms of food: "Ate lots here. Apple pie à la mode!" What higher praise could a man born into poverty give for the good life in America?

AN ARTIST FOREVER

As "Dr. Drosselmeyer" in Tulsa Ballet Theatre's production of *The Nutcracker.*

Photo by R.J. Hudson. Courtesy Archives, Tulsa Ballet.

# Epilogue: Tulsa

CRACKED, DRY LIPS PLAGUED THE FRAIL OLD GENTLEMAN in the hospital bed. The doctor brought in a soothing salve with instructions to apply it to the lips for three minutes.

"Three minutes? Why, Jasha, that's as long as Dying Swan!" And for three golden minutes the bleak hospital room was transformed into a theatre as the ballerina-wife began to dance, and the figure on the bed, within days of death, softly hummed the measure and beat the air in time to the music.

What an incredible team.

Partners in life as in their art, inseparable, they faced this last great gulf together, both more fearful for the other than for themselves. They had shared so much. Nearly forty-eight years of memories and delight. The joy of dancing together, traveling together, raising their son together. Ballet was the binding force in their lives as performers, artists, teachers, directors. Each filled and completed the other, making "the Jasinskis" a single unit.

The morning of 15 April 1991, the Jasinskis were separated by death. Jasha succumbed at eighty-three from multiple failures—heart, kidney, a body that simply had no more to give. The enormity of the loss for wife and son was shared by hundreds, perhaps thousands, who had loved and learned from him through the years.

How strange the road from a young boy's wriggling foot at a Polish garden party to a sterile hospital bed in Tulsa—and how wonderful the meandering path between.

Starving student, acclaimed performer, teacher, director, choreographer. Husband, father, American citizen. Czeslaw Roman Jasinski, both personally and professionally, was an ideal prince in all but royal blood—dignified, compelling, creative, kind. He took young bodies and gave them ballet grace. He took young minds and taught them to thirst for beauty. He took young souls and molded them into something rare, unique, and wonderful through discipline—changing his adopted state, changing his art, changing lives.

> I was given an unusual chance. I have had a good life. I was born in Poland but I die in America. God gave me everything.
>
> Ate lots here.
>
> Apple pie à la mode!

CZESLAW ROMAN JASINSKI, 1907–1991

© Jon B. Petersen, Tulsa. Courtesy Archives, Tulsa Ballet.

## A GIFT TO THE PLAINS

Jack Anderson

This couple, they chose
To settle down here,
Here on the Plains.
No one knew why.
They'd danced in New York,
In London, in Paris,
In Rome, Barcelona, and Buenos Aires.
Now it was time for their dancing to stop.
So they came out here
To this town on the Plains.
No one knew why.

They didn't quite, either.
But something called them across the map
To settle here
In this of all towns
And open their little Academy of Ballet.
Here is where something told them to stay.

So they stayed, this couple,
Year after year,
Years stretching onward into decades,
Years teaching ballet in their school—

To which students came,
Girls giggling in pink,
Plus a few brave inquisitive boys,
To have their lives

Touched by ballet,
And by more than ballet,
By what these teachers had known—had lived—
In New York, London, Vienna, and Brussels,
A gift of grace bestowed on the Plains.

Teaching there, all those years,
They civilized squirming
And energized torpor
Until every leg raised in arabesque
Extended beyond the City Limits.

What was that town? Who were those teachers?
It's possible you know.
Or, maybe, you don't.
You might not even recognize their names.
Or you might know ones like them,
For there are other ones like them
Scattered out there,
Gifts to the Plains
In other Plains towns
To which somehow
Lives were called and gifts were given.

No one knows why.
But this did happen
And grace remains grace.

Mr. Anderson, a dance critic for *The New York Times,* wrote "A Gift to the Plains" in honor of Roman Jasinski and Moscelyne Larkin.

# Cast of Characters

| | |
|---|---|
| ALICIA ALONSO | Cuban ballerina |
| A. EVERETT AUSTIN | Nicknamed "Chick," a great friend and associate of Lincoln Kirstein |
| GEORGE BALANCHINE | ("Georgi Melitonovich") The great twentieth-century choreographer who founded New York City Ballet. Roman Jasinski was Balanchine's first principal dancer and a lifelong friend. |
| BALLET RUSSE | (Or Ballets Russes) The name of three major ballet companies, existing from 1909 to 1964 and based variously in Paris, Monte Carlo, London, and New York, sometimes sequentially and oftentimes overlapping |
| IRINA BARONOVA | One of three original "baby ballerinas" with the second Ballet Russe |
| RENÉ BLUM | Director of ballet and opera at Monte Carlo |
| EDOUARD BOROVANSKY | Ballet Russe dancer and founder of company that became the Australian Ballet |
| ALEXANDRA DANILOVA | Ballet Russe ballerina with all three companies, frequently partnered by Roman Jasinski |
| COLONEL VASSILY DE BASIL | Impresario and director of the second Ballet Russe |
| SERGE DENHAM | Director of the third Ballet Russe |
| ANDRÉ DERAIN | Set designer for Les Ballets 1933, George Balanchine's first solo company |
| SERGE DIAGHILEV | Impresario and founder of the first Ballet Russe (The Ballets Russes) |
| LUBOV EGOROVA | (Princess Nikita Troubetzkoy)—Russian ballerina with prominent studio in Paris |

| | |
|---|---|
| MICHEL FOKINE | Early twentieth-century Russian choreographer who became well known in the West through his association with the first Ballet Russe and subsequent companies |
| FREDERIC FRANKLIN | Principal dancer with the third Ballet Russe |
| SERGE GRIGORIEV | Regisseur General of the first and second Ballet Russe companies |
| JAN HOYER | Polish Ballet Russe dancer |
| SOL HUROK | Balletomane and Russian impresario based in New York |
| EDWARD JAMES | Sponsor of Les Ballets 1933, a leading patron of the Surrealist movement, and husband of Viennese actress-dancer Tilly Losch |
| ROMAN LARKIN JASINSKI | Son of Roman Jasinski and Moscelyne Larkin, soloist with American Ballet Theatre, and principal dancer with Cincinnati Ballet and Tulsa Ballet Theatre, who succeeded his parents as artistic director of the Tulsa company |
| BARBARA KARINSKA | Famous costume maker of Paris and New York |
| LINCOLN KIRSTEIN | Writer and balletomane who brought Balanchine to the United States and with him co-founded the New York City Ballet and the School of American Ballet |
| BORIS KNIASEV | Company director and choreographer in Roman Jasinski's early career |
| BORIS KOCHNO | Knowledgeable artistic director of Les Ballets 1933, advisor to the first two Ballet Russe companies, and mentor to Roman Jasinski |
| MARIAN LADRE | Polish Ballet Russe dancer |
| EUGENE LAPITSKY | Soloist with the first Ballet Russe, and with the companies of Bronislava Nijinska and Ida Rubinstein |
| MOSCELYNE LARKIN | ("Moussia")—Roman Jasinski's wife of forty-seven years, dancer with the second and third Ballet Russe companies, and one of Oklahoma's five American Indian Ballerinas |
| YUREK LAZOWSKI | Polish character dancer and godfather to Roman Jasinski's son |

| | |
|---|---|
| DAVID LICHINE | Dancer with Ida Rubinstein and the second Ballet Russe, and later a choreographer |
| SERGE LIFAR | Principal dancer of the first Ballet Russe, star of the Paris ballet world, choreographer, and director of the Paris Opera Ballet, who saved Roman Jasinski's life |
| TILLY LOSCH | Viennese actress-dancer featured in Les Ballets 1933, and wife of Edward James |
| ALICIA MARKOVA | Great English ballerina later partnered by Roman Jasinski |
| LÉONIDE MASSINE | Star of all three Ballet Russe companies and renowned choreographer |
| EVA MATLAGOVA | Mother of Moscelyne Larkin |
| LUDOVIC MATLINSKY | Dancer with the Ida Rubinstein company who came out of Poland with Roman Jasinski |
| BRONISLAVA NIJINSKA | Dancer with the first Ballet Russe, renowned choreographer, artistic director, teacher, and sister of the famed dancer Vaslav Nijinsky |
| VASLAV NIJINSKY | Legendary star and choreographer of the first Ballet Russe |
| NINA NOVAK | Polish ballerina with the third Ballet Russe |
| SONO OSATO | Japanese-American soloist with second Ballet Russe |
| ANNA PAVLOVA | Legendary Russian ballerina |
| PAUL PETROFF | Principal dancer with the second Ballet Russe |
| TATIANA RIABOUCHINSKA | One of the three original "baby ballerinas" with the second Ballet Russe |
| IDA RUBINSTEIN | Actress-dancer with the first Ballet Russe, and impresario and star of her own subsequent companies |
| GERRY SEVASTIANOV | Husband of "baby ballerina" Irina Baronova, administrator of the second Ballet Russe and assistant to Sol Hurok |
| YUREK SHABELEVSKY | Dancer with the Ida Rubinstein company and the second Ballet Russe, who came out of Poland with Roman Jasinski |
| IGOR STRAVINSKY | The great twentieth-century composer who often collaborated with George Balanchine |
| PAVEL TCHELITCHEV | Twentieth-century painter and set designer of Les Ballets 1933 and Balanchine's ballet *Balustrade* |

| | |
|---|---|
| LUBOV TCHERNICHEVA | Wife of Serge Grigoriev and ballerina with the first two Ballet Russe companies |
| TAMARA TOUMANOVA | ("Tamarishka")—One of the three original "baby ballerinas" with the second Ballet Russe, principal dancer with Les Ballets 1933, and frequent partner of Roman Jasinski |
| SERGE UNGER | Dancer with the first Ballet Russe, and the companies of Bronislava Nijinska and Ida Rubinstein |
| ALEXANDRE VOLININE | Well-known teacher in Paris and partner of the famous ballerina Anna Pavlova |
| LÉON WOIZIKOWSKI | Polish character dancer with the first two Ballet Russe companies |
| PIOTR ZAILICH | Director of the Warsaw Opera Ballet in the early twentieth century |

## Known Repertoire of Roman Jasinski

*principal role

**principal role created on Roman Jasinski

L'Amour Sorcier, choreographed by Romanov

Amphion, choreographed by Massine

L'Après-midi d'un faune* (Afternoon of a Faun), choreographed by Nijinsky

Aurora's Wedding* (Le Mariage d'Aurore) after Pétipa (one-act version of The Sleeping Beauty)

La Baiser de la fée, choreographed by Nijinska

Balustrade**, choreographed by Balanchine

Le Beau Danube*, choreographed by Massine (Le Danube Bleu*) (Lifar)

Belkis, choreographed by Massine

Les Biches, choreographed by Nijinska

La Bien-Aimée, choreographed by Nijinska

Boléro, choreographed by Nijinska

Le Bourgeois Gentilhomme, choreographed by Balanchine

La Boutique fantasque, choreographed by Massine

Carnaval*, choreographed by Fokine

Cendrillon (Cinderella), choreographed by Fokine

Les Cent Baisers, choreographed by Nijinska

Choreartium*, choreographed by Massine

Chout, choreographed by Romanov

Cimarosiana, choreographed by Massine

Les Comédiens jaloux, choreographed by Nijinska

La Concurrence, choreographed by Balanchine

Coppélia, after Petipa

Le Coq d'or, choreographed by Fokine

Cotillon, choreographed by Balanchine

David (Le Roi David), choreographed by Massine

Les Dieux mendiants* (The Gods Go A-begging), choreographed by Lichine

Les Enchantments d'Alcine, choreographed by Massine

L'Errante**, choreographed by Balanchine

Etude*, choreographed by Nijinska

Fastes**, choreographed by Balanchine

Un Faune**, choreographed by Kniasev

Francesca da Rimini, choreographed by Lichine

Fue una vez…**, choreographed by Psota and S. Pueyrredón de Elizalde

Gaîté Parisienne*, choreographed by Massine

Giselle*, after Coralli

Graduation Ball*, choreographed by Lichine

Icare*, choreographed by Lifar

Jardin public, choreographed by Massine

Jeux d'enfants, choreographed by Massine

Légende de Berioska (La Légende du Bouleau; The Silver Birch; The Birch Trees), choreographed by Kniasev

Mademoiselle Fifi*, choreographed by Solov

Mozart Violin Concerto*, choreographed by Balanchine

Mozartiana**, choreographed by Balanchine

Night Shadow* (La Sonnambula), choreographed by Balanchine

Les Noces de Psyché et de l'Amour, choreographed by Nijinska

Nocturne, choreographed by Nijinska

The Nutcracker, after Ivanov

Obsession, choreographed by Kniasev

L'Oiseau de feu (The Firebird), choreographed by Fokine

Paquita*, after Petipa

Le Pavillon*, choreographed by Lichine

Paysage Enfantin, choreographed by Nijinska

Petrouchka, choreographed by Fokine

Polovtsian Dances from Prince Igor, choreographed by Fokine

Les Présages*, choreographed by Fokine

La Princesse Cygne, choreographed by Nijinska

Prodigal Son* (Le Fils prodigue), choreographed by Lichine

Protée*, choreographed by Lichine

Pulcinella, choreographed by Romanov

Raymonda (variations), after Pétipa

Rendez-vous Manqué, choreographed by Kniasev

Reverie Lunaire, choreographed by Kniasev

Rouge et Noir, choreographed by Massine

Schéhérazade, choreographed by Fokine

The Seven Deadly Sins** (Les Sept Péchés Capitaux), choreographed by Balanchine

Les Songes**, choreographed by Balanchine

Le Spectre de la Rose*, choreographed by Fokine

Swan Lake* (Le Lac des cygnes) (one-act version), after Pétipa

Les Sylphides*, choreographed by Fokine

Symphonie fantastique*, choreographed by Massine

Au Temps des Tartares, choreographed by Kniasev

Le Tricorne, choreographed by Massine

Tziganes, choreographed by Kniasev

Union Pacific, choreographed by Massine

La Valse, choreographed by Nijinska

Les Valses de Beethoven**, choreographed by Balanchine

Variations*, choreographed by Nijinska

## Selected Ballet Russe Repertoire of Tulsa Ballet

Afternoon of a Faun (L'Après-midi d'un faune)
Aurora's Wedding (Le Mariage d'Aurore)
Le Beau Danube
Les Biches
Choreartium
Cirque de Deux
Coppélia
Cotillon ("Hand of Fate" pas de deux)
The Firebird (L'Oiseau de feu)
Frankie and Johnny
Gaîté Parisienne
Giselle
Graduation Ball
Icare
Night Shadow (La Sonnambula)
The Nutcracker
Paganini
Paquita (excerpts)
Pas de quatre
Petrouchka (excerpts)
Polovtsian Dances from Prince Igor
The Prodigal Son (Le Fils Prodigue)
Raymonda (variations)
Rodeo
Schéhérazade
Swan Lake
Les Sylphides
Le Tricorne

## Selected Original Choreography of Roman Jasinski

Bach for a Hep Margrave
Bamboo Princess
Classical Symphony
Concerto in D
Convolutions
Divertissement Classique
Eurythmics
La Forêt Enchantée
Khachaturiana
The Four Moons (two variations)
Grande Tarantelle
Mozartiana
Pas de Paderewski
A Polish Tribute to Oklahoma
Rhapsodic Variations
Romanian Rhapsody
Romanze auf Wien
The Seasons
Soirée Musicale
Spanish Dance Suite
Tchaikovsky Divertissement
Variations on a Polish Theme
Zingara

# Notes

*All narratives quoting Czeslaw Roman Jasinski are taken from personal interviews conducted by Cheryl Forrest, Tulsa, Oklahoma, between the years 1988-1991 with the exception of those noted below. All translations from the French are by the authors with the exception of those noted below.*

## PROLOGUE: WARSAW

### EVERYTHING HAPPENED A MIRACLE IN MY LIFE

18. ***By scavenging newspapers:*** Roman Larkin Jasinski, in discussion with Cheryl Forrest, Tulsa, 28 March 2006.

22. ***each had choreographed:*** Czeslaw Roman Jasinski, interview by Doris Hering, July 1976, written transcript, Oral History Project, Dance Collection, Library and Museum of the Performing Arts, Lincoln Center, New York, 17.

## BOOK ONE: A GYPSY IN EUROPE 1928-1932

### 1928: SETTING THE STAGE

28. ***Born to a wealthy:*** Michael de Cossart, *Ida Rubinstein (1885-1960): A Theatrical Life* (Great Britain: Liverpool University Press, 1987), 7-9.

28. ***She was plucked by Diaghilev:*** S. L. Grigoriev, *The Diaghilev Ballet: 1909-1929,* trans. and ed. Vera Bowen (Harmondsworth, UK: Penguin Books, 1960), 20.

28. ***"Her long…peculiarly angular body:*** Peter Lieven, *The Birth of the Ballets-Russes,* trans. L. Zarine (London: George Allen and Unwin, 1936; New York: Dover Publications, 1973), 97. Citation is to the Dover edition.

### PARIS!

34. ***Serge Unger, born in Russia:*** "Presstime News," *Dance Magazine,* April 1969, 14.

34. ***Nijinska recommended:*** Lydia Sokolova, *Dancing for Diaghilev: The Memoirs of Lydia Sokolova,* ed. Richard Buckle (San Francisco: Mercury House, 1960), 202.

34. ***Diaghilev paid:*** Richard Buckle, *Diaghilev* (New York: Atheneum, 1979), 408.

34. ***"We were disappointed*:** Grigoriev, *Diaghilev Ballet,* 190.

35. ***Massine was given:*** David Vaughan, *Frederick Ashton and his Ballets*, 2nd ed. (London: Dance Books, 1999), 26.

38. ***"La Compagnie:*** Ibid.

39. ***She sought to rival:*** Serge Lifar, *Le Livre de la Danse* (Paris: Société Française de Diffusion Musicale et Artistique, 1954), 124-125.

39. ***"as a static Goddess:*** Keith Lester, "Rubinstein Revisited," *Dance Research: Journal of the Society for Dance Research* 1, no. 2 (Autumn 1983): 30.

39. ***"Madame Rubinstein can do anything:*** Vaughan, *Frederick Ashton*, 28. *"Madame Rubinstein peut faire tout sauf la virtuosité."* Translation assistance provided by Cecile Tuzii.

40. ***spent over a million:*** De Cossart, *Ida Rubinstein*, 32.

40. ***agonies of onstage insecurity:*** Lester, "Rubinstein Revisited," 28.

40. ***her friends:*** Ibid., 31.

40. ***"astonishingly provincial:*** Serge Lifar, *Serge Diaghilev: His Life, His Work, His Legend* (New York: G. P. Putnam's Sons, 1940), 337.

41. ***"had nothing of the dancer:*** Lifar, *Le Livre*, 124-125.

41. ***"The theater was full:*** Lifar, *Serge Diaghilev*, 339.

41. ***in more original works:*** De Cossart, *Ida Rubinstein*, 142.

41. ***"like a Pavlova swan:*** Lifar, *Serge Diaghilev*, 341.

41. ***"With an almost demonic indifference:*** Willi Reich, "Vienne: In Memoriam Maurice Ravel," Numéro Spécial, *La Revue Musicale: Hommage à Maurice Ravel*, December 1938, 467.

41. ***the best production of the season:*** Lynn Garafola, "Bronislava Nijinska's 'Bolero,'" *Dance in Hispanic Cultures: Proceedings of the Society of Dance History Scholars* (Riverside, CA: University of California, 1991): 254.

41. ***"was treading in the steps:*** Henri Pruniéres, "Chronique et Notes: La Musique en France et à l'Etranger—Les Ballets d'Ida Rubinstein à l'Opéra," *La Revue Musicale* 10, no. 3 (January 1929): 242 and 245.

41. ***"Stravinsky was seen:*** Lifar, *Serge Diaghilev*, 337.

42. ***in Monte Carlo, Rome, Vienna:*** Vaughan, *Frederick Ashton*, 30.

### THE GYPSY YEARS

47. ***I never met Diaghilev:*** Connie Cronley, "Roman Jasinski Bio," (press release, Tulsa Ballet Theatre, March 1991).

48. ***"Diagilev died this morning:*** Grigoriev, *Diaghilev Ballet*, 265.

49. ***"the Black Hole of Calcutta:*** Diana Menuhin, "Les Ballets 1933," *Dance Research: Journal of the Society for Dance Research* (London) 6, no. 2 (Autumn 1988): 65.

51. ***"The girls wear bathing suits:*** "Volinine at Work," *The Dancing Times* (London), January 1928, 551.

52. ***Once again, Jasinski, Unger, and Lapitsky:*** Program, "London Coliseum," 28 April 1930, collection Czeslaw Roman Jasinski.

### KNIASEV: NOT CROOK BUT MAGIC

58. ***such words as "elegance:*** Review, Paul Gregorio, *Comedia*, 1 July 1930.

60. ***Truth to tell:*** Program, "Saison Les Ballets Russes de Monte-Carlo" (Monaco: Théâtre de Monte-Carlo, 1934), collection Archives Société des Bains de Mer, Monte Carlo.

### A CHANCE TO DANCE

61. ***Again, they pawed:*** Program, "Les Ballets de Madame Ida Rubinstein" (Paris: Académie Nationale de Musique et de Danse, 25 June 1931), collection Bibliothèque nationale de France, Opéra; program, "Madame Ida Rubinstein Season" (London: The Covent Garden Opera Syndicate, 1930, 6-17 July 1931), reprint courtesy Royal Opera House Archives, Covent Garden.

61. ***Again, they presented:*** Ibid.

61. ***"How sad:*** *Candide*, 2 July 1931, as quoted in Vicente García-Márquez, *Massine: A Biography* (New York: Alfred A. Knopf, 1995), 214.

61. ***By 18 July:*** Czeslaw Jasinsky, contract to dance with Ida Rubinstein, 25 April–18 July 1931, collection Roman Larkin Jasinski.

61. ***and after one more brief:*** Ceslav [*sic*] Jasinski, contract to dance with Boris Kniasev, 3 August 1931, collection Roman Larkin Jasinski.

63. ***His name was in the Rubinstein:*** Program, "Madame Ida Rubinstein Season," Covent Garden.

## BOOK TWO: THE BALLETS RUSSES AND BALANCHINE 1932-1939

### DE BASIL'S BALLETS RUSSES DE MONTE-CARLO

73. ***Alexandra Danilova, in London:*** Alexandra Danilova, *Choura: The Memoirs of Alexandra Danilova* (New York: Alfred A. Knopf, 1986), 113. Roman Jasinski told his son that Balanchine called older ballerinas "yesterday's flowers." Roman Larkin Jasinski, in discussion with Cheryl Forrest, Tulsa, 4 May 2006.

76. ***a prime example:*** "Palaces of Princess Grace," *Mansions, Monuments, and Masterpieces,* televised broadcast, produced by Arts and Entertainment Television, 2002.

81. **COTILLON *broke new:*** Kathrine Sorley Walker, *De Basil's Ballets Russes* (New York: Atheneum, 1983), 10.

81. ***From 9 June:*** Vicente García-Márquez, *The Ballets Russes: Colonel de Basil's Ballets Russes de Monte Carlo, 1932-1952* (New York: Alfred A. Knopf, 1990), xiii.

82. ***Jacques Yassinsky:*** "Les Participants au Concours de Choreographie 1932," *Les Archives Internationales de la Danse* (Paris), 15 January 1933, 24; program, "3 Grandes Epreuves Internationales de Danses Artistiques: Théâtre des Champs-Elysées, du 2 au 4 juillet," *Les Archives Internationales de la Danse* (Paris), July 1932-May 1936. For this competition, *Berioska* was renamed *La Légende du Bouleau.*

82. ***For six cold weeks:*** García-Márquez, *Colonel de Basil's Ballets Russes,* xiii and 9.

### BALANCHINE AND LES BALLETS 1933

85. ***But I lost the lawsuit:*** Jasinski actually may have won this lawsuit: "I have heard that Toumanova and Jasinski, both of them, have won the suits brought against them by Monte Carlo for violation of contract." Edward James to "Master Bernstein," 31 January 1934, by the kind permission of the Trustees of the Edward James Foundation. It appears that Jasinski and the other former de Basil dancers declined to renew their contracts, which gives credence to Jasinski's assertion that "Colonel de Basil just didn't want to lose me." Stella Beddoe, "Edward James and Les Ballets 1933," *A Surreal Life: Edward James 1907-1984,* ed. Nicola Coleby (Brighton and Hove, UK: The Royal Pavilion, Libraries and Museums / London: Philip Wilson Publishers, 1998), 41.

87. ***Coco Chanel and Cole Porter:*** Boris Kochno, "Les Ballets 1933," *Les Ballets 1933* (Saratoga Springs, NY: National Museum of Dance, 1990).

87. ***Painter André Derain quipped:*** Tamara Finch, "Les Ballets 1933," *Dancing Times* 78, no. 930 (March 1988): 532-533.

87. ***painted in the style:*** Boris Kochno, in collaboration with Maria Luz, *Le Ballet en France: du quinzième siècle à nos jours* (France: Librairie Hachette, 1954), 300.

88. ***An Englishman called Edward James:*** According to Irina Baronova, Jasinski already was acquainted with Edward James. She states that James sponsored Serge Lifar's tour of seaside resorts in 1932, the year prior to his involvement with Les Ballets 1933, and in his reminiscences Jasinski spoke of a Lifar tour to Biarritz and other destinations in the south of France. Jasinski partnered Baronova on this tour. Irina Baronova, *Irina: Ballet, life and love* (Gainesville: University Press of Florida, 2005), 83; M. Jasinsky, contract with Arnold Meckel to dance with Serge Lifar, 27 June 1932.

88. ***he was the illegitimate son:*** Others gave credence to this rumor. Laurence Benaïm, *Marie Laure de Noailles: La vicomtesse du bizarre* (Paris: Bernard Grasset, 2001), 265.

However, years later Edward James stated that he believed that he was actually the *grandson* of Edward VII. In his autobiography, he claims that his grandmother, Helen Forbes, was the mistress of Edward VII, and that his mother gave him a bundle of letters written by both Edward VII and George V acknowledging her paternity. Edward James, *Swans Reflecting Elephants: My Early Years*, ed. George Melly (London: Weidenfeld and Nicolson, 1982), 5-6.

92. ***Before Edward James's arrival:*** Finch, "Les Ballets 1933," 534.

92. ***There was no room:*** Shelley Tobin, "A Complete Catalogue of the Collection at Brighton Museum and Art Gallery," *Les Ballets 1933* (Brighton, UK: The Royal Pavilion and Museum, 1987), 51, 59, 69, and 74.

92. ***all were so varied:*** Philip Dyer, "Recollections of Les Ballets 1933," *Les Ballets 1933* (Brighton, 1987), 35.

92. ***Composer Igor Stravinsky:*** James, *Swans Reflecting Elephants*, 140. According to Jasinski, Stravinsky was "a very kind man, soft spoken. He liked to dress casually, no tie." Cronley, "Roman Jasinski Bio."

94. ***James bore most:*** Jane Pritchard, "Les Ballets 1933," *Les Ballets 1933* (Brighton, 1987), 12-13.

94. ***they were being paid:*** Finch, "Les Ballets 1933," 533.

94. ***"danced with fussy hand movements:*** Ibid., 534.

94. ***"was the despair of Balanchine:*** Menuhin, "Les Ballets 1933," 64.

94. ***He had worked at least once:*** Pritchard, "Les Ballets 1933" (Brighton, 1987), 13.

94. ***Three Penny Opera:*** "Kurt Weill," *Les Ballets 1933* (Brighton, 1987), 94.

94. ***"hugely acclaimed:*** Olga Maynard, *The American Ballet* (Philadelphia: MacRae Smith Company, 1959), 72.

96. ***"Les Ballets 1933 was presented by Edward James:*** Janet Flanner, *Paris Was Yesterday: 1925-1939*, ed. Irvin Drutman (London: Virago, 2003), 113, originally published under Ms. Flanner's *nom de plume*, Genêt, in "Letter From Paris," *New Yorker*, 8 June 1933. According to Lincoln Kirstein, Ms. Flanner was not actually present at the premiere; he states that she wrote her account based upon a conversation following his own attendance. Lincoln Kirstein, *By With To and From: A Lincoln Kirstein Reader*, ed. Nicolas Jenkins (New York: Farrar, Straus, & Giroux, 1991), 142.

97. ***the least successful:*** Rebecca Quinton, ed. and rev., "Les Valses de Beethoven," *Les Ballets 1933: Cast List and Notes* (Brighton, UK: The Royal Pavilion and Museum, 1999), adapted from various earlier notes by Shelley Tobin.

97. ***It gave full creative license:*** Kochno, "Les Ballets 1933" (Saratoga Springs, 1990).

97. ***It is also to André Derain:*** Ibid.

97. ***London's MORNING POST:*** Quinton, *Les Ballets 1933*, 1999.

97. ***performed nearly nude:*** John Percival, "The Golden Summer," *Dance and Dancers* (London), June 1983, 33.

97. ***twenty feet in length:*** Ibid.

97. ***The final falling cloudburst:*** Pritchard, "Les Ballets 1933" (Brighton, 1987), 18.

97. ***Balanchine hidden:*** Jane Pritchard, "A Surreal Life: Edward James, 1907-1984," *Dancing Times* (London) 88, no. 1054 (July 1988): 914.

98. ***pure classical dance:*** Kochno, "Les Ballets 1933" (Saratoga Springs, 1990).

98. ***couldn't get it out of his mind:*** William MacKay, "Edwin Denby, 1903-1983," in *Edwin Denby: Dance Writings,* ed. Robert Cornfield and William McKay (New York: Alfred A. Knopf, 1986), 22.

98. ***"Tamara Toumanova and Roman Jasinsky:*** Review, *Evening News* (London), June 1933, by the kind permission of the Edward James Foundation.

98. ***Corps members played multiple roles:*** Finch, "Les Ballets 1933," 534.

99. ***Parisians had their choice:*** Lincoln Kirstein, "Ballet," *American Vogue*, 1 November 1933, as quoted in *Les Ballets 1933* (Saratoga Springs, 1990).

99. ***including Igor Stravinsky:*** Ibid.

99. ***"Roman Yasinsky [sic]:*** Review, *Paris Weekly*, 9 June 1933, by the kind permission of the Edward James Foundation.

99. ***"From the moment of our debut:*** Kochno, "Les Ballets 1933" (Saratoga Springs, 1990).

99. ***and as he watched:*** Eugene R. Gaddis, *Magician of the Modern: Chick Austin and the Transformation of the Arts in America* (New York: Alfred A. Knopf, 2000), 200.

100. ***"introduced to us a brilliant male dancer:*** "The Ballets of 1933: Brilliant Dancing by Tilly Losch," *Daily Telegraph*, 29 June 1933, Dance Collection, Library and Museum of the Performing Arts, Lincoln Center, New York.

100. ***"calling him 'nothing but an amateur:*** Tamara Tchinarova Finch, *Dancing Into the Unknown: My Life in the Ballets Russes and Beyond* (Hampshire, UK: Dance Books, 2007), 72.

100. ***Lifar danced LE SPECTRE DE LA ROSE:*** Pritchard, "Les Ballets 1933" (Brighton, 1987), 15.

101. ***Kirstein had found his man:*** Gaddis, *Magician of the Modern*, 200.

103. ***a "short, adventurous and passionate spell:*** Boris Kochno, "Preface," *Les Ballets 1933* (Brighton, 1987), 5.

104. ***the idea of an American company:*** Gaddis, *Magician of the Modern*, 200.

104. ***"This will be the most important:*** Lincoln Kirstein to A. Everett Austin, 16 July 1933, as quoted in Gaddis, *Magician of the Modern,* 198 and 203.

105. ***Kirstein extols George Balanchine:*** Ibid., 198-201.

105. ***Kirstein in Europe:*** Richard Buckle, in collaboration with John Taras, *George Balanchine: Ballet Master* (New York: Random House, 1988), 69.

105. ***"iron-clad contract:*** Ibid.

105. ***"will arrange everything:*** Lincoln Kirstein, telegram to A. Everett Austin, 8 August 1933, Special File, Wadsworth Atheneum Archives, as quoted in Gaddis, 208.

105. ***"Guaranteed living expenses:*** Buckle, *George Balanchine*, 69-70.

105. ***on 11 August:*** Ibid., 70.

106. ***"what the hell Dimitriev did:*** Ibid., 71.

106. ***"Await your decision:*** George Balanchine, telegram to Lincoln Kirstein, 29 August 1933, School of American Ballet, as quoted in Buckle, *George Balanchine*, 71.

106. ***to visit a French countess:*** Balanchine and Jasinski most likely visited Marie Laure, the Vicomtesse de Noailles, who was an early supporter of Les Ballets 1933 and had a villa at Hyères, only a few miles from Toulon. Benaim, *Marie Laure de Noailles*, Chapter 6 and 265-266; and James, *Swans Reflecting Elephants*, 135. According to Stéphane Boudin-Lestienne, Historian of Art and Architecture at the Villa Noailles, the Noailles built the villa with its fifteen bedrooms to accommodate their visiting artist friends and entertained there frequently, counting painters, composers, and dancers among their guests. Stéphane Boudin-Lestienne, in discussion with Cheryl Forrest, Hyères, France, 13 September 2006.

107. ***"He is extremely beautiful:*** Lincoln Kirstein to A. Everett Austin, 16 July 1933, as quoted in Gaddis, *Magician of the Modern*, 200-201.

107. ***"presence Jasinsky:*** George Balanchine, telegram to Lincoln Kirstein, 14 September 1933, as quoted in Buckle, *George Balanchine*, 72.

107. ***"Presence now Toumanova:*** Ibid., 15 September 1933, 73.

**MY STARVING**

110. ***My mother would say:*** Roman Larkin Jasinski, in discussion with Cheryl Forrest, Tulsa, 4 May 2006.

110. ***My mother, Stefania:*** Ibid.

112. ***I remember that I saw:*** Ibid.

113. ***clean the oil lamps:*** Ibid. This was Roman Jasinski's designated job as a child.

113. ***Still, Jasha once told:*** Ibid.

116. ***The Germans swarmed:*** *The World Book*, ed., M. V. O'Shea (Chicago and Kansas City: Roach and Fowler, 1922), s.v. "Poland."

117. ***I remember one time:*** R. L. Jasinski, discussion, 4 May 2006.

### LIFAR TO THE RESCUE

120. ***The contract that Jasinski signed:*** Czeslaw Jasinsky, contract to dance with Serge Lifar, 15 October 1933.

121. ***Another original contract:*** M. Jasinsky, contract with Arnold Meckel, 27 June 1932.

123. ***"My dear friend:*** Serge Lifar, *Ma Vie: From Kiev to Kiev*, trans. James Holman Mason (Hutchinson of London, 1970), 147.

123. ***For a mere $10,000:*** Gaddis, *Magician of the Modern,* 222-224. It seems that perhaps not all of the collection was Lifar's to sell. In his memoirs, Edward James claims that a Christian Bérard backdrop was stolen from him by Lifar. James states that he eventually proved it was his, and that the Wadsworth Atheneum returned the drop to him. James, *Swans Reflecting Elephants,* 148-149. Gallery owner Julian Levy hinted that the rest of the collection had been appropriated by Lifar after Diaghilev's death. Julien Levy, "The Lifar Collection," *The Serge Lifar Collection of Ballet Set and Costume Designs* (Hartford, CT: Wadsworth Atheneum, 1965), 7, as quoted in Gaddis, *Magician of the Modern*, 452, note 4.

123. ***"In one bound:*** Levy, "The Lifar Collection," 7, as quoted in Gaddis, *Magician of the Modern*, 224.

### DE BASIL AND BLUM: THE BEGINNING OF THE END

127. ***Şol Hurok, who added:*** Walker, *De Basil's Ballets Russes*, 34.

127. ***Bronislava Nijinska's Théâtre de la Danse:*** Baer, Nancy Van Norman, *Bronislava Nijinska: A Dancer's Legacy* (San Francisco: The Fine Arts Museums of San Francisco, 1986), 63, and Walker, *De Basil's Ballets Russes,* 35-36.

131. ***exotic young Asian-American girl:*** Sono Osato, *Distant Dances* (New York: Alfred A. Knopf, 1980), 28-30.

131. ***"J'ai l'honneur:*** Roman Jasinski to Monsieur W. de Basil, 12 June 1934, collection Roman Larkin Jasinski.

131. ***His company now danced:*** García-Márquez, *Colonel de Basil's Ballets Russes*, xvi.

132. ***"I should love to see you:*** Czeslaw Jasinski to Edward James, 30 July 1934, by the kind permission of the Trustees of the Edward James Foundation. Translation from the French provided by the Foundation.

133. ***"As I have had no reply:*** Ibid., 7 August 1934.

133. ***Jasinski's "excellent dancing:*** Edward James, letter to a friend, 7 August 1934, by the kind permission of the Trustees of the Edward James Foundation.

134. ***"Thank you very much:*** Jasinski to Edward James, 11 August 1934, by the kind permission of the Trustees of the Edward James Foundation.

#### A GYPSY ONCE MORE

146. ***"la bombe:*** Kochno, *Le Ballet en France,* 303.

#### THE AMERICAN DREAM

161. ***Petroff bled like a bull:*** Roman Larkin Jasinski, in discussion with Cheryl Forrest, Tulsa, 4 May 2006.

#### THE WORLD DARKENS

167. ***Here lies a point:*** For this brief discussion of the nomenclature of the various related companies, we are indebted to Kathrine Sorley Walker's *De Basil's Ballets Russes,* Vicente García-Márquez' *The Ballets Russes: Colonel de Basil's Ballets Russes de Monte Carlo 1932-1952,* and Jack Anderson's *The One and Only: The Ballet Russe de Monte Carlo.*

169. ***The opposing directors:*** Walker, *De Basil's Ballets Russes,* 86.

#### DOWN UNDER

172. ***He screamed at us:*** Cronley, "Roman Jasinski Bio."

### BOOK THREE: THE WAR YEARS 1939-1947

#### INTERMEZZO

181. ***12 June to 29 July:*** García-Márquez, *Colonel de Basil's Ballets Russes,* xiv.

181. ***under the name…company was elsewhere:*** García-Márquez, *Colonel de Basil's Ballets Russes, xvii;* and Jack Anderson, *The One and Only: The Ballet Russe de Monte Carlo* (New York: Dance Horizons, 1981), 34.

184. ***a letter in French:*** W. de Basil to "mes chères Sono et Jacha [sic]," 14 October 1939, collection Roman Larkin Jasinski.

184. ***in another letter:*** N. Bouchonnet to "Sono and Jasha," 2 November 1939, collection Roman Larkin Jasinski.

186. ***16 Rue de Gramont:*** Bouchonnet, letter; and García-Márquez, *Colonel de Basil's Ballets Russes,* 244. The company address.

#### A STAR IN HIS OWN RIGHT

188. ***The company was now called:*** Newspaper clippings and programs, collection Czeslaw Roman Jasinski.

189. ***Their domestic skills:*** Ibid.

190. ***"best-looking man:*** "Fashion and Society" (Sydney), clipping, 1 February 1940, 11, collection Czeslaw Roman Jasinski.

192. ***The English, French, and Polish:*** Program, "Midnight Performance for Polish Relief," Theatre Royal (Sydney), 12 March 1940, collection Czeslaw Roman Jasinski.

193. ***found it "outstanding:*** Basil Burdett, "Successful Ballet for Hospital Funds," *Sydney Morning Herald*, 19 July 1940.

193. ***RAYMONDA....seventeen pieces:*** Program, "Midnight Performance."

193. ***Recipients included:*** Burdett, "Successful Ballet," and various programs and newspaper clippings, collection Czeslaw Roman Jasinski.

193. ***"sheer joyous rapture:*** Fan letters addressed to Roman Jasinski, collection Roman Larkin Jasinski.

195. ***"[The] accenting of [Jasinsky's] big allegro dance:*** Newspaper clipping, 23 April 1940, collection Czeslaw Roman Jasinski.

195. ***"Roman Jasinsky, a signal success:*** Ibid., 2 April 1940.

195. ***"the house thundered its applause:*** "Opening of Ballet," newspaper clipping (1940), collection Czeslaw Roman Jasinski.

195. ***"pure classical style:*** Basil Burdett, "Notable Ballet Opening," *The Herald* (Sydney), 15 March 1940.

195. ***"I have never seen:*** Fan letters, collection Roman Larkin Jasinski.

196. ***"the surprise of the season:*** "Stronger Ballet Programme," newspaper clipping, (1940), collection Czeslaw Roman Jasinski.

196. ***"The outstanding thing:*** "Return of Ballet Welcomed," *The Sun* (Sydney), 15 July 1940.

196. ***"enlarged the scope:*** "The Ballet Returns. Brilliant 'Icare.' Jasinsky's Success." *Sydney Morning Herald,* 15 July 1940.

196. ***"magnificent," "brilliant:*** Newspaper clippings, collection Czeslaw Roman Jasinski.

198. ***twenty curtain calls:*** Geoffrey Hutton, " 'Icare' Wins 20 Curtains," *The Argus* (Melbourne), (1940), collection Czeslaw Roman Jasinski.

198. ***PRODIGAL SON and ICARE were two ballets:*** Lichine's *Prodigal Son* became a staple in de Basil's Ballets Russes. Roman Jasinski danced the role for many years and in fact danced the lead in the company's final performance of the piece in 1947. Lili Cockerille Livingston, "Prodigal's Return," *Dance Magazine*, February 1986, 62.

199. "***I am always enchanted:*** Fan letters, collection Roman Larkin Jasinski.

200. ***"Your work:*** Ibid.

**DARK DAYS**

204. ***Original Ballet Russe, hit the continental shores:*** García-Márquez, *Colonel de Basil's Ballets Russes*, 267-269.

206. ***choreography as a maturation:*** Ibid., 278.

206. ***On 22 January 1941, Balustrade premiered:*** Ibid., 277.

207. ***"As is so often the case:*** S. Hurok, *S. Hurok Presents: A Memoir of the Dance World* (New York: Hermitage House, 1953), 143.

207. ***"Among the men:*** Denby, *Dance Writings*, 70-71.

207. ***resumed its tour, but without:*** Walker, *De Basil's Ballets Russes*, 105 and 107.

207. ***Baronova, under a separate contract:*** Hurok, *S. Hurok Presents*, 143.

208. ***later admissions by Baronova:*** Baronova states that Hurok withheld payment to de Basil, causing the dancers to go unpaid, and that her husband Sevastianov asked her to strike as well, while he recruited those dancers Hurok wanted for Ballet Theatre. De Basil eventually sued Hurok for "conspiracy and sabotage." The case was dismissed when the Colonel, traveling with his company, was unable to appear in court. Baronova, *Ballet, life and love*, 323-325.

209. ***Hurok was looking for a way:*** Walker, *De Basil's Ballets Russes*, 110.

210. ***the strike was caused:*** "Statement" document of dancers' grievances, 25 March 1941, collection Roman Larkin Jasinski.

#### UH! OH! BAD EYE!

217. ***Eva Matlagova's story:*** Eva Matlagova Larkin, "There Goes My Bread," unpublished memoir as told to Thelma D. Garpner, n.d., collection Roman Larkin Jasinski.

#### SOUTH AMERICAN SAGA

222. ***We also traveled by train:*** Roman Larkin Jasinski, in discussion with Cheryl Forrest, Tulsa, 11 May 2006.

222. ***arm-wrestling champion:*** Roman Larkin Jasinski, telephone conversation with Cheryl Forrest, 13 June 2006.

230. ***Marian Ladre:*** Moscelyne Larkin, "Private Musings", unpublished memoir as told to Georgia Snoke, Tulsa, 2002, 37.

232. ***he gave some thought:*** Hurok, *S. Hurok Presents*, 190.

232. ***Alicia Alonso stepped in:*** Larkin, "Private Musings," 43-44.

232. ***Hurok sent new dancers:*** Lili Cockerille Livingston, *American Indian Ballerinas* (Norman, OK and London: University of Oklahoma Press, 1997), 142-143 and 178.

232. ***the company was stranded:*** Walker, *De Basil's Ballets Russes*, 137-138.

#### TATTERED SHADOW

233. ***sapped, for a time:*** Walker, *De Basil's Ballets Russes*, 138-139.

233. ***He decried:*** Hurok, *S. Hurok Presents*, 194-196.

234. ***The Original Ballet Russe was no longer:*** Ibid., Chapter 10 and 183-200.

236. ***when the building above her exploded:*** Roman Larkin Jasinski, in discussion with Cheryl Forrest, Tulsa, 11 May 2006.

239. ***Impresario Sol Hurok:*** Hurok, *S. Hurok Presents*, 194-196.

241. ***"gentle, cultured intellectual:*** Ibid., 108.

241. ***he refused:*** Ibid.

241. ***final, fatal move:*** Barbara Naomi Cohen-Stratyner, *Biographical Dictionary of Dance* (New York: Schirmer Books, 1982), s.v. "René Blum."

243. ***"an instinct for the theatre:*** Hurok, *S. Hurok Presents*, 137.

245. ***"a mere tyro:*** Ibid.

## BOOK FOUR: LIFE IN AMERICA 1948-1991

### FALLING STAR

251–252. ***She danced the "Cowgirl":*** Anatole Chujoy and P.W. Manchester, comp. and ed., *The Dance Encyclopedia*, rev. ed., (New York: Simon and Schuster, 1967), s.v. "Moscelyne Larkin."

252. ***"She was remarkable:*** Maynard, *The American Ballet*, 92.

252. ***at the suggestion of Agnes de Mille:*** Roman Larkin Jasinski, in discussion with Cheryl Forrest, Tulsa, 4 May 2006.

253. ***"Why you cry:*** Larkin, "Private Musings," 58.

255. ***her heart would stop:*** Yvonne Chouteau, telephone conversation with Georgia Snoke, 15 February 2006.

255. ***Programs from this period:*** Various programs, The Ballet Russe de Monte Carlo, 1938-1962, Dance Collection, Library and Museum of the Performing Arts, Lincoln Center, New York.

256. ***For one six-month period:*** Larkin, "Private Musings," 59-60.

258. ***"You are apt to think:*** Hurok, *S. Hurok Presents*, 144-145.

258. ***"By one means or another:*** Ibid., 197.

### GYPSY PRINCE

261. ***that Jasinski held South America:*** Pablo de Madalengoitia, in discussion with Georgia Snoke, Lima, Peru, 8 June 1968.

261. ***"During 8 years:*** Fan letter to Roman Jasinski, 30 August 1952, collection Roman Larkin Jasinski.

262. ***"Please try to pacify:*** Serge Denham to Roman Jasinski, 5 February 1953, collection Czeslaw Roman Jasinski.

263. ***"I hope that peace reigns:*** Serge Denham to Roman Jasinski, (1953).

263. ***"That Moussia is a terrific secretary:*** Doris Luhrs to Roman Jasinski, 23 January 1953, collection Czeslaw Roman Jasinski.

264. ***"Here is another appraisal:*** Serge Denham to Roman Jasinski, (1953), collection Czeslaw Roman Jasinski. This letter includes excerpts from a letter written by Marian Ladre to "Sergei Ivanovitch" (Serge Denham).

265. ***Columbia Artists wanted to renew the ballet's contract:*** Serge Denham to Roman Jasinski, February 1953, collection Czeslaw Roman Jasinski.

265. ***Its own publicity crowed:*** Program, Concert Company, *Ballet Russe de Monte Carlo*, (1953), collection Czeslaw Roman Jasinski.

265. ***"Judging from the hundreds of letters:*** Serge Denham to Roman Jasinski, February 1953, collection Czeslaw Roman Jasinski.

269. ***Roman Larkin Jasinski was accepted:*** Roman Larkin Jasinski, in discussion with Cheryl Forrest, Tulsa, 11 May 2006.

269. ***That he, too, would become:*** Roman Larkin Jasinski's dancing genes were indeed strong. After early training with his parents, young Roman moved to New York and was taken under the wing of George Balanchine, who previously had told Jasha on several occasions that if Roman were left with him, he would raise him as his son, taking him to museums, placing him with the best teachers and the greatest musicians, and training him "the way we were trained." After dancing as an apprentice with Balanchine's New York City Ballet, Jasha's son danced with American Ballet Theatre, eventually attaining the rank of soloist. Roman returned to Tulsa as a principal dancer when his parents' company became fully professional. Subsequently he was a principal dancer with Cincinnati Ballet before returning to Tulsa Ballet Theatre to serve as ballet master and eventually as artistic director. He resigned that post in 1995. R. L. Jasinski, discussion, ibid.

270. ***When I came in the door:*** R. L. Jasinski, discussion, ibid.

### A HOME OF HIS OWN

280. ***"Young talent must have an audience:*** Benedict J. Lubell to "Celebrity Series" members ("Dear Member,") 1 December 1956, collection Georgia Snoke.

280. *a* ***"bonus attraction:*** "Civic Ballet Debut is Saturday," Tulsa newspaper article, 12 December 1956, collection Georgia Snoke.

280. ***With the Jasinskis in leading roles:*** Program, "The Tulsa Civic Ballet," *The Celebrity Series,* Tulsa, 15 December 1956, collection Georgia Snoke.

280. ***The newborn Tulsa Civic Ballet:*** Program, "Oklahoma Indian Ballerina Festival," Ballet Arts and the Semi-Centennial Commission of the State of Oklahoma, 1957, collection Tulsa Ballet.

282. ***It was time to trumpet:*** Larkin, "Private Musings," 70.

282. ***each of whom possessed an American Indian heritage:*** Livingston, 4, 29, 32, and 56; and Yvonne Chouteau, telephone conversation with Georgia Snoke, 15 February 2006.

282. ***"a corn-fed corps de ballet:*** *The Times* (London), 24 October 1957, as quoted in a (1957) Tulsa newspaper clipping, collection Georgia Snoke.

282. ***Headlines shouted:*** Reviews of the 1957 Indian Ballerina Festival, all collection Georgia Snoke: P. W. Manchester, "Oh! What a Beautiful Evening!" *Dance News*, December 1957; *The Times* (London), 24 October 1957, as quoted in a (1957) Tulsa newspaper clipping; Jean Simson, "Ballerinas Present Top Performance," *Tulsa Tribune,* (1957); and Maurice DeVinna, "Ballerinas Offer Brilliant Centennial Contribution," *Tulsa World*, (1957).

285. ***The National Foundation:*** Program, "Oklahoma Indian Ballerina Festival," Oklahoma Arts and Humanities Council and the National Foundation on the Arts and Humanities, Tulsa, 28 October 1967, collection Tulsa Ballet.

285. ***Again the festival was reviewed:*** Reviews of the 1967 Indian Ballerina Festival: Walter Terry, "The Four Moons," *Saturday Review*, 18 November 1967, 60; Marion Simon, "Indian Ballerinas Dance for State's Birthday Party," *National Observer*, 30 October 1967; "Moon Maidens," *Newsweek*, 6 November 1967, 101; and P.W. Manchester, "Indian-Ballerina Festival Climaxes Oklahoma Jubilee," *Dance News*, December 1967.

285. ***"what honor you have brought:*** Walter Terry to "My beautiful Moussia," collection Moscelyne Larkin Jasinski.

286. ***"They always want something new:*** Barry Laine, "The Ballet Star as Guest . . . " *New York Times*, 26 July 1981.

286. ***"How bright my memories:*** Excerpts from the Jasinskis' *Memory Book*, collection Moscelyne Larkin Jasinski.

288. ***Balanchine told me:*** Roman Larkin Jasinski, in discussion with Cheryl Forrest, Tulsa, 11 May 2006.

290. ***eventually attained "major company" status:*** Ann Barzel, "National Reports: Six NARB Members Upgraded," *Dance News* 60, no. 5 (January 1975): 7.

291. ***NEW YORK TIMES critic:*** Jack Anderson, "Dance View: Sometimes a Revival Is More Rewarding Than a Premiere," *New York Times*, 25 August 1985.

291. ***"Tulsa did American dance proud:*** Jennifer Dunning, "Ballet: Tulsa in a Salute," *New York Times*, 15 November 1982.

291. ***"a leading American regional ballet company:*** Dunning, "The Tulsa Ballet Leaps Into New York," *New York Times*, 6 November 1983.

291. ***"There isn't a company:*** David C. MacKenzie, "Tulsa Ballet's Directors 'Indestructibles,'" *Tulsa World*, 20 June 1982.

291. ***"Tulsa Ballet is one of the best:*** Clive Barnes, *New York Post*, 19 November 1983.

291. ***"not only Ballet Russe-style:*** Walter Terry, "Tulsa," *Ballet News* 3, no. 7 (January 1982): 37-38.

292. ***"pure classical line:*** Lili Cockerille Livingston, "Tulsa Ballet Theatre's Ballet Russe Renaissance," *Dance Magazine*, February 1986, 60.

292. ***"A mistake was made:*** Larkin, "Private Musings," 54; and Roman Larkin Jasinski, in discussion with Cheryl Forrest, Tulsa, 11 May 2006.

293. ***"shining example:*** Excerpt from text of *Dance Magazine* Award plaque, as read to Georgia Snoke by Moscelyne Larkin during a telephone conversation, (2000).

## Selected Bibliography

*Bibliography contains books, programs, documents, and those articles consulted but not cited.*


Anderson, Jack. *The One and Only: The Ballet Russe de Monte Carlo*. New York: Dance Horizons, 1981.

Baer, Nancy Van Norman. *Bronislava Nijinska: A Dancer's Legacy*. San Francisco: The Fine Arts Museums of San Francisco, 1986.

Baronova, Irina. *Ballet, life and love*. Gainesville, FL: University Press of Florida, 2006.

Beaumont, Cyril W. *Complete Book of Ballets*. London: Putnam, 1951.

Beevor, Antony, and Artemis Cooper. *Paris after the Liberation: 1944-1949*. New York: Penguin Books, 1994.

Benaïm, Laurence. *Marie Laure de Noailles: La vicomtesse du bizarre*. Paris: Bernard Grasset, 2001.

Bentley, Toni. *Costumes by Karinska*. New York: Harry N. Abrams, 1995.

Buckle, Richard. *Diaghilev*. New York: Atheneum, 1979.

_________, in collaboration with John Taras. *George Balanchine: Ballet Master*. New York: Random House, 1988.

_________. *In the Wake of Diaghilev*. New York: Holt, Rinehart and Winston, 1982.

_________. *Nijinsky*. New York: Simon and Schuster, 1971.

Charles-Roux, Edmonde. *Chanel and her world: Friends, Fashion, and Fame*. New York: The Vendome Press, 2004.

Chujoy, Anatole, and P.W. Manchester, editors. *The Dance Encyclopedia*. Rev. ed. New York: Simon and Schuster, 1967.

Cohen, Selma Jeanne, editor. *International Encyclopedia of Dance*. Vol. 4. New York and Oxford: Oxford University Press, 1998.

Cohen-Stratyner, Barbara Naomi. *Biographical Dictionary of Dance*. New York: Schirmer Books, 1982.

Coleby, Nicola, editor. *A Surreal Life: Edward James, 1907-1984*. Brighton and Hove, UK: The Royal Pavilion, Libraries and Museums / London: Philip Wilson Publishers, 1998.

Contracts:

Ceslav [*sic*] Jasinski—Boris Kniaseff, 3 August 1931.

Czeslaw Jacinsky [*sic*]—Teatro alla Scala, 6 November 1931.

Czeslaw Jasinski—M. Carolus Duran, 18 July 1930.

Czeslaw Jasinski—Spessivtzeva, 8 April 1930.

Czeslaw Jasinsky—Ida Rubinstein, 25 April–18 July 1931.

Czeslaw Jasinsky—Serge Lifar and Arnold Meckel, 15 October 1933.

M. Jasinsky—Arnold Meckel, 27 June 1932.

Cross, Julia Vincent. "A Volinine Vignette." *Dance Magazine* 31, no. 2 (February 1957): 42, 43 and 79.

Danilova, Alexandra. *Choura: The Memoirs of Alexandra Danilova*. New York: Alfred A. Knopf, 1986.

De Andia, Béatrice, editor. *Paris et ses Théâtres: architecture et décor*. Paris: Action Artistique de la Ville de Paris, 1998.

De Cossart, Michael. "Ida Rubinstein and Diaghilev: A One-Sided Rivalry." *Dance Research: Journal of the Society for Dance Research* 1, no. 2 (Autumn 1983): 3-20.

_________. *Ida Rubinstein (1885-1960): A Theatrical Life*. Great Britain: Liverpool University Press, 1987.

De Mille, Agnes. *Dance to the Piper*. New York: Grosset and Dunlap, 1952.

Denby, Edwin. *Dance Writings*. Edited by Robert Cornfield and William MacKay. New York: Alfred A. Knopf, 1986.

Depaulis, Jacques. *Paul Claudel et Ida Rubinstein: Une collaboration difficile*. Paris: Annales Litteraires de l'Université de Besançon, 1994.

Duberman, Martin. *The Worlds of Lincoln Kirstein*. New York: Alfred A. Knopf, 2007.

Dukes, Ashley. "The Scene in Europe: Russian Ballet—Malvern—Salzburg." *Theatre Arts Monthly* 17, No. 10 (October 1933): 765-769.

Finch, Tamara Tchinarova. *Dancing Into the Unknown: My Life in the Ballets Russes and Beyond*. Hampshire, UK: Dance Books, 2007.

Flanner, Janet. *Paris Was Yesterday 1925-1939.* 2nd ed. Edited by Irving Drutman. London: Verago Press, 2003. Originally published in a series of articles for *The New Yorker,* 1925–1939, under the title "Letter from Paris."

Fonteyn, Margot. *Pavlova: Portrait of a Dancer.* New York: Viking, 1984.

Gaddis, Eugene R. "The Hartford Catastrophe." *Ballet Review* 28, no. 2 (Summer 2000): 54-74.

_________. *Magician of the Modern: Chick Austin and the Transformation of the Arts in America.* New York: Alfred A. Knopf, 2000.

Garafola, Lynn. *Diaghilev's Ballets Russes.* New York and Oxford: Oxford University Press, 1989.

_________, and Nancy Van Norman Baer, editors. *The Ballets Russes and its World.* New Haven, CT and London: Yale University Press, 1999.

García-Márquez, Vicente. *The Ballets Russes: Colonel de Basil's Ballets Russes de Monte Carlo, 1932–1952.* New York: Alfred A. Knopf, 1990.

_________. *Massine: A Biography.* New York: Alfred A. Knopf, 1995.

Grigoriev, S. L. *The Diaghilev Ballet: 1909-1929.* Translated and edited by Vera Bowen. Harmondsworth, Middlesex, UK: Penguin Books, 1960.

Haskell, Arnold. *Ballet: A Complete Guide to Appreciation—History, Aesthetics, Ballets, Dancers.* Harmondsworth, Middlesex, UK: Penguin Books, 1938.

_________, editor. *Ballet—to Poland: In Aid of the Polish Relief Fund.* London: Adam and Charles Black, 1940.

Hurok, S. *S. Hurok Presents: A Memoir of the Dance World.* New York: Hermitage House, 1953.

James, Edward. *Swans Reflecting Elephants: My Early Years.* Edited by George Melly. London: Weidenfeld and Nicolson, 1982.

Jasinski, Roman. "A Communication: Some Recollections of *Swan Lake* in Warsaw." *Dance Chronicle* 14, no. 1 (1991): 102–105.

Kirstein, Lincoln. *By With To and From: A Lincoln Kirstein Reader.* Edited by Nicholas Jenkins. New York: Farrar, Straus and Giroux, 1991.

_________. *Mosaic: Memoirs.* New York: Farrar, Straus and Giroux, 1994.

Kniaseff, Boris. "The Reminiscences of Boris Kniaseff." Part Three. *Ballet Today* 10, no. 8 (October 1957): 21.

Kochno, Boris, in collaboration with Maria Luz. *Le Ballet.* France: Librairie Hachette, 1954.

_________. *Diaghilev and the Ballets Russes.* Translated by Adrienne Foulke. New York and Evanston: Harper and Row, 1970.

Larkin, Edna Moscelyne. "Private Musings." Unpublished memoir as told to Georgia Snoke, Tulsa, 2002.

Larkin, Eva Matlagova. "There Goes My Bread." Unpublished memoir as told to Thelma D. Garpner, Tulsa, n.d.

Lieven, Peter. *The Birth of the Ballets-Russes*. Translated by L. Zarine. London: George Allen and Unwin, 1936. Reprinted with minor corrections and a new foreward by Catherine Lieven Ritter. New York: Dover Publications, 1973.

Lifar, Serge. *Serge Diaghilev: His Life, His Work, His Legend*. New York: G. P. Putnam's Sons, 1940.

_________. *Le Livre de la Danse*. Paris: Société Française de Diffusion Musicale et Artistique, 1954.

_________. *Les Memoires d'Icare*. Monaco: Éditions Sauret, 1993.

_________. *Du temps que j'avais faim*. Paris: Librairie Stoch, 1935.

_________. *Ma Vie. From Kiev to Kiev*. Translated by James Holman Mason. London: Hutchinson, 1970.

Livingston, Lili Cockerille. *American Indian Ballerinas*. Norman, OK and London: University of Oklahoma Press, 1997.

Malherbe, Henri. "Chronique musicale." *Le Temps* (5 December 1928): 3.

Markova, Alicia. *Markova Remembers*. Boston and Toronto: Little, Brown and Co., 1986.

Mason, Francis. *I Remember Balanchine: Recollections of the Ballet Master by Those Who Knew Him*. New York: Doubleday, 1991.

Maynard, Olga. *The American Ballet*. Philadelphia: MacRae Smith Company, 1959.

Documents, collection Roman Larkin Jasinski:

Identity card. M. Czeslaw Jasinski, Paris: 2 May 1937.

Certificate confirming residency and employment. Commissaire de Police —N. Bouchonnet, Paris: 2 May 1935.

Certificate confirming residency and employment. Czeslaw Jasinsky—Ida Rubinstein, Paris: 10 May 1931.

Certificate confirming residency and employment. Roman Jassinsky [*sic*] — N. Bouchonnet for W. de Basil, Paris : 28 March 1935.

Entry permit. Czeslak [*sic*] Jasinski, Argentina: (1942).

"Statement" document outlining striking dancers' grievances. Havana: 25 March 1941.

Work permit. Czeslaw Jasinski—Stanislaw Kara, Polish Consul, Paris: 31 August 1935.

Work permit. Roman Jassinsky [*sic*]—Ministère du Travail, Paris: May 1934.

National Museum of Dance. *Les Ballets 1933*. Saratoga Springs, NY: National Museum of Dance, 1990.

The National Film and Sound Archive and The National Library of Australia. *The Ballets Russes in Australia 1936-1940: An Avalanche of Dancing*. VHS recording, 1999.

Nijinska, Bronislava. *Early Memoirs*. Translated and edited by Irina Nijinska and Jean Rawlinson. New York: Holt, Rinehart and Winston, 1981.

Nijinsky, Romola. *Nijinsky*. New York: Simon and Schuster, 1934.

Osato, Sono. *Distant Dances*. New York: Alfred A. Knopf, 1980.

Programs:

"Ballet Russe de Monte Carlo," various, 1938-52. Collection New York Public Library.

"Ballet Russe de Monte Carlo," 1959–1960. Collection Tulsa Ballet.

"Ballet Russe de Monte Carlo Concert Company," various, 1952-1954. Collection Czeslaw Roman Jasinski.

"Les Ballets de Boris Kniaseff," Théâtre de Monte-Carlo: 17, 18, 19, and 20 January 1931. Collection Archives Société des Bains de Mer.

"Les Ballets de Boris Kniaseff," L'Opéra-Comique: July 1930. Collection Bibliothèque nationale de France.

"Les Ballets de Boris Kniaseff," Théâtre de Monte-Carlo: 10, 14, 15, and 16 April 1931. Collection Archives Société des Bains de Mer.

"Les Ballets de Boris Kniaseff," Théâtre de Monte-Carlo: 28 November 1930. Collection Bibliothèque nationale de France.

"Les Ballets de Madame Ida Rubinstein," Académie Nationale de Musique et de Danse (Paris): November 1928. Collection Bibliothèque nationale de France.

"Les Ballets de Madame Ida Rubinstein," Académie Nationale de Musique et de Danse (Paris): May 1929. Collection Bibliothèque nationale de France.

"Les Ballets de Madame Ida Rubinstein," Académie Nationale de Musique et de Danse (Paris): 22, 23, 24, and 25 June 1931. Collection Bibliothèque nationale de France.

"Ballets de Monte-Carlo," Théâtre de Monte-Carlo: 1936. Collection Archives Société des Bains de Mer.

"Ballets Nijinska," Théâtre National Opéra-Comique (Paris): June 1932. Collection Bibliothèque nationale de France.

"Les Ballets 1933," Théâtre des Champs-Elysées (Paris): 1933. Collection Roman Larkin Jasinski.

"Ballets Russes de Monte-Carlo" (Paris): 28 May 1934. Collection Cheryl Forrest.

"Les Ballets Russes de Monte-Carlo," Théâtre de Monte-Carlo: 14, 16, 23,and 30 April 1932. Collection Archives Société des Bains de Mer.

"Les Ballets Russes de Monte-Carlo," Théâtre de Monte-Carlo: 3 and 5 May 1932. Collection Archives Société des Bains de Mer.

"Les Ballets Russes de Monte-Carlo," Théâtre des Champs-Elysées (Paris): June 1932. Collection Bibliothèque nationale de France.

"Les Ballets Russes de Monte-Carlo," Théâtre de Monte-Carlo: 1933. Collection Archives Société des Bains de Mer.

"Col. W. de Basil's Ballets Russes (de Monte-Carlo)," Royal Opera House Covent Garden, London: June-September 1936. Collection Cheryl Forrest.

"Col. DeBasil's [*sic*] Ballet Russe de Monte Carlo," Memorial Hall (Springfield, Ohio): 14 March 1935. Collection New York Public Library.

"Galas Ida Rubinstein," 23-25 June 1931. Collection New York Public Library.

"Madame Ida Rubinstein Season," The Covent Garden Opera Syndicate (1930) (London): 6-17 July 1931. Collection Royal Opera House.

"London Coliseum," 28 April 1930. Collection Czeslaw Roman Jasinski.

"Oklahoma Indian Ballerina Festival," Ballet Arts and the Semi-Centennial Commission of the State of Oklahoma: 1957. Collection Tulsa Ballet.

"Oklahoma Indian Ballerina Festival," Oklahoma Arts and Humanities Council and the National Foundation on the Arts and Humanities, Tulsa: 28 October 1967. Collection Tulsa Ballet.

"Original Ballet Russe," Season 1940–1941. Collection Tulsa Ballet.

"Russian Ballet," Royal Opera House, London: June-September 1938. Collection Cheryl Forrest.

"Représentations de Ballets Russes," Théâtre de Monte Carlo: 22 January 1925. Collection Bibliothèque nationale de France.

"Saison Les Ballets Russes de Monte-Carlo," Théâtre de Monte-Carlo: 7, 10, 17, 24, 26, and 28 April 1934. Collection Archives Société des Bains de Mer.

"Saison Les Ballets Russes de Monte-Carlo," Théâtre de Monte-Carlo: 4, 6, 9, 11, 23, 25, and 27 April 1935. Collection Archives Société des Bains de Mer.

"3 Grandes Epreuves Internationales de Danses Artistiques," Théâtre des Champs-Elysées: 2-4 July 1932. Collection Bibliothèque nationale de France.

"Tulsa Civic Ballet," The Celebrity Series (Tulsa): 15 December 1956. Collection Georgia Snoke.

Quinton, Rebecca, editor. *Les Ballets 1933: Cast Lists and Notes.* Catalogue of Les Ballets 1933, adapted from various earlier notes by Shelley Tobin. Brighton, UK: The Royal Pavilion, Art Gallery and Museums, 1999.

The Royal Pavilion, Art Gallery and Museums. *Complete Catalogue of the Collection at Brighton Museum and Art Gallery: Les Ballets 1933.* Brighton, UK: The Royal Pavilion, Art Gallery and Museums, 1987.

Schouvaloff, Alexánder. *The Art of Ballets Russes: The Serge Lifar Collection of Theater Designs, Costumes, and Paintings at the Wadsworth Atheneum, Hartford, Connecticut.* New

Haven, CT and London: Yale University Press / Hartford, CT: Wadsworth Atheneum, 1997.

Severn, Margaret. "Dancing with Bronislava Nijinska and Ida Rubinstein," *Dance Chronicle* 11, no. 3 (1988): 333-364.

Severn, Merlyn. *Ballet in Action.* New York: Oxford University Press, 1938.

Smakov, Gennady. *The Great Russian Dancers.* New York: Alfred A. Knopf, 1984.

Sokolova, Lydia. *Dancing for Diaghilev: The Memoirs of Lydia Sokolova.* Edited by Richard Buckle. San Francisco: Mercury House, 1960.

Taper, Bernard. *Balanchine: A Biography.* Berkeley, Los Angeles, and London: University of California Press, 1984.

Twysden, A. E. *Alexandra Danilova.* New York: Kamin Dance Publishers, 1947.

Tyler, Parker. *The Divine Comedy of Pavel Tchelitchew.* New York: Fleet Publishing Corporation, 1967.

Vaughan, David. *Frederic Ashton and His Ballets.* 2nd ed. London: Dance Books, 1999.

"M. Alexandre Volinine." *The Dancing Times*, no. 539 (August 1955): 707.

"Volinine at Work." *The Dancing Times,* no. 208 (January 1928): 548-551.

Walker, Kathrine Sorley. *De Basil's Ballets Russes.* New York: Atheneum, 1983.

# Index

E